EARLY REPUBLIC

D0556555

RELIGION AND POLITICS
IN THE
EARLY REPUBLIC

=➤●◄=

Jasper Adams and the
Church-State Debate

DANIEL L. DREISBACH
EDITOR

THE UNIVERSITY PRESS OF KENTUCKY

Frontispiece: Portrait of Jasper Adams, courtesy of the Archives, Warren Hunting Smith Library, Hobart and William Smith Colleges, Geneva, New York 14456.

The editor gratefully acknowledges permission to publish material in the archives of the William L. Clements Library.

A brief excerpt from the Introduction first appeared, in slightly different form, in *Liberty* 90, no. 4 (July/August 1995): 16-19, and is reprinted by permission.

Scholarly publisher for the Commonwealth, serving Bellarmine College, Berea College, Centre College of Kentucky, Eastern Kentucky University, The Filson Club, Georgetown College, Kentucky Historical Society, Kentucky State University, Morehead State University, Murray State University, Northern Kentucky University, Transylvania University, University of Kentucky, University of Louisville, and Western Kentucky University.

Editorial and Sales Offices:
The University Press of Kentucky
663 South Limestone Street
Lexington, Kentucky 40508-4008

Library of Congress Cataloging-in-Publication Data
Religion and politics in the early republic : Jasper Adams and the church-state debate / Daniel L. Dreisbach, editor.
    p.   cm.
    Includes bibliographical references and index.
    ISBN 0-8131-1950-2 (cloth : alk. paper) — ISBN 0-8131-0880-2 (pbk. : alk. paper)
    1. Church and state—United States. 2. Adams, J. (Jasper), 1793-1841. Relation of Christianity to civil government in the United States. 3. Christianity and politics. 4. Church and state —United States—Sermons. 5. Episcopal Church—Sermons.
I. Dreisbach, Daniel L. II. Adams, J. (Jasper), 1793-1841. Relation of Christianity to civil government in the United States.
BR516.R346 1996
322'.1'097309034—dc20   95-37861

This book is printed on acid-free recycled paper meeting the requirements of the American National Standard for Permanence of Paper for Printed Library Materials.

∞

Manufactured in the United States of America

For Joyce and Mollie Abigail

CONTENTS

ILLUSTRATIONS

PREFACE

"A page of history," Justice Oliver Wendell Holmes opined, "is worth a volume of logic."[1] Thus, jurists and scholars have consistently turned to the pages of history to inform their interpretations of the constitutional provisions governing relations between religion and civil government. James Madison agreed that any discussion of church and state was appropriately and profitably illuminated by history. "[O]n this question," he wrote, "experience will be an admitted umpire."[2] The U.S. Supreme Court has long relied on history, especially the dramatic disestablishment struggle in revolutionary Virginia, to guide its interpretation of the First Amendment provisions concerning religion.[3] As Justice Wiley Rutledge observed: "No provision of the Constitution is more closely tied to or given content by its generating history than the religious clause of the First Amendment. It is at once the refined product and the terse summation of that history."[4]

A sermon preached at St. Michael's Church in Charleston, South Carolina, on 13 February 1833 by the Reverend Jasper Adams provides valuable insight into the historical understanding of the First Amendment religion provisions and the social and intellectual forces that shaped church-state relations in the early republic. In an address before a convention of the South Carolina Diocese of the Protestant Episcopal Church, Adams argued that the Christian religion is an indispensable support for civil government, essential to social order and stability. A published version of the sermon, entitled *The Relation of Christianity to Civil Government in the United States* (1833), was distributed widely across the country. This was among the first major works controverting Thomas Jefferson's vision of a secular polity and absolute church-state separation. Although Adams's remarkably prescient discourse is noteworthy in its own right, its principal importance lies in the exchange of ideas it promulgated. Eager to confirm his interpretation of American church-state doctrine, Adams circulated his pamphlet among scores of leading intellectuals and public figures of the day. Letters written in response to Adams's sermon provide a vivid portrait of early nineteenth-century thought on the constitutional role of religion in American politics and public life.

This book for the first time brings together Adams's sermon, a critical review of the sermon published anonymously in 1835, and complete and reliable transcripts of letters written in 1833 in response to the sermon by John Marshall, Joseph Story, James Madison, and John Smythe Richardson. These previously unpublished letters are of particular importance, since Madison is generally credited with drafting the First Amendment religion provisions, and Chief Justice Marshall and Associate Justice Story were eminent jurists whose legal opinions during their distinguished careers on the Supreme Court illuminated the meaning of the federal Constitution. Richardson was a respected and influential South Carolina judge who, at Adams's request, supplied his opinion on technical legal matters addressed in the sermon.

During the colonial and early national periods, ministers often preached sermons addressing the nature of divine intervention in the life of the nation. Religion, it was frequently argued, was an essential component of social harmony, civic virtue, and good government. Among the compilations of political sermons of this era are the edited collections of John Wingate Thornton, *The Pulpit of the American Revolution* (1860); Frank Moore, *The Patriot Preachers of the American Revolution, 1766-1783* (1860); and Ellis Sandoz, *Political Sermons of the American Founding Era, 1730-1805* (1991). Other excellent anthologies contain important political sermons, including the first volume of Bernard Bailyn's edited collection, *Pamphlets of the American Revolution, 1750-1776* (1965); and Charles S. Hyneman and Donald S. Lutz's two-volume edition of *American Political Writing during the Founding Era, 1760-1805* (1983).

Political sermons and similar writings of the era have also been the subjects of a rich library of secondary works. The literature reveals that a vibrant religious culture influenced the early republic and its institutions. It is difficult to overestimate the power of the pulpit in molding public opinion, shaping cultural values, and building social and political institutions. A selected bibliography of outstanding scholarship on the role of religion in the late colonial, revolutionary, and early national periods is provided at the end of this book.

Although Adams's sermon is the product of a later generation, its spirit and tone are very much in the tradition of the political sermons of the founding period. Moreover, it is principally concerned with the design and goals of the founders in creating a new arrangement for church-state relations. The sermon was written in the age of Andrew Jackson, but it focuses on the founding era.

Adams's sermon and the responses to it confirm that the relationship between religion and civil government was the subject of lively debate in the early republic. The material compiled here has been arranged to emphasize the content and intensity of that debate. An introductory essay seeks to place the sermon and the attendant discussion within a historical and intellectual context. This sets the stage for Adams's sermon, the centerpiece of the volume. The sermon and Adams's notes are accompanied by a bibliography of the major works cited by Adams. This is followed by letters written in response to the sermon and an unsigned review published in an 1835 edition of the *American Quarterly Review*. The review essay celebrates the Jeffersonian vision of a secular polity and enthusiastically endorses the separation of church and state. Adams's sermon and the review essay illustrate two sharply contrasting interpretations of the constitutional role of religion in American public life. The Epilogue reflects briefly on the principal themes of the collected documents and the continuing church-state debate in the United States. Four appendices provide background on the life and work of the Reverend Jasper Adams. Appendix 4, in particular, discusses the preparation, publication, and distribution of the sermon and identifies the many luminaries who, according to Adams's records, were sent a copy of the sermon. Finally, the Selected Bibliography offers a guide to leading literature on religion and church-state relations in American political culture.

If Justice Holmes was correct that "a page of history is worth a volume of logic," then there is great advantage in making frequent reference to our past. The church-state debate today is strikingly similar to that of the 1830s. The increasing secularization of American public life and the role of religion in a pluralistic society were concerns that dominated the debate then, as they do now. Thus, I hope that this unique collection of documents will cast light not only on the past but also on the future of church-state relations in the United States.

This book was made possible by the support of many individuals and institutions. Grants from the National Endowment for the Humanities and the Religion and Public Policy Research Fund enabled me to visit several archives in the summer of 1992. A Faculty Senate research award and a School of Public Affairs summer research stipend from the American University afforded me the time and resources to devote myself to this project.

I wish to acknowledge the courtesy and assistance of archivists, curators, and reference librarians at the College of Charleston Libraries, the South Caroliniana and Thomas Cooper Libraries at the University of South Carolina, the Franklin Trask Library at Andover Newton Theological School, the Howard-Tilton Memorial Library at Tulane University, the John Hay Library at Brown University, the University of Virginia Library, the Van Pelt Library at the University of Pennsylvania, the Warren Hunting Smith Library at Hobart and William Smith Colleges, Yale University Library, the

Office of the Secretary and Butler Library at Columbia University, the American Antiquarian Society, the Chicago Historical Society, the Massachusetts Historical Society, the New-York Historical Society, the South Carolina Historical Society, the Charleston Library Society, the Huntington Library, the New York Public Library, the South Carolina State Library, the State Library of Massachusetts, the South Carolina Department of Archives and History, the Massachusetts Archives at Columbia Point, the Pendleton District Commission, the Sumter County Museum, the National Archives and Records Administration, the Supreme Court of the United States, and the Library of Congress. I would be remiss if I did not also thank the staff of the Bender Library at the American University who handle interlibrary loan transactions, for their patience and good humor in processing my seemingly endless requests for obscure documents. Editors of the Adams family, Calhoun, Jackson, Madison, and Marshall papers kindly and promptly responded to my requests for information. J.C.A. Stagg and Charles F. Hobson, editors of the papers of James Madison and John Marshall respectively, provided valuable assistance in identifying and transcribing manuscripts. Above all, thanks are due to the William L. Clements Library at the University of Michigan for generous assistance and permission to print materials in their collection. In particular, I wish to express my appreciation to curator of books Richard W. Ryan for his help.

I am grateful for the support and advice of teachers, colleagues, and friends. A special thanks goes to Professor Thomas E. Buckley of Loyola Marymount University, an extraordinary scholar of church and state in colonial and revolutionary Virginia, who has been a source of wisdom for this project and my other research endeavors. Professor Buckley first suggested to me the idea for this book and encouraged me to see it through to completion. I am much indebted to Dr. James McClellan, who many years ago recognized the importance of the documents presented here and their place in American intellectual history. He generously shared with me his unpublished research on and analysis of the Adams manuscript and offered incisive suggestions on the project. My appreciation also extends to the staff of the University Press of Kentucky for their help and encouragement in bringing this volume to print. Professor Douglas Kries of Gonzaga University helped me decipher and translate lines from Latin. The project benefited from the contributions of Peter Byrd, Joyce Dreisbach, Dr. Peter B. Dreisbach, and Cliff Larsen. I am also grateful for the able research assistance of Megan Baksh, Dan Hofherr, Mary Kopczynski, Jordana Schmier, and Tad Stephenson.

The views expressed in the introduction, epilogue, and editorial notes, as well as any errors, are mine alone and should not be ascribed to the individuals and institutions whose assistance I acknowledge.

Finally, my deepest appreciation is reserved for my wife, Joyce Cowley, and daughter, Mollie Abigail, for their patience, encouragement, and endless good humor. They unselfishly gave up much so that this book could become a reality. It is dedicated to them.

NOTES

1. *New York Trust Co. v. Eisner,* 256 U.S. 345, 349 (1921). Although Justice Holmes was not addressing a religion clause controversy when he wrote this, several justices of the Supreme Court have noted that Holmes's aphorism is particularly relevant to this area of the law. See, for example, *Committee for Public Education and Religious Liberty v. Nyquist,* 413 U.S. 756, 777 n. 33 (1973) ("Our Establishment Clause precedents have recognized the special relevance in this area of Mr. Justice Holmes' comment that 'a page of history is worth a volume of logic'"); *Walz v. New York Tax Commission,* 397 U.S. 664, 675-76 (1970). See also *Kovacs v. Cooper,* 336 U.S. 77, 95 (1949) (Frankfurter, J.) ("In law also, doctrine is illuminated by history").

2. Letter from James Madison to Jasper Adams, Sept. 1833, reprinted below, p. 117.

3. See, for example, *Reynolds v. United States,* 98 U.S. 145, 162-64 (1878).

4. *Everson v. Board of Education,* 330 U.S. 1, 33-34 (1947) (Rutledge, J., dissenting).

NOTES ON THE TEXTS

Two editions of Jasper Adams's sermon were published in 1833 by the Charleston printer A.E. Miller. The first edition has fifty-six numbered pages, and the second reaches page 64 (the text of the second edition is actually sixty-two pages long, since page numbers 2 and 3 were skipped in an apparent printer's error). The few substantive differences in the editions are mainly in the copious notes attached to the printed sermon. The second edition is republished in its entirety in this book.

Bound into Adams's personal copy of the first edition are his handwritten notes detailing the preparation, revision, publication, and distribution of the sermon. This copy of the sermon is in the archives of the William L. Clements Library at the University of Michigan. The notes reveal that Adams consulted colleagues on various points addressed in the sermon and that he found their comments useful in revising the sermon for the second edition. He also recounted the manner in which the tract was distributed and, more important, to whom it was sent. Adams meticulously reproduced endorsements that were sent to prominent figures soliciting comments on the printed sermon. He copied in his own hand letters written to him in response to the sermon by Madison, Marshall, Story, and J.S. Richardson. These notes provide a valuable documentary record of the printed sermon and the national discussion it generated.

The documents compiled in this book have been lightly annotated. Translations of non-English phrases and the full names and titles of persons who may not be familiar to some readers are provided in brackets. Since emendations can become more of a distraction than a help, bracketed material has been kept to a minimum.

Adams's sermon and sermon notes have been edited to preserve their original style and character. Nineteenth-century typography, spelling, and punctuation are often confusing to the modern eye. Nevertheless, the original convention of punctuation, grammar, capitalization, italicization, and anglicized and archaic spelling have been, for the most part, retained. Obvious misspellings and typesetter's errors have been silently corrected. Most other changes to the original text, however, including the addition of punctuation marks, editorial comments, and translations, have been placed in brackets. Similar editorial considerations governed the preparation of the review essay and the letters of response.

The sermon notes, both footnotes and endnotes, are Adams's own. Superscript note references have been changed from assorted symbols—stars, daggers, and so on—to Arabic numerals. Adams's abbreviated and non-uniform citation style is unchanged. To assist the modern reader, however, a bibliography of many of the works cited by Adams is provided following the sermon notes.

Cross-references in Adams's sermon and notes and all page references to the sermon are to the second edition. The numbers in brackets following page references indicate parallel citations to the sermon in the present volume.

As was common in published works of the era, Adams occasionally interpolated his own words into quotations without closing and reopening quotation marks. Since this practice is usually obvious, no marks have been added. Wherever quotation marks or other punctuation marks were deemed necessary or helpful in conveying the writer's thoughts, though, they have been added in brackets. Adams occasionally added comments in quotations, usually enclosed in parentheses. In two instances, however, he used brackets; in order to avoid confusing Adams's emendations and the editor's, these brackets have been silently changed to parentheses.

In the course of the editorial process, the wording of most direct quotations was checked in the original sources. Adams silently edited some passages, and he made a few transcription errors. Quotations and citations, however, are reproduced here as they appear in the second edition of the sermon, correct or incorrect.

Reproducing Adams's handwritten notes and transcriptions of letters presented interesting challenges. Not only has the ink faded and the paper deteriorated since 1833, but also Adams's handwriting is at times nearly illegible. Paleographers with expertise in nineteenth-century script were consulted in an effort to ensure the accuracy of the transcription of notes and letters in Adams's hand. Also, editors of the Madison and Marshall papers reviewed the transcriptions of the Madison and Marshall letters respectively. They generously offered insight on each writer's manner of expression and writing style, provided information concerning the provenance of the letters, and shared unpublished notes in their files related to the letters.

A few words in the handwritten material remain undecipherable. After close examination of each letter in these words and the context in which the words were used, the best determination was made. Each doubtful reading is followed by a question mark in brackets.

All editorial decisions were governed by a desire to preserve the in-

tegrity and character of the original documents. The reader will note in-
consistencies in the texts, especially in the idiosyncratic spelling and use of
punctuation marks. The adherence to archaic conventions may at times be
distracting to a modern audience; however, this is the cost of producing
authentic replicas and transcriptions of documents with the minimum number of changes to the original texts.

INTRODUCTION

A Debate on Religion and Politics in the Early Republic

In February 1833 the Reverend Jasper Adams, president of the College of Charleston, delivered a sermon before the South Carolina Convention of the Protestant Episcopal Church. A published version of his address, entitled *The Relation of Christianity to Civil Government in the United States*, was distributed widely across the country.[1] The sermon and reactions to it by leading intellectuals of the era provide valuable insights into the historical understanding of the First Amendment religion provisions and the social and intellectual forces that shaped church-state relations in the founding era.

American history, Adams argued in his sermon, confirmed that religion—specifically Christianity—was the central pillar of social order and stability. He believed that if a nation and its people were to prosper, civil government must conform to basic Christian precepts and maintain a public and influential role for religion as the foundation of all civil, legal, and political institutions. He disavowed, however, the Old World pattern of formal, exclusive ecclesiastical establishment. He similarly rejected the invitation to create a secular political order. The First Amendment to the U.S. Constitution, he concluded, created an environment in which religion could flourish and inform public values. It merely proscribed legal preference for one religious sect over all others.

The colonial and early national periods were replete with political sermons addressing the nature of divine intervention in the life of the country.[2] Religion, speakers frequently argued, provided indispensable support for a free and stable society. Although Adams's sermon was but one contribution to this extensive body of literature addressing the relation between religion and civil government, it is noteworthy for several reasons.

First, Adams wrote a trenchant, thoroughly researched treatise that constitutes a significant contribution to constitutional scholarship. Its insights confirm that he was a sage observer of American politics and society, a scholar of philosophy, theology, history, and law who was endowed with great powers of foresight.[3] This remarkably prescient discourse anticipated the emergence of a dominant secular culture and the inevitable conflict with the formerly ascendant religious establishments. The sermon was among the first major polemics from the embattled religious traditionalists that through skillful use of legal and historical arguments controverted the secular political vision attributed to Thomas Jefferson. Adams's tract was recognized by contemporaries, as well as by subsequent commentators, as a learned and useful dissertation.[4]

Second, Adams was an eminent educator and moral philosopher who circulated in influential political and intellectual fora of his time. He was a member of the renowned Adams family of Massachusetts, whose contributions to the founding of the republic are well known. A graduate of Brown University (1815), he held faculty appointments at his alma mater and the U.S. Military Academy. Adams was also an ordained minister in the Protestant Episcopal Church, and at the time he delivered this sermon he was president of the College of Charleston, a post he held for a decade (1825–26, 1828–36).[5] As an acquaintance of many of the nation's leading intellectuals, including architects of the republic and its institutions, Adams was well placed to comment on the intentions of the individuals who drafted, enacted, and implemented the constitutional arrangement for church-state relations. Published in 1833, the sermon was written within living memory of the drafting of the First Amendment and, it could be argued, provides documentary evidence of the historical understanding of the religion clauses.

Third, perhaps most important, Adams circulated his tract among scores of leading intellectuals and statesmen of the day, including James Madison, John Quincy Adams, Andrew Jackson, Martin Van Buren, John Marshall, Roger B. Taney, Joseph Story, James Kent, John C. Calhoun, Henry Clay, Robert Y. Hayne, Richard M. Johnson, and Daniel Webster. The recipients were the nation's preeminent intellectuals, politicians, jurists, and clerics.[6] Adams requested some to comment on his thesis. Unpublished letters written in response to Adams's discourse, which Adams compiled and annexed to his personal copy of the sermon, provide a vivid portrait of early nineteenth-century thought on American church-state relations.[7] Of particular importance are the comments of former president Madison, who is generally credited with framing the First Amendment religion provisions, and the views of Chief Justice Marshall and Associate Justice Story, two eminent jurists whose legal opinions illuminated the meaning of the Constitution.[8]

In this essay I will analyze Adams's sermon, examine the discussion it promulgated, and set this exchange in the context of church-state debate in the early republic. The first part of the essay will review sources of church-state controversy at the time the sermon was written and developments that may have inspired Adams. Following this, I will briefly examine the arguments advanced in the sermon. Attention will then be focused on letters written in response to Adams's sermon by Madison, Marshall, and Story.

These documents, written more than a century ago, offer a unique and compelling commentary on influential interpretations of the First Amendment in the early national period.

CHURCH AND STATE IN THE AGE OF ANDREW JACKSON

The early 1830s was a turbulent era in South Carolina and, indeed, in the nation. The ascendancy of Jacksonian democracy and a rancorous nullification debate engendered political turmoil that threatened the very soul of the Union. The appropriate role of religion in society increasingly became a subject of public controversy. Adams perceived a destabilizing secular drift in American culture. A growing indifference toward, and a diminishing role for, religion were disconcerting to him. He lamented the sentiment, "gradually gaining belief among us, that Christianity has no connexion with the law of the land, or with our civil and political institutions."[9] Several controversies of a specifically religious nature, which Adams referenced in his sermon, attracted public attention in the late 1820s and early 1830s and may have inspired Adams to engage his state and nation in a debate on the relation of religion to civil government.

Jacksonian Democracy

The inauguration of Andrew Jackson as the seventh president of the United States in 1829 revived long-standing controversies of interest to organized religion. These issues were among the concerns addressed in Adams's sermon. With its emphasis on the "common man" and its ardent Americanism, Jacksonian democracy prompted a shift in ecclesiastical influence from clerics trained in the staunchly conservative, aristocratic, and staid Episcopal and Congregational Churches on the eastern seaboard to those in nonconformist, democratic, and evangelical congregations on the frontier, such as the Baptist, Methodist, and Western Presbyterian denominations. Members in the latter churches would eventually exercise great influence in shaping public policy and, more specifically, in sweeping away remaining vestiges of the old religious establishments.[10] Since the president was a champion of equalitarianism, Anson Phelps Stokes wrote, "[i]t was natural that Jackson should stoutly oppose special favors for any religious body, and that he should stand for the principle of strict separation of Church and State and of religious freedom, even to opposing the issuing of a Thanksgiving Day proclamation."[11] Jackson's opposition to the anti–Sunday mail campaign, coupled with his refusal to issue religious proclamations, led many to accuse him, like Jefferson before him, of being antireligious.[12] These developments arguably "assisted the growing secularization of society" and confirmed that a strictly religious ethos had a diminishing influence on social values.[13]

Disestablishment in Massachusetts

A noteworthy development of 1833 was the formal disestablishment of the Congregational Church in the old Puritan Commonwealth of Massachusetts.[14] This transition, which Adams noted in his sermon only in passing, may have sharpened his focus on church-state relations.[15] In 1831 the state legislature voted in favor of disestablishment, and two years later a constitutional amendment embodying the proposal was overwhelmingly ratified by the people.[16] Massachusetts was the last state, following Connecticut in 1818 and New Hampshire in 1819, to sever formal legal ties with an established church, and this development generated considerable debate concerning the appropriate relationship between ecclesiastical and civil authorities. Disestablishment was welcomed by Adams, who denounced legal preference for one form of Christianity over all others.[17] He was concerned, however, that discontinuation of legal preference for the formerly established church in his native state might be misinterpreted as a sign of indifference toward the Christian religion and its general claims in shaping social, civil, and political institutions.[18] The Christian religion in general, Adams believed, sustained civil institutions and was essential to social order and good government.

The Sunday Mail Controversy

The transportation and delivery of mail on Sundays was a source of recurring church-state controversy in the early nineteenth century. This practice heightened conservative Protestant fears about the rise of anti-Christian sentiment and the growing secularization of public life. It also brought into focus contrasting views of the appropriate relationship between civil government and religion. Religious traditionalists, on the one hand, emphasized the obligation of civil government to preserve and protect fundamental Christian institutions. Jacksonians, on the other hand, warned that acknowledgment by law of religious observances might invade liberty of conscience and foster a dangerous and entangling alliance between religious and political institutions.

Ancient English and colonial laws that imposed restraints on Sunday travel were at the root of the Sunday mail controversy.[19] Variant forms of these laws survived well into the nineteenth century, creating problems for the U.S. government in mail delivery. The issue, as it affected postal services, was addressed in a congressional act of 30 April 1810. The statute required postmasters "at all reasonable hours, on every day of the week, to deliver, on demand, any letter, paper or packet, to the person entitled to or authorized to receive the same."[20] Before the passage of this legislation, no uniform policy governed Sunday business in U.S. post offices. Although no affront to the Christian community was intended, the statute set off an avalanche of protests and petitions from a multitude of religious leaders, denominations, and citizens' committees demanding legislation to discontinue Sunday postal operations. Petitions were generally referred to the postmaster general, but Congress was eventually moved to report on the issue. In 1815 both the Senate and the House of Representatives resolved that it would be "inexpedient" to grant the request of the petitioners to prohibit postal services on Sunday.[21]

The controversy subsided for a decade and then exploded in the late 1820s. In March 1825 Congress enacted legislation reaffirming postal obligations spelled out in the 1810 law.[22] Once again, Congress was inundated with petitions and counterpetitions revealing strong sentiment on all sides of the issue.[23] On 19 January 1829 Senator Richard M. Johnson of Kentucky, chairman of the Senate Committee on Post Offices and Post Roads, released a report setting forth fundamental reasons why it would be inappropriate for the U.S. government to yield to demands of religious traditionalists to disallow Sunday mail. Senator Johnson, who later served as vice-president of the United States under Martin Van Buren (1837–41), argued that proposed legislation to stop the mails on Sunday "was improper, and that nine hundred and ninety-nine in a thousand were opposed to any legislative interference, inasmuch as it would have a tendency to unite religious institutions with the government." He further opined "that these petitions and memorials in relation to Sunday mails, were but the entering wedge of a scheme to make this government a religious, instead of a social and political, institution."[24] Jacksonian democrats and liberal groups embraced the report as a reasoned and eloquent affirmation of religious liberty and church-state separation.[25] To detractors, however, the report confirmed the triumph of political atheism and secularism endorsed by the Jackson Administration.[26]

The report was a classic defense of church-state separation and a powerful manifesto for a secular political order:

If kept within its legitimate sphere of action, no injury can result from its [Sunday] observance. It should, however, be kept in mind, that the proper object of government is, to protect all persons in the enjoyment of their religious, as well as civil rights; and not to determine for any, whether they shall esteem one day above another, or esteem all days alike holy.

We are aware, that a variety of sentiment exists among the good citizens of this nation, on the subject of the Sabbath day; and our government is designed for the protection of one, as much as for another. . . . With these different religious views, the committee are of opinion that Congress cannot interfere. It is not the legitimate province of the legislature to determine what religion is true, or what is false. Our government is a civil, and not a religious, institution. Our constitution recognises in every person, the right to choose his own religion, and to enjoy it freely, without molestation. Whatever may be the religious sentiments of citizens, and however variant, they are alike entitled to protection from the government, so long as they do not invade the rights of others. . . .

Extensive religious combinations, to effect a political objective, are, in the opinion of the committee, always dangerous. . . .

Let the national legislature once perform an act which involves the decision of a religious controversy, and it will have passed its legitimate bounds. The precedent will then be established, and the foundation laid for that usurpation of the Divine prerogative in this country, which has been the desolating scourge to the fairest portions of the old world. Our Constitution recognises no other power than that of persuasion, for enforcing religious observances. Let the professors of Christianity recommend their religion by deeds of benevolence—by Christian meekness— by lives of temperance and holiness. . . . Their moral influence will then do infinitely more to advance the true interests of religion, than any measures which they may call on Congress to enact.[27]

The report provoked lively debate in the chambers of Congress. The most ardent opponents of Johnson's secular vision were Senator Theodore Frelinghuysen of New Jersey and Representative William McCreery of Pennsylvania. McCreery drafted a minority report, released on 5 March 1830, that outlined the themes of the anti–Sunday mail campaign:

All Christian nations acknowledge the first day of the week, to be the Sabbath. Almost every State in this Union has, by positive legislation, not only recognized this day as sacred, but has forbidden its profanation under penalties imposed by law.

It was never considered, by any of those States, as an encroachment upon the rights of conscience, or as an improper interference with the opinions of the few, to guard the sacredness of that portion of time acknowledged to be holy by the many.

The petitioners ask not Congress to expound the moral law; they ask not Congress to meddle with theological controversies, much less to interfere with the rights of the Jew or the Sabbatarian, or to treat with the least disrespect the religious feelings of any portion of the inhabitants of the Union; they ask the introduction of no religious coercion into our civil institutions; no blending of religion and civil affairs; but they do ask that the agents of Government, employed in the Post Office Department, may be permitted to enjoy the same opportunities of attending to moral and religious instruction, or intellectual improvement, on that day, which is enjoyed by the rest of their fellow citizens.[28]

An even more articulate defense of the conservative, evangelical Protestant position was offered by Senator Frelinghuysen on 8 May 1830 in a celebrated speech on the Senate floor.[29] Despite these efforts, Senator Johnson's view ultimately prevailed, and the campaign to prevent the Sunday mails failed.[30]

Adams was a staunch advocate of laws preserving Sabbath observances.[31] In his sermon notes, he echoed the conservative Protestant position that postal service policy revealed an anti-Christian bias and diminished the role of religion in public life. He objected to the Sunday mail legislation because "[i]t employs some thousands in desecrating and destroying an institution peculiar to Christianity." Indeed, Adams described it as "the first statute enacted by Congress, authorizing and requiring a violation of the religion of the country."[32] Recognition of the Christian Sabbath in the public calendar was important to religious traditionalists like Adams, because it "furnished one of the strongest proofs that the United States was truly a Christian nation."[33] Moreover, from Adams's perspective, the controversy symbolized the Jackson Administration's alleged hostility toward traditional religion and the efforts to strip the public arena of stabilizing religious influences. These fundamental concerns prompted Adams's sermon.

A Christian Party in Politics

The propriety and constitutionality of Christian political activism was the subject of rancorous debate in the late 1820s and early 1830s. The defeat of the anti–Sunday mail campaign strengthened the conviction of many religious citizens that infidelity and radical secularism had gained ascendancy in national politics under a banner of liberal political reform. This was a bitter reversal for religious traditionalists who believed that the United States was a Christian nation, and it impressed upon them the urgency of mobilizing all their resources, including a potential army of conservative Christian voters and partisan activists, to save the country from political atheism and to reestablish Christian values and morality in public life.

The Reverend Ezra Stiles Ely (1786–1861), an influential Presbyterian clergyman in Philadelphia, addressed the role of Christians in politics in a Fourth of July oration in 1827.[34] In a discourse entitled "The Duty of Christian Freemen to Elect Christian Rulers," Ely proposed "a new sort of union," which he called "a Christian party in politics."[35] It was not entirely clear what he meant by this phrase.[36] He described an electoral alliance composed of "three or four of the most numerous denominations of Christians in the United States," including Presbyterians, Baptists, Methodists, and Congregationalists.[37] Ely also allowed that the Protestant Episcopal Church, as well as the Lutheran and Dutch Reformed Churches, could add to this informal political union.[38] But this was a party without strict political or sectarian definition and without membership rolls or subscriptions.[39] Rather, Ely envisioned a loose coalition of Christian activists, transcending sectarian lines, united to elect moral candidates for public office and to restore Christian values in a society awash in a sea of infidelity. This was a reform movement, spiritual in its mission and socially conservative in its policies, formed voluntarily by pious citizens "adopting, avowing, and determining to act upon, truly religious principles in all civil matters."[40] The immediate goal was to give a coherent political voice and electoral clout to conservative, evangelical Protestants.

Ely's proposal rested on the premise that every citizen—"from the highest to the lowest," both ruler and ruled—"ought to serve the Lord with fear, and yield his sincere homage to the Son of God."[41] The religious criteria by which Ely measured fitness for public office were clearly identified: "Every ruler *should be* an avowed and a sincere friend of Christianity. He should know and believe the doctrines of our holy religion, and act in conformity with its precepts. . . . [O]ur civil rulers ought to act a religious part in all the relations which they sustain."[42]

Having established the duty of civil rulers to serve the Lord, Ely argued that righteous citizens had the duty "to honour the Lord Jesus Christ and promote christianity by electing and supporting as public officers the friends" of Christ. Accordingly, "every Christian who has the right and the opportunity of exercising the elective franchise ought to do it," Ely counseled.[43] He acknowledged that many pious constituents were disillusioned, even disgusted, by politics and thus relinquished their right to vote; but "[i]f all *good men* are to absent themselves from elections, then the *bad* will have the entire transaction of our public business."[44] If morality in public life is to be restored, he concluded, then all righteous citizens must be "Christian politicians," and "as conscientiously religious at the polls as in the pulpit, or house of worship."[45] Ely exhorted all who professed to be Christians to "unite and co-operate with *our Christian party*" and, in so doing, to "agree that they will support no man as a candidate for any office, who is not professedly friendly to Christianity, and a believer in divine Revelation."[46] He entreated Christians to "abstain from supporting by their suffrages" candidates given to Sabbath-breaking, intemperance, profane swearing, adultery, debauchery, lewdness, gambling, and profligate living.[47] "Let us never support by our votes any immoral man, or any known contemner of any of the fundamental doctrines of Christ, for any office: and least of all for the Presidency of these United States. . . . We are a Christian nation: we have a right to demand that all our rulers in their conduct shall conform to Christian morality; and if they do not, it is the duty and privilege of Christian freemen to make a new and a better election."[48] If pious citizens would unite on voting day, he argued, they could by sheer weight of numbers dominate every public election in America.[49]

Ely's proposal drew immediate and vehement denunciation from liberal religionists (including Unitarians and Universalists), skeptics, rationalists, and freethinkers.[50] It was attacked as an undemocratic expression of religious intolerance and bigotry that threatened to extinguish civil and religious liberties and to Christianize every aspect of public life. Some critics described it as a Presbyterian plot to organize evangelical sects into a special-interest political bloc that would subject the secular state to ecclesiastical domination.[51] Adversaries of the "Christian party" were urged to unite in opposition to "the disciplined forces of the enemy," lest, in the words of one critic, "the unprecedented efforts which are now employed, will ultimately succeed in the utter subversion of all the principles of civil and religious liberty."[52] Describing himself "as a sentinel upon the watch-tower of liberty," Universalist minister William Morse denounced the "theological tyrants" who "are always studying to extend their influence by seeking alliance with the civil power, and debasing the human mind, in order to accomplish their ends." Political liberty and the right of suffrage, he warned, would be little more than "a name to such as belonged not to the union, if five of the most popular religious sects in this country should unite, and succeed in getting the reins of government into their own hands."[53] Zelotes Fuller similarly warned of "a deep and artful scheme" that, if consummated, would "tend to infuse the spirit of religious intolerance and persecution into the political institutions of our country, and in the end, completely to annihilate the political and religious liberty of the people." Fuller, a Universalist, called on enlightened and intelligent patriots to "speedily and vigorously" oppose this plan.[54] He urged them

to repel every encroachment upon your sacred rights and privileges—to see that the equal rights of conscience—the freedom of religious opinion—the provisions and the spirit of the constitutions of the political government of our country, are never trampled in the dust, by bigotry, fanaticism, or superstition. Let not the base spirit, of civil and religious intolerance, that bane of our free institutions and misfortune of our country, ever receive from you the least encouragement. Forbid that clerical ambition should ever obtain a leading influence in the political councils of the nation. Keep down that spirit, where it ought to be kept, *in silence and darkness,* that would overthrow the liberty of our country, and establish on its ruins an ecclesiastical hierarchy. Crush the demon of tyranny in the very embryo of his existence. Certain it is, that you *now* have power to do this, and it is no less certain, that it is your imperious *duty* to do it.

Never I beseech of you, encourage a certain *"Christian party in politics,"* which under moral and religious pretences, is officiously and continually interfering with the religious opinions of others, and endeavouring to effect by law and other means, equally exceptionable, a systematic course of measures, evidently calculated, to lead to a union of Church and State. If a union of church and state should be effected, which may God avert, then will the doctrines of the prevailing sect, become the creed of the country, to be enforced by fines, imprisonment, and doubtless death! Then will superstition and bigotry frown into silence, everything which bears the appearance of liberality; the hand of genius will be palsied, and a check to all further improvements in our country, will be the inevitable consequence. If we now permit the glorious light of liberty to be extinguished, it may never more shine to cheer a benighted world with the splendour of its rays.[55]

Much criticism of the "Christian party in politics" extended far beyond Ely's specific and limited suggestions. Liberal religionists and secularists used his discourse to denounce the political stirrings of conservative Protestants as evidenced by the "Christian party" and the anti–Sunday mail campaign. To critics, these developments represented an intolerance that threatened nascent secular interpretations of freedom of conscience and church-state separation.

Ely anticipated and answered the principal criticisms of his proposal. He disavowed, for example, the establishment of any religious sect by law and denied vehemently that his proposal transgressed the rights of conscience, violated the constitutional ban on religious tests, or promoted a union of church and state.[56] "Are Christians," he asked, "the only men in the community who may not be guided by their judgment, conscience, and choice, in electing their rulers?" He responded, "Christians have the same rights and privileges in exercising the elective franchise" as are "accorded to Jews and Infidels."[57] Although he acknowledged that Christianity may not be "a constitutional test of admission to office," Ely argued that Christians retained the right in casting their ballots to "prefer the avowed friends of the Christian religion to Turks, Jews, and Infidels."[58] He saw no constitutional impediment to Christians exercising their political liberty to support Christian candidates and causes by their votes, just as infidels had the political liberty to support anti-Christian candidates and measures.[59]

The national furor sparked by Ely's suggestion did not subside for decades, and it nourished the suspicion of many that Presbyterian clerics were "attempting to control the state to further their own schemes" and to exclude non-Christians from full participation in the political process.[60] The impact of Ely's plan was contrary to that which was intended. Not only did the cohesive electoral bloc Ely envisioned never materialize, but also the proposal unified and energized opponents of orthodox Protestant influence in secular politics. The idea of a "Christian party" marked the decline of traditional religious influence in society. It confirmed that a Christian ethic was no longer shared by all in public life; rather, Christians were just one more partisan pressure group competing with others in the political arena for the allegiance of the American electorate.[61]

Although Adams did not expressly comment on Ely's "Christian party," he was undoubtedly aware of the debate it generated. The delicate constitutional issues raised by Ely's proposal were intertwined with other church-state controversies of the day and tested the constitutional limits of participation by religious citizens in the political system. Adams's sermon, like Ely's "Christian party" and the anti–Sunday mail campaign, was the product of conservative Protestant consternation with the growing secularization of public life.

The Thomas Cooper Controversy

Perhaps the most direct inspiration for Adams's convention sermon is found in "the momentous events of 1832 [that] combined to make this particular year one of the most confused and exciting in South Carolina's history."[62] The bitter nullification controversy came to a head when opposing conventions met in Columbia late in the year. Conspicuously entangled in this debate was the aged controversialist Thomas Cooper (1759–1839), president of South Carolina College and "one of the best known figures in South Carolina."[63] He was a zealous, indeed radical, advocate of laissez-faire principles, free trade, states' rights and decentralization, slavery, and other causes that came to be known as the South Carolina Doctrines.[64]

Cooper was also an unabashed critic of orthodox Christianity and, like his old friend Thomas Jefferson, contemptuous of the Presbyterian clergy.[65] He denounced state support for religious practices and observances and denied that America was in any legal sense a Christian nation.[66] Staunch opponents of Cooper's political campaign for states' rights conveniently "aligned themselves with his vocal religious critics, and when the attack [on Cooper's putative leadership of the nullification campaign] came it was almost entirely of a religious nature, even though it was to a large degree political in motivation."[67] Cooper, for his part, energetically joined the fray with even greater invective against the clergy and church doctrine.[68] The cynical injection of Cooper's religious views into the nullification debate was incendiary, and the ensuing melee brought the state to "the verge of civil war."[69]

A motion to remove Cooper from the college presidency was introduced in the state legislature by his opponents in 1831. Among the charges leveled against him were that "[h]e had interfered with the religious opinions of his students, taught them doctrines highly offensive to parents and guardians, and had sneered at observance of the Sabbath, public prayers, and certain religious sects."[70] During public hearings in the state house in December 1832, Cooper vigorously defended his right under the state constitution to profess and maintain his controversial religious and political opinions.[71] He escaped dismissal by the legislature, but his standing in the state was sufficiently eroded that he was soon forced to resign.

With its profound implications for academic freedom and religious liberty, the Cooper controversy undoubtedly touched Jasper Adams in Charleston.[72] It is difficult to imagine that Adams, who composed and delivered his convention address during the tumultuous days of the Cooper affair, was not inspired, in part at least, by this unprecedented statewide debate on religious liberty and the uneasy relationship between church and state.[73]

Christianity and the Common Law

Adams was also moved by a long-simmering debate that flared up in the late 1820s and early 1830s on whether Christianity was a part of the common law. This issue went to the very heart of Adams's thesis that Christianity was a fundamental component of American law. Adams recognized the implications of this debate and used his sermon to issue a public opinion on the subject.

The principal discussants in this debate were Thomas Jefferson and Joseph Story. The former argued with irreverent flourish "that Christianity neither is, nor ever was, a part of the common law," while the latter maintained that "[t]here never has been a period in which the common law did not recognize Christianity as lying at its foundations."[74] Adams, aligned with Story, repudiated Jefferson's unorthodox view.[75] In his sermon he scrutinized constitutional, statutory, and case law, as well as published commentaries on the subject, affirming that in adopting the common law of England the American people had made Christianity part of their fundamental law.[76] Adams and fellow conservatives complained bitterly that Jefferson's vision of a secular polity "was never accredited until Jefferson gave it currency, executed it in Virginia, and read it into the United States Constitution."[77] They lamented that Jefferson's radical doctrine emboldened like-minded successors, especially Andrew Jackson, to eschew public prayers, fast day proclamations, religious oaths, Sabbath day observances, and other manifestations of a Christian nation.[78]

In a private letter to the English radical John Cartwright, which Cartwright published in England and which shortly thereafter appeared in American papers, Jefferson argued that the widely held belief among English and American lawyers that Christianity was a part of the common law was a "judiciary forgery" promulgated by a mistranslation in Sir Henry Finch's magnum opus on the common law.[79] Finch (1558–1625) had cited an earlier opinion written in Norman French by Sir John Prisot (d. 1460), Chief Justice of the Common Pleas. Prisot said it was proper to give credence to such laws as the people of the Holy Church have in "ancient scripture," for this is common law on which all manner of laws are founded.[80] Jefferson alleged that Finch erroneously construed *ancien scripture* as *holy scripture,* or the Holy Bible, whereas the term should have been translated as the ancient "written laws of the church."[81] According to Jefferson, this led Finch to conclude falsely that church law, having warrant in Christian scriptures, was accredited by the common law of England. Finch argued, in short, that the common law incorporated the Christian scriptures, and nothing in the common law was valid that was not consistent with divine revelation. As Jefferson saw it, however, the issue addressed by Prisot was not whether Christianity was a part of common law of England, but rather to what extent ecclesiastical law was to be recognized and enforced (given faith and credit) by the common law courts.[82] Jefferson proceeded to trace Finch's "error" through Sir Matthew Hale, Sir William Blackstone, Lord Mansfield, and other English jurists, who gave this new doctrine respectability, and finally to its transmission to America.

Jefferson's rejection of the virtually undisputed connection between Christianity and the common law confirmed to his detractors that he was an infidel, contemptuous of established judicial, legal, and religious authority that uniformly recognized the Christian basis of the common law. More important, his thesis undermined the acknowledgment of Christian precepts in law and public policy and arguably accelerated the secularization of public life. Jefferson's argument, in short, challenged the notion that America was in any legal sense a Christian nation.

Jefferson defiantly concluded the Cartwright letter with a provocative invitation to any lawyer "to produce another scrip of authority for this judiciary forgery."[83] Conservative jurists and religious traditionalists, mindful of Jefferson's influence and the radical implications of his theory for American church-state relations, were eager to expose his sophistry. Justice Story took up the challenge, demolishing Jefferson's thesis in a published opinion in the *American Jurist and Law Magazine.*[84] After consulting English authorities, Story concluded that Jefferson's commentary was "so manifestly erroneous" that it could only be regarded as a willful "mistake."[85] Story argued that Prisot, the authority cited by Finch, had referred to a superior law, having a foundation in nature or divine appointment, and not merely to an ancient written code of the Church, as Jefferson contended. Clearly, it would be absurd to say that Prisot meant that the positive code of the Church was the foundation of *all* human laws. It was the common law, which recognized revealed religion, upon which all manner of laws were founded.[86] Thus, the more plausible translation was Finch's, which held that the common law credited the Holy Scriptures and professed to be built upon them.

Adams cited with approval Story's rebuttal of Jefferson's thesis.[87] Unlike Story, however, Adams drew on American case law and concluded that it provided additional authorities refuting Jefferson's theory. Adams quoted "with an unsparing hand" from New York judge James Kent's precedent-setting opinion in the 1811 blasphemy case of *People v. Ruggles,* and from the influential 1824 opinion of the Supreme Court of Pennsylvania in *Updegraph v. Commonwealth.*[88] These and other cases affirmed the proposition that general Christianity is and always has been a part of the common law.[89] Clearly, this debate touched the very core of Adams's thesis, and while more immediate events may have encouraged Adams in his enterprise, none framed the issue at hand more succinctly and none moved him more passionately.[90]

JASPER ADAMS ON THE RELATION OF CHRISTIANITY TO CIVIL GOVERNMENT

Jasper Adams was a devout Christian whose principal interest was to preserve the traditional influence of Christian morality in American public life. The belief promulgated by alleged adversaries of "Christian Truth," such as Jefferson, "that Christianity has no connexion with the law of the land, or with our civil and political institutions . . . is considered by me," Adams wrote, "to be in contradiction to the whole tenor of our history, to be false in fact, and in the highest degree pernicious in its tendency, to all our most valuable institutions, whether social, legal, civil or political."[91] He lamented the growing indifference of his country toward the public observance of and reverence for Christianity. Adams was convinced that religion could not flourish without the support of civil government, nor could civil government be sustained absent the indispensable support of religious principle.[92]

An inescapable premise of Adams's discourse is that no state of ancient or modern times has ever prospered unless it was built on a religious foundation.[93] Moreover, the American experience, he argued, demonstrated that a free government could not long endure unless Christianity was acknowledged as the cornerstone of its fundamental law. Christian principles and morals in a general, nondenominational sense provided the foundation upon which a stable civil government must be built. Significantly, however, Adams disavowed the Old World pattern of religious establishment in which one particular form of Christianity was given legal preference over all others.[94] Such church-state unions, he conceded, had "given rise to flagrant abuses and gross corruptions."[95]

In their state and federal constitutions, Adams wrote, Americans seized the opportunity to introduce profound changes in church-state relations.[96] By the time of independence, the American people were convinced of "the impolicy of a further union of Church and State *according to the ancient mode.*"[97] Thus, virtually "all the States in framing their new constitutions of government, either silently or by direct enactment, discontinued the ancient connexion."[98]

Having rejected the ancient model of exclusive ecclesiastical establishment, Adams observed,

A question of great interest here comes up for discussion. In thus discontinuing
the connexion between Church and Commonwealth;—did the people of these
States intend to renounce all connexion with the Christian religion? Or did they
only intend to disclaim all preference of one sect of Christians over another, as far
as civil government was concerned; while they still retained the Christian religion
as the foundation of all their social, civil and political institutions?[99]

Clearly, answered Adams, the American people adopted the latter position.
In any case, he believed the answers to these questions were of vital importance "to the religion, the morals, the peace, the intelligence, and in fact, to
all the highest interests of this country."[100]

According to Adams, "[t]he originators and early promoters of the
discovery and settlement of this continent, had the propagation of Christianity before their eyes, as one of the principal objects of their undertaking."[101] Colonial charters abound with the sentiment that the Christian
religion was intended by pious forefathers to be the cornerstone of the social
and political structures they created.[102] Adams reported that all twenty-four
state constitutions at the time, nourished by this colonial heritage, recognized "Christianity as the well known and well established religion of the communities."[103] This historical survey, Adams concluded, confirms that "THE
PEOPLE OF THE UNITED STATES HAVE RETAINED THE CHRISTIAN RELIGION
AS THE FOUNDATION OF THEIR CIVIL, LEGAL AND POLITICAL INSTITU-
TIONS; WHILE THEY HAVE REFUSED TO CONTINUE A LEGAL PREFERENCE
TO ANY ONE OF ITS FORMS OVER ANY OTHER. In the same spirit of practical wisdom, moreover, they have consented to tolerate all other religions."[104]

The "Constitution of the United States was formed directly for political, and not for religious objects," Adams conceded. Thus, "it contains
but slight references of a religious kind."[105] However, by dating the instrument "in the year of our Lord, 1787," and by excepting Sunday in the ten
days in which a president may consider a veto, the people of the United
States "professed themselves to be a Christian nation."[106] The First Amendment, he continued,

leaves the entire subject [of religion] in the same situation in which it found it; and
such was precisely the most suitable course. The people of the United States having, in this most solemn of all their enactments, professed themselves to be a Christian nation; and having expressed their confidence, that all employed in their service
will practice the duties of the Christian faith;—and having, moreover, granted to all
others the free exercise of their religion, have emphatically declared, that Congress
shall make no change in the religion of the country. This was too delicate and too

important a subject to be entrusted to their guardianship. It is the duty of Congress, then, to permit the Christian religion to remain in the same state in which it was, at the time when the Constitution was adopted. They have no commission to destroy or injure the religion of the country. Their laws ought to be consistent with its principles and usages. They may not rightfully enact any measure or sanction any practice calculated to diminish its moral influence, or to impair the respect in which it is held among the people.[107]

The soundness of his view, Adams insisted, was confirmed by the historic recognition of and reverence for the Christian religion in public life:

The public authorities both in our State and National Governments, have always felt it to be required of them, to respect the peculiar institutions of Christianity. . . . From the first settlement of this country up to the present time, particular days have been set apart by public authority, to acknowledge the favour, to implore the blessing, or to deprecate the wrath of Almighty God. In our Conventions and Legislative Assemblies, daily Christian worship has been customarily observed. All business proceedings in our Legislative halls and Courts of justice, have been suspended by universal consent on Sunday. Christian Ministers have customarily been employed to perform stated religious services in the Army and Navy of the United States. In administering oaths, the Bible, the standard of Christian truth is used, to give additional weight and solemnity to the transaction. A respectful observance of Sunday, which is peculiarly a Christian institution, is required by the laws of nearly all, perhaps of all the respective States. My conclusion, then, is sustained by the documents which gave rise to our colonial settlements, by the records of our colonial history, by our Constitutions of government made during and since the Revolution, by the laws of the respective States, and finally by the uniform practice which has existed under them.[108]

Adams thus aligned himself with jurist Joseph Story. Citing Story's recently published *Commentaries on the Constitution of the United States* (1833), Adams contended that the First Amendment adopted the common law definition of *establishment:* "The meaning of the term 'establishment' in this amendment unquestionably is, the preference and establishment given by law to one sect of Christians over every other."[109] The First Amendment nonestablishment clause, in short, proscribed Congress from giving any religious sect or denomination a preferred legal status or conferring upon one church special favors and advantages that are denied others. This provision, however, was not meant to silence religion or restrict its influence in society. To the contrary, Adams argued, the amendment created an environment in which religion could flourish and inform the public ethic.

Adams feared that Jefferson's vision of a secular polity, in which Christianity received "no regard and no countenance from our civil institutions," would "tend to degrade [Christianity] and to destroy its influence among the community." This, in turn, would prove detrimental to our national standing. "Christianity," he wrote, "has been the chief instrument by which the nations of Christendom have risen superior to all other nations;—but if its influence is once destroyed or impaired, society instead of advancing, must infallibly retrograde."[110] Adams further cautioned "that if our religion is once undermined, it will be succeeded by a decline of public and private morals, and by the destruction of those high and noble qualities of character, for which as a community we have been so much distinguished[.]"[111] The preservation of Christian moral influence, therefore, was essential to social order and stability. In short, "[n]o power less efficacious than Christianity, can permanently maintain the public tranquillity of the country, and the authority of law. We must be a Christian nation, if we wish to continue a free nation."[112]

Adams believed, as did many religious traditionalists of the day, that if religion is denied "the sustaining aid of the civil Constitutions and law of the country," then religion's influence in the community will be destroyed.[113] On this point Jefferson and Madison could not have disagreed with Adams more strenuously. They believed, in contrast, that true and genuine religion flourished in the marketplace of ideas; and there was little warrant for the fear that without the support of civil government, religion would decline and cease to buttress social order and good government. "[T]ruth," Jefferson argued in his celebrated Bill for Establishing Religious Freedom, "is great and will prevail if left to herself."[114] Madison similarly rejected Adams's position "that Religion, if left to itself, will suffer from a failure" of public pecuniary aid.[115] It is a contradiction, Madison noted, to argue that discontinuing state support for Christianity will precipitate its demise, since "this Religion both existed and flourished, not only without the support of human laws, but in spite of every opposition from them." Moreover, a religion not invented by human machinations must have preexisted and been sustained before state subsidy. If Christianity depends on the support of civil government, then the pious confidence of the faithful in its "innate excellence and the patronage of its Author" will be undermined.[116] The best and purest religion, Madison thus concluded, relies on the spontaneous, voluntary support of the devoted and eschews all corrupting endorsements of the state.[117]

Adams did not describe the precise nature and scope of governmental aid for religion that he thought appropriate. Significantly, however, he drew a distinction, profound in its day, between an exclusive sectarian establishment and a public acknowledgment of nondenominational Christianity as the foundation of civil institutions. He denounced the former and espoused the latter. He also rejected Jefferson's invitation to erect a "wall of separation between Church and State."[118] Adams believed that Jefferson's secular vision manifested an indifference toward the faith that Americans had professed and cherished since the discovery and settlement of the continent. The American people, he argued, had declined both the ancient model of exclusive establishment and Jefferson's "wall of separation." Instead, "[t]hey wisely chose," in Adams terms, "the middle course." The American people "rightly considered their religion as the highest of all their interests, and refused to render it in any way or in any degree, subject to governmental interference or regulations. Thus, while all others enjoy full protection in the profession of their opinions and practice, Christianity is the established religion of the nation, its institutions and usages are sustained by legal sanctions, and many of them are incorporated with the fundamental law of the country."[119] This was the vision Adams celebrated—a vision he found embodied in state constitutions and the First Amendment. This was America's inheritance and, as Adams saw it, the only course for a free and united people.

A Debate on Church and State

Adams solicited and received responses to his sermon. Letters from prominent correspondents provide insight into the constitutional provisions governing church-state relations. The most noteworthy preserved responses to the sermon came from James Madison, John Marshall, and Joseph Story. The Story and Madison letters are among these authors' most perceptive pronouncements on a delicate constitutional matter. The views of these men are significant, since Madison has long been recognized as the Father of the Bill of Rights, and Marshall and Story are among the most venerated jurists in American history. The Story letter, on the one hand, and the Madison letter, on the other, present two contrasting interpretations of the distinctively American doctrine of church-state relations. The Madison letter articulated a separationist church-state position, while the Story letter argued that religion was an essential support for good government and that it must inform the public ethic. Significantly, these contrasting views persist in the modern church-state debate.

Affirming Adams's thesis, Chief Justice Marshall declared: "One great object of the colonial charters was avowedly the propagation of the Christian faith. Means have been employed to accomplish this object, & those means have been used by government."[120] Marshall concluded his brief address of courtesy with a qualified endorsement of Adams's discourse:

No person, I believe, questions the importance of religion to the happiness of man even during his existence in this world. It has at all times employed his most serious meditation, & had a decided influence on his conduct. The American population is entirely Christian, & with us, Christianity & Religion are identified. It would be strange, indeed, if with such a people, our institutions did not presuppose Christianity, & did not often refer to it, & exhibit relations with it. Legislation on the subject is admitted to require great delicacy, because fredom [sic] of conscience & respect for our religion both claim our most serious regard. You have allowed their full influence to both.[121]

Justice Story was more effusive in his praise for Adams's dissertation. "I have read it with uncommon satisfaction," he wrote, "& think its tone & spirit excellent."[122] He then reiterated the position articulated in his recently published *Commentaries:*

My own private judgement has long been, (& every day's experience more & more confirms me in it,) that government can not long exist without an alliance with religion *to some extent;* & that Christianity is indispensable to the true interests & solid foundations of all free governments. I distinguish, as you do, between the establishment of a particular sect, as the Religion of the State, & the Establishment of Christianity itself, without any preference of any particular form of it. I know not, indeed, how any deep sense of moral obligation or accountableness can be expected to prevail in the community without a firm persuasion of the great Christian Truths promulgated in your South Carolina constitution of 1778. I look with no small dismay upon the rashness & indifference with which the American People seem in our day to be disposed to cut adrift from old principles, & to trust themselves to the theories of every wild projector in to [?] religion & politics.[123]

Story could not resist taking a swipe at Jefferson, his old nemesis on sensitive church-state issues:

M^r. Jefferson has, with his accustomed boldness, denied that Christianity is a part of the common Law, & D^r. [Thomas] Cooper has with even more dogmatism, maintained the same opinion. I am persuaded, that a more egregious error never was uttered by able men. And I have long desired to find leisure to write a dissertation to establish this conclusion. Both of them rely on authorities & expositions which are wholly inadmissible. And I am surprised, that no one has as yet exposed the shallowness of their enquiries. Both of them have probably been easily drawn into the maintenance of such a doctrine by their own skepticism. It is due to truth, & to the purity of the Law, to unmask their fallacies.[124]

In closing, Story raised the specter of encroaching apostasy, presumably promulgated by Jefferson and Cooper, that he feared threatened Christian truth: "These are times in which the friends of Christianity are required to sound the alarm, & to inculcate sound principles. I fear that infidelity is make [sic] rapid progress under the delusive guise of the freedom of religious opinion & liberty of conscience."[125]

Madison, then in his eighty-third year and afflicted with chronic rheumatism that rendered his "hands & fingers, as averse to the pen as they are awkward in the use of it," was the last to respond.[126] Despite the former president's advanced age, his faculties were undiminished, and his thoughtful response reflected an abiding interest in the subject to which he had devoted so much of his public life. Interestingly, Madison marked his frank and informal epistle "private"; thus, as Adrienne Koch concluded, it "cannot . . . be interpreted as a stance taken for public notice."[127]

The simple but critical question, as Madison saw it, was "whether a support of the best & purest religion, the Christian Religion itself, ought not, so far at least as pecuniary means are involved, to be provided for by the Government, rather than be left to the voluntary provisions of those who profess it."[128] Although he conceded the difficulty in delineating the appropriate jurisdictions of church and state, Madison adopted a separationist stance in this last of his major pronouncements on church-state relations, unapologetically dissenting from Adams's thesis and the views of Marshall and Story.

Madison concurred with Adams that any discussion of American church-state relations was appropriately informed by history. "[O]n this question," he wrote, "experience will be an admitted umpire."[129] His historical narrative and the conclusions he drew from it, however, differed greatly from Adams's. After briefly surveying church-state arrangements in European and American history, Madison challenged the core of Adams's thesis. In his native Commonwealth of Virginia, he argued,

the existing character [of the community], distinguished as it is by its religious features, & the lapse of time, now more than fifty years, since the legal support of Religion was withdrawn, sufficiently prove, that it does not need the support of Government. And it will scarcely be contended that government has suffered by the exemption of Religion from its cognizance, or its pecuniary aid.

The apprehension of some seems to be, that Religion left entirely to itself, may run into extravagances injurious both to Religion & social order; but besides the question whether the interference of Government *in any form*, would not be more likely to increase than controul the tendency, it is a safe calculation that in this, as in other cases of excessive excitement, reason will gradually regain its ascendency. Great excitements are less apt to be permanent than to vibrate to the opposite extreme.[130]

Having examined the effects of various church-state models on religious freedom, Madison proceeded to controvert Adams's thesis. He was unmoved by the claim that only religion provided a sound basis for morality and good government. Moreover, he found little warrant for the fear "that Religion left entirely to itself" would demoralize society, undermine respect for authority, and unleash individual and collective licentiousness destructive of social harmony. In the final analysis, Madison believed that the Old World system of exclusive, legal establishment of a particular church was favorable neither to true religion nor to the legitimate ends of civil government. Genuine religion flourished best, he thought, when "left to the voluntary provisions of those who profess it," without entanglements of any sort with civil government—including those fostered by financial support, regulation, or compulsion.[131]

Madison further counseled in conclusion: "The tendency to a usurpation on one side, or the other, or to a corrupting coalition or alliance between them, will be best guarded against by an entire abstinence of the Government from interference, in any way whatever, beyond the necessity of preserving public order, & protecting each sect against trespasses on its legal rights by others."[132] Interestingly, Madison placed the emphasis, as did the First Amendment, on restraining civil government "from interference" with religion rather than on limiting the influence of religion and ecclesiastical authorities in public life.

Significantly, Madison jettisoned Jefferson's rigid "wall of separation" in favor of a more subtle metaphor that acknowledged the complex and shifting intersection of church and state: "I must admit, moreover, that it may not be easy, in every possible case, to trace the *line of separation,* between the rights of Religion & the Civil authority, with such distinctness, as to avoid collisions & doubts on unessential points."[133] Madison's metaphor is more precisely descriptive of the actual church-state relationship in the United States than Jefferson's "wall." A wall conjures up the image of "two distinct and settled institutions in the society once and for all time separated by a clearly defined and impregnable barrier."[134] It also tends to set "the two sides at odds with one another, as antagonists."[135] Madison's "line," unlike Jefferson's "wall," is fluid, more adaptable to changing relationships. A line has length but not breadth. It can move constantly, even zigzag, and unlike a wall, it can be overstepped.[136] Therefore, as Madison noted, it is not easy to "trace the line of separation . . . with such distinctness, as to avoid collisions & doubts on unessential points."[137]

The Marshall, Story, and Madison letters represent a diversity of views on the constitutional relationship between religion and civil government in the United States. Few individuals in the founding era had a more profound influence on the shaping of constitutional values and institutions of the young republic than these three men. Their opinions, offered in response to Adams's printed sermon, thus merit close attention.

THE MODERN CHURCH-STATE DEBATE

From colonial days to the present, relations between religious and civil authorities have been the subject of a vital, frequently vociferous debate. Emerging from this discussion has been a distinctively American approach to church-state relations shaped by the profoundly religious experience and character of the American people. A central feature of the church-state debate has been an inquiry into the historical and constitutional role of religion in American public life. Indeed, if there is one constant in this discussion, it is the broad agreement among jurists and scholars that the constitutional relationship between church and state is informed by and must accord with America's experience and religious heritage.

Adams's sermon together with the preserved responses to it richly document early nineteenth-century thought on the relation of religion to civil government in the United States. They provide a remarkable commentary on influential interpretations of church-state relations and the First Amendment in the formative era of the republic. Regrettably, Adams's prescient tract and the responses it generated have not received the attention they merit.[138] A belated review of Adams's sermon is appropriate, given renewed interest in the historical foundations of the Bill of Rights and the continuing controversy concerning the constitutional role of religion in public life.

Antagonists in modern church-state controversies have found support for their respective positions in these documents. James McClellan, a biographer of Justice Story, observed that Adams's sermon "deals with this very issue of the absolutist [i.e., strict separationist] versus the no preference theories at both the state and federal levels." A nonpreferentialist, McClellan described Adams as "an informed critic of the wall of separation theory" whose sermon "offers an abundance of evidence to refute the notion that church-state relations in early nineteenth century America ever followed the absolutist example offered by Jefferson and Madison."[139] Story's letter further buttresses the nonpreferentialist position. Separationist advocates, in sharp contrast, have found succor in Madison's strong dissent to Adams's thesis. For example, reflecting on Madison's letter, Adrienne Koch concluded that Madison "tried to establish a *secular* moral order as the American political system, and thought it might be good, perhaps even the best order ever devised."[140] These contrasting views persist to modern times.

Collectively, the papers reproduced in this book are a unique artifact of an important debate that took place in the early republic. They are also thoroughly modern documents that anticipated the inevitable church-state conflict precipitated by disestablishment and the secularization of American culture. The contours of current church-state debate are strikingly similar to those represented by Adams's convention address and the responses to it. Reflection on this national discussion more than 150 years ago casts light not only on the past but also, it is hoped, on the future of church-state arrangements and the constitutional role of religion in American public life.

NOTES

1. Jasper Adams, *The Relation of Christianity to Civil Government in the United States. A Sermon, Preached in St. Michael's Church, Charleston, February 13th, 1833, before the Convention of the Protestant Episcopal Church of the Diocese of South-Carolina*, 2d ed. (Charleston, S.C.: A.E. Miller, 1833). The text of the second edition reaches page 64, but page numbers 2 and 3 were skipped. The actual sermon is twenty-six pages in length with footnotes, followed by thirty-six pages of endnotes, also with footnotes.

2. For useful compilations of political sermons of this era, see John Wingate Thornton, ed., *The Pulpit of the American Revolution: or, The Political Sermons of the Period of 1776* (Boston: Gould and Lincoln, 1860; New York: Da Capo, 1970); Frank Moore, ed., *The Patriot Preachers of the American Revolution, 1766-1783* (New York, 1860); and Ellis Sandoz, ed., *Political Sermons of the American Founding Era: 1730-1805* (Indianapolis: Liberty, 1991).

3. James McClellan, *Joseph Story and the American Constitution: A Study in Political and Legal Thought* (Norman: Univ. of Oklahoma Press, 1971), p. 136.

4. See, for example, B.F. Morris, *Christian Life and Character of the Civil Institutions of the United States, Developed in the Official and Historical Annals of the Republic* (Philadelphia: George W. Childs, 1864), pp. 237-38, 256-57, 264-65. Adams's printed sermon was noticed in publications of the time, including the Charleston, South Carolina, *Gospel Messenger, and Southern Episcopal Register* 10, no. 113 (May 1833): 156-58, and no. 120 (Dec. 1833): 380-81; *American Quarterly Register* 5, no. 4 (May 1833): 334; and *Churchman* 3, no. 10 (25 May 1833): 455.

5. For a biographical sketch of Adams's life, see Appendix 1. See also [Charles Cotesworth Pinckney], *The Sermon, Delivered at Pendleton, by the Rector of Christ Church, Greenville, on the Occasion of the Death of the Rev. Jasper Adams, D.D.* (Charleston, S.C.: A.E. Miller, 1842), reprinted in full in this volume as Appendix 3; and Allen Johnson, ed., *Dictionary of American Biography*, vol. 1 (New York: Scribner's, 1928), p. 72.

6. The list of recipients, according to Adrienne Koch, included "almost every important figure of the day." See Koch, *Madison's "Advice to My Country"* (Princeton, N.J.: Princeton Univ. Press, 1966), p. 43. The complete list of the recipients of Adams's sermon is provided in Appendix 4.

7. Several responses to the sermon, including letters from James Madison, John Marshall, and Joseph Story, were copied by Adams and bound into his personal copy of the first printed edition of the sermon. This copy of the sermon is located in the William L. Clements Library, University of Michigan. (The handwritten material bound into the author's copy of the sermon is hereinafter cited as Author's Notes.) For further information on the preparation, publication, and distribution of Adams's sermon, see Appendix 4.

8. On the cover of copies sent to Madison and Marshall, Adams reported, he placed the following endorsement: "If it suits the much respected patriot & statesman to whom this is sent, to write the author a few lines expressive of his opinion of the validity of the argument herein contained, it will be received as a distinguished favour." Similar requests were extended to Justice Story and others. Author's Notes, pp. 15, 8.

9. Adams, *Relation*, p. 7 [42].

10. Anson Phelps Stokes, *Church and State in the United States*, 3 vols. (New York: Harper and Brothers, 1950), 1:700.

11. Ibid., 1:697.

12. Ibid., 1:702. See also Arthur M. Schlesinger Jr., *The Age of Jackson* (Boston: Little, Brown, 1945), p. 352 (noting the criticism of Jackson in the popular tract [by Henry Whiting Warner?], *An Inquiry into the Moral and Religious Character of the American Government* [New York: Wiley and Putnam, 1838]). For a brief summary of evangelical Protestant concerns during the Jacksonian era, see Richard J. Carwardine, *Evangelicals and Politics in Antebellum America* (New Haven, Conn.: Yale Univ. Press, 1993), pp. 55-58.

President Jackson's refusal to appoint a fast day in 1832 disappointed religious traditionalists. In a letter dated 12 June 1832, addressed to the General Synod of the Dutch Reformed Church, the president explained his position. Restating Jefferson's stance in the Danbury Baptist letter of 1802, Jackson argued that while he believed "in the efficacy of prayer," he thought a presidential fast day proclamation would be unconstitutional, disturbing "the security which religion now enjoys in this country, in its complete separation from the political concerns of the General Government." Letter from Andrew Jackson to the Synod of the Reformed Church, 12 June 1832, reprinted in John Spencer Bassett, ed., *Correspondence of Andrew Jackson*, vol. 4 (Washington, D.C.: Carnegie Institution, 1929), p. 447. Senator Henry Clay, Jackson's political nemesis, introduced a resolution requesting Jackson to reconsider his decision not to designate a national day of public fasting, humiliation, and prayer in order to avert a threatening cholera epidemic. See the remarks of Henry Clay in the U.S. Senate on 27 and 28 June 1832, in Robert Seager II, ed., *The Papers of Henry Clay*, vol. 8 (Lexington, Ky.: Univ. Press of Kentucky, 1984), pp. 545-46. Clay's motion was arguably a cynical political ploy designed to embarrass and discredit Jackson among conservative Protestants and to appeal to religious constituents in the upcoming 1832 election. In any case, this episode confirmed the suspicions of many conservative Protestants that Jackson, like Jefferson, was an advocate of irreligion and the growing secularization of public life. See Stokes, *Church and State* 3:181-83; Schlesinger, *Age of Jackson*, pp. 350-52; Perry Miller, *The Life of the Mind in America: From the Revolution to the Civil War* (New York: Harcourt, Brace and World, 1965), pp. 38-39. The consternation of conservative Protestants was heightened when the Democratic governor of New York followed Jackson's lead in declining to proclaim a fast day. See Merrill D. Peterson, *The Jefferson Image in the American Mind* (New York: Oxford Univ. Press, 1960), p. 94. Adams devoted several pages of his sermon notes to cataloging the voluminous precedents in American history for executive and legislative proclamations of days of public fasting, thanksgiving, and prayer. See Adams, *Relation*, pp. 35-39, n. E [66-73]. For a general examination of the controversy concerning thanksgiving and fast day proclamations, see Stokes, *Church and State* 3:176-200.

13. Schlesinger, *Age of Jackson*, p. 360.

Conservative, evangelical Protestants also found themselves at odds with the Jackson Administration over the forced removal of American Indians to western lands. Protestant missionary societies had long devoted great resources to proselytizing and educating the Indians. They had also vigorously opposed brutal efforts to dispossess native peoples of what remained of their ancestral lands.

The Indian land controversy gained national attention in 1831, when the state of Georgia prosecuted missionaries for violating a state law—part of a legislative strategy to abolish the Cherokee Nation's political existence in Georgia—that required all white persons residing in the Cherokee Nation to obtain a license and to take an oath of allegiance to the state of Georgia. The missionaries were found guilty and sentenced to four years at hard labor in the state penitentiary. The Reverend

Samuel A. Worcester appealed his conviction to the U.S. Supreme Court, arguing "that he entered the aforesaid Cherokee nation in the capacity of a duly authorised missionary of the American Board of Commissioners for Foreign Missions, under the authority of the president of the United States, and . . . that he was, at the time of his arrest, engaged in preaching the gospel to the Cherokee Indians, and in translating the sacred scriptures into their language, with the permission and approval of the said Cherokee nation, and in accordance with the humane policy of the government of the United States for the civilization and improvement of the Indians; and that . . . this prosecution the state of Georgia ought not to have or maintain, because . . . several treaties have, from time to time, been entered into between the United States and the Cherokee nation of Indians, . . . [that] acknowledge the said Cherokee nation to be a sovereign nation, authorised to govern themselves, and all persons who have settled within their territory, free from any right of legislative interference by the several states composing the United States of America." *Worcester v. Georgia,* 31 U.S. (6 Peters) 515, 538-39 (1832). In an opinion written by Chief Justice John Marshall, the Court recognized the Cherokee Nation as "a distinct community occupying its own territory, with boundaries accurately described, in which the laws of Georgia can have no force, and which the citizens of Georgia have no right to enter, but with the assent of the Cherokees themselves, or in conformity with treaties, and with the acts of congress" (at 561). Thus the Georgia law under which the missionaries were prosecuted was void, and consequently the convictions were annulled. Georgia ignored the decision, and President Jackson, who had no sympathy for Indian territorial claims, declined to enforce it. Worcester and a fellow missionary languished in prison for another eighteen months, and the stage was set for the scandalous episode known as the Trail of Tears. For many conservative Protestants, Jackson's refusal to intercede on behalf of the missionaries was further evidence of the administration's hostility to orthodox Christianity.

See generally Stokes, *Church and State* 1:708-13; John R. Bodo, *The Protestant Clergy and Public Issues, 1812-1848* (Princeton, N.J.: Princeton Univ. Press, 1954; Philadelphia: Porcupine, 1980), pp. 85-111; William G. McLoughlin, *Cherokees and Missionaries, 1789-1839* (New Haven, Conn.: Yale Univ. Press, 1984), pp. 239-99; Francis Paul Prucha, introduction to *Cherokee Removal: The "William Penn" Essays and Other Writings,* ed. Francis Paul Prucha (Knoxville: Univ. of Tennessee Press, 1981), pp. 3-40; Theda Perdue and Michael D. Green, eds., *The Cherokee Removal: A Brief History with Documents* (Boston: Bedford Books, 1995); and William L. Anderson, "Bibliographical Essay," in *Cherokee Removal: Before and After,* ed. William L. Anderson (Athens: Univ. of Georgia Press, 1991), pp. 139-47.

14. Massachusetts historian John D. Cushing observed: "The Congregational churches of Massachusetts during the provincial and early constitutional periods formed a system that has often been described as an 'establishment.'" This description, while not altogether accurate, is useful if it is understood that individual congregations were largely autonomous, they were bound by no articles of faith by the civil authority, and they formed a "system" only insofar as they shared a common theological heritage. See Cushing, "Notes on Disestablishment in Massachusetts, 1780-1833," *William and Mary Quarterly,* 3d ser., 26 (1969): 169. For excellent examinations of disestablishment in Massachusetts, see William G. McLoughlin, *New England Dissent, 1630-1833: The Baptists and the Separation of Church and State,* 2 vols. (Cambridge, Mass.: Harvard Univ. Press, 1971); and Jacob C. Meyer, *Church and State in Massachusetts: From 1740 to 1833* (Cleveland: Western Reserve Univ. Press, 1930).

15. Adams, *Relation,* p. 7 [42].

16. Stokes, *Church and State* 1:418-27.

17. Adams, *Relation*, pp. 5-7, 15-16 [41-42, 48-49].

18. Ibid., pp. 7, 15 [42, 48].

19. Sabbath observances commemorate the Creator's sanctification of the seventh day for rest (Genesis 2:1-3); the Fourth Commandment, which stipulates that the Sabbath be kept free from secular defilement (Exodus 20:8-11); and, in the Christian dispensation, the resurrection of Jesus Christ (Matthew 28:1-8; Mark 16:1-8; Luke 24:1-10; John 20:1-8). The Sabbath has been set aside by custom and law for rest, worship, and spiritual improvement. Sabbath desecration was an offense under common law, and the charters, statutes, and public policy of colonial, state, and national governments preserved this solemn observance. See generally Richard C. Wylie, *Sabbath Laws in the United States* (Pittsburgh: National Reform Association, 1905); and William Addison Blakely, ed., *American State Papers Bearing on Sunday Legislation*, rev. ed. (Washington, D.C.: Religious Liberty Association, 1911).

20. "An Act regulating the Post-office Establishment," *Statutes at Large*, vol. 2, sec. 9, 592, at 595 (30 April 1810).

21. Blakely, ed., *American State Papers Bearing on Sunday Legislation*, pp. 182-86.

22. "An Act to reduce into one the several acts establishing and regulating the Post-office Department," *Statutes at Large*, vol. 4, sec. 11, 102, at 105 (3 March 1825).

23. A House committee report on the issue commented: "It is believed that the history of legislation in this country affords no instance in which a stronger expression has been made, if regard be had to the numbers, the wealth or the intelligence of the petitioners." U.S. Congress, House, *Report from the Committee on the Post Office and Post Roads*, 20th Cong., 2d sess., House Rept. 65, 3 Feb. 1829; reprinted in *American State Papers. Documents, Legislative and Executive, of the Congress of the United States*, Class 7, *Post Office Department* (Washington, D.C.: Gales and Seaton, 1834), p. 212, hereinafter cited as *American State Papers*.

24. U.S. Congress, Senate, 20th Cong., 2d sess., *Register of Debates in Congress* (19 Jan. 1829), 5:42.

25. See Stokes, *Church and State* 2:20: "The Senate report, based on the sound theory that our government is 'a civil and not a religious institution,' made Senator Johnson a national hero of the more liberal-minded and radical groups."

26. See Schlesinger, *Age of Jackson*, pp. 350-52.

27. U.S. Congress, Senate, *Report on Stopping the United States Mail, and closing the Post-offices on Sunday, January 19, 1829*, 20th Cong., 2d sess., Senate Doc. 46, 19 Jan. 1829; reprinted in *American State Papers*, Class 7, pp. 211-12. See also *Review of a Report of the Committee, to whom was Referred the Several Petitions on the Subject of Mails on the Sabbath, Presented to the Senate of the United States, January 16 [sic], 1829* (Boston: Peirce and Williams, 1829).

28. U.S. Congress, House, *Report of the Minority of the Committee on Post Offices and Post Roads, to whom the memorials were referred for prohibiting the transportation of the Mails, and the opening of Post Offices, on Sundays*, 21st Cong., 1st sess., House Rept. 271, 5 March 1830; reprinted in *American State Papers*, Class 7, p. 231.

29. "Speech of Mr. Frelinghuysen, on the Subject of Sunday Mails," U.S. Congress, Senate, 21st Cong., 1st sess., *Register of Debates in Congress* (8 May 1830) 6: Appendix, pp. 1-4. The speech was published and distributed widely. See Theodore Frelinghuysen, *Speech of Mr. Frelinghuysen, on His Resolution Concerning Sabbath Mails. In the Senate of the United States, May 8, 1830* (Washington, D.C.: Rothwell and Ustick, 1830).

30. For further discussion of the Sunday mail controversy, see Oliver W.

Holmes, "Sunday Travel and Sunday Mails: A Question Which Troubled Our Fore-fathers," *New York History* 20 (Oct. 1939): 413-24; Richard R. John, "Taking Sabba-tarianism Seriously: The Postal System, the Sabbath, and the Transformation of American Political Culture," *Journal of the Early Republic* 10 (1990): 517-67; James R. Rohrer, "Sunday Mails and the Church-State Theme in Jacksonian America," *Journal of the Early Republic* 7 (1987): 53-74; and Bertram Wyatt-Brown, "Prelude to Abolitionism: Sabbatarian Politics and the Rise of the Second Party System," *Journal of American History* 58 (1971): 316-41. See generally Frederick L. Bronner, "The Observance of the Sabbath in the United States, 1800-1865," Ph.D. diss., Harvard Univ., 1937; and Harmon Kingsbury, *The Sabbath: A Brief History of Laws, Petitions, Remonstrances and Reports, with Facts and Arguments, Relating to the Christian Sabbath* (New York, 1840).

31. See, for example, Jasper Adams, *Elements of Moral Philosophy* (Cambridge, Mass.: Folsom, Wells and Thurston, 1837), pp. 86-98.

32. Adams, *Relation,* pp. 33-34, n. D [65].

33. Bodo, *Protestant Clergy,* p. 39. See also Fred J. Hood, *Reformed America: The Middle and Southern States, 1783-1837* (University: Univ. of Alabama Press, 1980), pp. 97-101.

34. Ezra Stiles Ely, *The Duty of Christian Freemen to Elect Christian Rulers: A Dis-course Delivered on the Fourth of July, 1827, in the Seventh Presbyterian Church, in Phila-delphia. With an Appendix, Designed to Vindicate the Liberty of Christians, and of the American Sunday School Union* (Philadelphia, 1828). Ely's discourse is reprinted in Joseph L. Blau, ed., *American Philosophical Addresses, 1700-1900* (New York: Colum-bia Univ. Press, 1946), pp. 551-62. Citations here refer to the 1828 edition.

Ely was pastor of Old Pine Street Church in Philadelphia. He also served as moderator of the Presbyterian General Assembly in the United States and was an influential figure in the American Sunday School Union. He wrote several popular theological treatises and for many years edited the weekly publication the *Philadel-phian.* For a biographical sketch, see "Notes: The Rev. Dr. Ezra Stiles Ely," *Journal of the Presbyterian Historical Society* 2 (Sept. 1904): 321-24.

35. Ely, *Duty of Christian Freemen,* p. 8; emphasis in the original.

36. Wyatt-Brown, "Prelude to Abolitionism," p. 324.

37. Ely, *Duty of Christian Freemen,* p. 11.

38. Ely candidly acknowledged that he would choose to be ruled by "a sound Presbyterian," but he "would prefer a religious and moral man, of any one of the truly Christian sects, to any man destitute of religious principle and morality." He concluded, "Let a civil ruler . . . be a Christian *of some sort,* . . . rather than not a Christian of any denomination" (ibid., p. 13; emphasis in the original).

39. Thomas Cooper reported that Ely wrote in his paper, the *Philadelphian:* "Membership in this party is commenced and continued, or discontinued, at the pleasure of each member, without any initiation, fee or ceremony. This party has neither time nor place of meeting, but the members of it exchange their sentiments whenever they please, through common conversation, or the instrumentality of the press." [Thomas Cooper], *The Case of Thomas Cooper, M.D. President of the South Carolina College. Submitted to the Legislature and the People of South Carolina. December 1831,* 2d ed. (Columbia, S.C.: Times and Gazette Office, 1832), Appendix 1, p. 3.

40. Ely, *Duty of Christian Freemen,* p. 8.

41. Ibid., p. 4.

42. Ibid.; emphasis in the original. Ely cited Proverbs 3:6 as biblical authority for this statement. See Joseph L. Blau, "'The Christian Party in Politics,'" *Review of Religion* 11 (1946-47): 22.

43. Ely, *Duty of Christian Freemen,* pp. 6, 7.

44. Ibid., p. 7; emphasis in the original.

45. Ibid., p. 14.

46. Ibid., pp. 9, 10; emphasis in the original.

47. Ibid., p. 10.

48. Ibid., p. 14.

49. Ibid., p. 11; Joseph L. Blau, ed., *Cornerstones of Religious Freedom in America,* rev. ed. (New York: Harper Torchbooks, 1964), p. 124.

50. For a description of the opposition aroused by Ely's proposal, see Blau, "'Christian Party in Politics,'" pp. 26-35; Schlesinger, *Age of Jackson,* pp. 136-40; [Cooper], *Case of Thomas Cooper,* Appendix 1.

51. This was the theme of Thomas Cooper's compilation of documents and analysis of the "[p]lans and schemes of the orthodox Clergy of the Presbyterian denomination in particular [i.e., the 'Christian party in politics'], to acquire a sectarian influence over the political government of the Country and all seminaries of education." See [Cooper], *Case of Thomas Cooper,* Appendix 1, p. 1.

52. David Pickering, *Address Delivered before the Citizens of Providence, in the Universalist Chapel, on the Fifty-second Anniversary of American Independence* (Providence, R.I., 1828), p. 15.

53. William Morse, *An Oration Delivered before the Citizens of Nantucket, July 4, 1829, being the Fifty-third Anniversary of the Declaration of the Independence of the United States of America* (Boston, 1829), p. 11.

54. Zelotes Fuller, *The Tree of Liberty. An Address in Celebration of the Birth of Washington, Delivered at the Second Universalist Church in Philadelphia, Sunday Morning, February 28, 1830* (Philadelphia, 1830), in Blau, ed., *Cornerstones,* pp. 134-35.

55. Ibid., p. 136; emphasis in the original.

56. See Ely, *Duty of Christian Freemen,* p. 5.

57. Ibid., pp. 15, 6.

58. Ibid., p. 10.

59. Ibid., p. 12. Ely argued that he claimed nothing more for Christians "than our political institutions secure alike to Christians and Infidels of every description; the liberty of thinking for themselves, of publishing their opinions, and of acting in conformity with them, in any such manner as will not interfere with the rights of others. An avowed enemy to Christ has *the political liberty* of being an infidel in his opinions; of preferring an infidel for his civil ruler; and of giving his vote in aid of the election of an infidel. I am a Christian in opinion, and claim the right of preferring a Christian to an infidel; and of giving my suffrage only in favour of persons whom I deem friendly to Christianity, and of good moral character." Nothing in his proposal, Ely concluded, constituted a religious establishment or a union of church and state (p. 15; emphasis in the original).

60. Albert Post, *Popular Freethought in America, 1825-1850* (New York: Columbia Univ. Press, 1943), p. 213.

61. See Hood, *Reformed America,* p. 111; and Charles I. Foster, *An Errand of Mercy: The Evangelical United Front, 1790-1837* (Chapel Hill: Univ. of North Carolina Press, 1960), pp. 57-60.

62. Daniel Walker Hollis, *University of South Carolina,* vol. 1, *South Carolina College* (Columbia: Univ. of South Carolina Press, 1951), p. 113.

63. Ibid., p. 77.

64. Dumas Malone, *The Public Life of Thomas Cooper* (New Haven, Conn.: Yale Univ. Press, 1926), pp. 332, 302. As a young man in England, Cooper had campaigned against slavery; see pp. 19-22, 76, 284.

65. Ibid., pp. 243, 259-64, 338-43; Hollis, *University of South Carolina* 1:98-99, 108. Malone noted: "Jefferson's point of view [regarding Presbyterians] was essentially the same as that of his friend [Cooper], although he was less easily affrighted, less prone to hysteria, and much more discreet in his public utterances" (*Public Life*, p. 262). For more on Jefferson's attitude toward the Presbyterians, see the letter from Thomas Jefferson to William Short, 13 April 1820, reprinted in Andrew A. Lipscomb and Albert Ellery Bergh, eds., *The Writings of Thomas Jefferson*, 20 vols., Library Ed. (Washington, D.C.: Thomas Jefferson Memorial Association, 1903-4), 15:246, hereinafter cited as *Writings of Jefferson*.

66. Malone, *Public Life*, pp. 340-41.

67. Hollis, *University of South Carolina* 1:109.

68. Malone wrote that Cooper "took the offensive against the hated clergy and fanned into flame their smoldering resentment" (*Public Life*, p. 338).

69. Hollis, *University of South Carolina* 1:113.

70. Ibid., p. 112. See also Malone, *Public Life*, p. 356.

71. For a contemporary discussion of the issues raised by the Cooper controversy and Cooper's constitutional defense, see *Dr. Cooper's Defence before the Board of Trustees. From the Times and Gazette of December 14, 1832* (Columbia, S.C.: Times and Gazette Office, n.d.); *Reply to Censor; or, An Appeal to the Good Sense of the People of South Carolina, by Justice* (Columbia, S.C.: Times and Gazette Office, n.d.); *An Appeal to the State. By Censor. Truth Is Great, and It Will Triumph* (N.p., n.d.); *An Appeal to the State by Censor, Continued* (Columbia, S.C.: Free Press and Hive Office, 1831); and [Cooper], *Case of Thomas Cooper.* The Cooper affair and some of these pamphlets are examined in Kenneth R. Platte, "The Religious, Political and Educational Aspects of the Thomas Cooper Controversy," M.A. thesis, Univ. of South Carolina, 1967; and James Lowell Underwood, *The Constitution of South Carolina*, vol. 3, *Church and State, Morality and Free Expression* (Columbia: Univ. of South Carolina Press, 1992), pp. 203-5. For further discussion of Dr. Cooper's tenure as president of South Carolina College, see Edwin L. Green, *A History of the University of South Carolina* (Columbia, S.C.: State Co., 1916), pp. 34-43; Maximilian LaBorde, *History of the South Carolina College, from Its Incorporation, Dec. 19, 1801, to Dec. 19, 1865, Including Sketches of Its Presidents and Professors*, rev. ed. (Charleston, S.C.: Walker, Evans and Cogswell, 1874), pp. 121-77; and Colyer Meriwether, *History of Higher Education in South Carolina* (Washington, D.C.: GPO, 1889; Spartanburg, S.C.: Reprint Co., 1972), pp. 143-56.

72. See J.H. Easterby, *A History of the College of Charleston, Founded 1770* (Charleston, S.C., 1935), p. 86.

73. Another church-state issue was the subject of public debate in South Carolina in 1833. The South Carolina Supreme Court ruled on a challenge to a Sunday closing ordinance. The high court reviewed the case of Alexander Marks and C.O. Duke, two Columbia merchants charged with violating a local ordinance requiring stores to close on Sundays. Marks, a Jew, and Duke, an avowed infidel, maintained that the ordinance infringed a state constitutional guarantee of religious liberty. The court rejected the claim, ruling that the ordinance "enjoins no profession of faith, demands no religious test, extorts no religious ceremony, confers no religious privilege or 'preference.'" *Town Council of Columbia v. C.O. Duke and Alexander Marks*, 2 Strobhart 530 (S.C. 1833). See also Joseph L. Blau and Salo W. Baron, eds., *The Jews of the United States, 1790-1840: A Documentary History*, 3 vols. (New York: Columbia Univ. Press, 1963), 1:24-26. Adams noted this case in a postscript to the second edition of his sermon; see *Relation*, p. 64 [104]. For a discussion of the legal impact of the case and a history of Sunday laws in South Carolina, see Underwood, *Constitution of South Carolina* 3:90-144.

74. Thomas Jefferson, "Whether Christianity Is Part of the Common Law?" in *Reports of Cases Determined in the General Court of Virginia. From 1730, to 1740; and From 1768, to 1772* (Charlottesville, Va., 1829), reprinted in Paul Leicester Ford, ed., *The Works of Thomas Jefferson*, 12 vols., Federal Ed. (New York: G.P. Putnam's Sons, 1904-5), 1:453-64, hereinafter cited as *Works of Jefferson;* Joseph Story, "The Value and Importance of Legal Studies," in *The Miscellaneous Writings of Joseph Story*, ed. William W. Story (Boston: Charles C. Little and James Brown, 1851), p. 517. Adams cited Story with approval; see *Relation*, p. 41, n. ★ [74, n. ★].

75. See Adams, *Relation*, p. 7 [42].

76. Ibid., pp. 40-57, nn. F-G [73-95].

77. Peterson, *Jefferson Image*, p. 94.

78. See *An Inquiry into the Moral and Religious Character of the American Government* (New York: Wiley and Putnam, 1838), pp. 10-13, 188-89. The author argued that Jefferson's exclusion of religion from public life was a policy eagerly followed by Jackson and others in national and state governments.

79. Letter from Thomas Jefferson to Major John Cartwright, 5 June 1824, reprinted in *Writings of Jefferson* 16:50. The Finch book in question is Henry Finch, *Law; or, A Discourse thereof; in Four Books* (1613; London, 1759), bk. 1, chap. 3, p. 7.

A legal compilation prepared by Jefferson and published posthumously in 1829, entitled *Reports of Cases Determined in the General Court of Virginia*, contained a six-page appendix that examined "whether Christianity is a part of the common law." See Jefferson, "Whether Christianity Is Part of the Common Law?" in *Reports of Cases*. Written in 1764, when Jefferson was twenty-one years of age, this short dissertation was apparently the original brief expounded in the Cartwright letter. See Peterson, *Jefferson Image*, pp. 95-96. For Jefferson's early reflections on the subject, see the letter from Jefferson to John Adams, 24 Jan. 1814; and the letter from Jefferson to Thomas Cooper, 10 Feb. 1814, both reprinted in *Writings of Jefferson* 14:71-76, 85-97 respectively. For an analysis of Jefferson's essay, see Johnson Brigham, "A Forgotten Chapter in the Life of Jefferson," *Green Bag* 12 (Aug. 1900): 441-44.

80. *Humfrey Bohun v. John Broughton, Bishop of Lincoln,* Year Book, 34 Henry VI, folio 38, 40 (1458).

81. Jefferson, "Whether Christianity Is Part of the Common Law?" in *Works of Jefferson* 1:455.

82. Ibid., 455-56.

83. Letter from Thomas Jefferson to Major John Cartwright, 5 June 1824, reprinted in *Writings of Jefferson* 16:50.

84. Joseph Story, "Christianity a Part of the Common Law," *American Jurist and Law Magazine* 9 (April 1833): 346-48, reprinted in William W. Story, ed., *Life and Letters of Joseph Story*, vol. 1 (Boston: Charles C. Little and James Brown, 1851), pp. 431-33.

85. Peterson, *Jefferson Image*, p. 96.

86. Story, "Christianity a Part of the Common Law," in *Life and Letters*, p. 432.

87. Adams cited this 1833 article, although it is not clear that he was aware the author was Justice Story. Adams, *Relation*, pp. 40-41, n. ★ [74, n. ★]. The magazine identified the writer by the initials "J.S."

88. Adams, *Relation*, p. 46 [81]. See *People v. Ruggles*, 8 Johnson 290 (N.Y. 1811); and *Updegraph v. Commonwealth*, 11 Sergeant & Rawle 394 (Pa. 1824). Adams cited these cases and provided extracts from them: *Relation*, p. 16, n. § [48-49, n. 25]; pp. 48-49 [84-85]; and pp. 46-48 [81-83].

89. See, for example, *Vidal v. Girard's Executors*, 43 U.S. (2 Howard) 127 (1844);

State v. Chandler, 2 Harrington 553 (Del. 1837); *Commonwealth v. Kneeland*, 20 Pickering 206 (Mass. 1838); and *Lindenmuller v. People*, 33 Barbour 548 (N.Y. 1861).

90. For further discussion of the relationship between Christianity and the common law, see Morton Borden, *Jews, Turks, and Infidels* (Chapel Hill: Univ. of North Carolina Press, 1984), pp. 97-129; Isaac A. Cornelison, *The Relation of Religion to Civil Government in the United States of America: A State without a Church, but not without a Religion* (New York: G.P. Putnam's Sons, 1895), pp. 120-63; Peterson, *Jefferson Image*, pp. 92-98; Miller, *Life of the Mind*, pp. 186-206; Stephen C. Perks, *Christianity and Law: An Enquiry into the Influence of Christianity on the Development of English Common Law* (Whitby, Eng.: Avant, 1993); P. Emory Aldrich, "The Christian Religion and the Common Law," *American Antiquarian Society Proceedings* 6 (April 1889–April 1890): 18-37; M.B. Anderson, "Relations of Christianity to the Common Law," *Albany Law Journal* 20 (4 Oct. 1879): 265-68, and (11 Oct. 1879): 285-88; Arthur William Barber, "Christianity and the Common Law," *Green Bag* 14 (1902): 267-73; Bradley S. Chilton, "Cliobernetics, Christianity, and the Common Law," *Law Library Journal* 83 (1991): 355-62; "Is Christianity a Part of the Common-Law of England?" *Quarterly Christian Spectator* 8 (March 1836): 13-22; Courtney Kenny, "The Evolution of the Law of Blasphemy," *Cambridge Law Journal* 1, no. 2 (1922): 127-42; Max J. Kohler, "The Doctrine That 'Christianity Is a Part of the Common Law,' and Its Recent Judicial Overthrow in England, with Particular Reference to Jewish Rights," *Publications of the American Jewish Historical Society* 31 (1928): 105-34; and Jayson L. Spiegel, "Christianity as Part of the Common Law," *North Carolina Central Law Journal* 14 (1984): 494-516.

91. Adams, *Relation*, pp. 22, 7 [52, 42].

92. Ibid., pp. 26, 17, 18 [56, 50]. Adams cited with approval the famous lines from George Washington's Farewell Address: "Of all the dispositions and habits, which lead to political prosperity, religion and morality are indispensable supports. . . . And let us with caution indulge the supposition, that morality can be maintained without religion. Whatever may be conceded to the influence of refined education on minds of peculiar structure, reason and experience both forbid us to expect, that national morality can prevail in exclusion of religious principle" (p. 60, n. I [99]). For the complete speech, see "Farewell Address," 19 Sept. 1796, in John C. Fitzpatrick, ed., *The Writings of George Washington*, vol. 35 (Washington, D.C.: GPO, 1940), pp. 214-38.

93. This is a paraphrase of a statement in a speech delivered by Alexander H. Everett, reprinted in part in Adams's endnotes. Adams, *Relation*, p. 55, n. G [93].

94. Ibid., p. 5 [40].

95. Ibid., p. 6 [41].

96. Ibid., pp. 6, 11 [41, 45].

97. Ibid., p. 6 [41]; emphasis in the original.

98. Ibid. [41].

99. Ibid., pp. 6-7 [42]. The same question, Adams noted, was raised by the First Amendment: "Did the people of the United States, when in adopting the Federal Constitution they declared, that 'Congress shall make no law respecting an establishment of religion or prohibiting the free exercise thereof,' expect to be understood as abolishing the national religion, which had been professed, respected and cherished from the first settlement of the country, and which it was the great object of our fathers in settling this then wilderness to enjoy according to the dictates of their own consciences?" (p. 7 [42]).

100. Ibid., p. 7 [42].

101. Ibid., p. 8 [43].

102. Ibid., pp. 8-9 [43-44]. Adams examined in detail the religious character of early colonial charters and constitutions (pp. 8-9, and 29-30, n. A [43-44, 59-60]).

103. Ibid., p. 11 [45].

104. Ibid., p. 12 [46]; emphasis in the original.

105. Ibid., p. 14, n. ‡ [47, n. 21]; p. 12 [46].

106. Ibid., p. 13 [46]; see also pp. 12, and 32-33, n. C [46, 63-64]. See the U.S. Constitution, Art. 7, and Art. 1, sec. 7, cl. 2. One of the most striking features of the Constitution is the absence of an invocation of the Deity or explicit Christian designation. In this respect the Constitution departed from the pattern of colonial charters, state constitutions, and other public documents of the era. Adams noted these constitutional provisions as refutation of the charge that the Constitution, because it lacked explicit Christian references, was atheistic or anti-Christian in character. See generally Daniel L. Dreisbach, "God and the Constitution: Reflections on Selected Nineteenth-Century Commentaries on References to the Deity and the Christian Religion in the United States Constitution," paper presented at the American Political Science Association annual meeting, Washington, D.C., 3 Sept. 1993.

107. Adams, *Relation*, p. 13 [46-47].

108. Ibid., pp. 14-15 [47-48].

109. Adams, *Relation*, p. 13, n. † [46, n. 20], citing Joseph Story, *Commentaries on the Constitution of the United States*, 3 vols. (Boston: Hilliard, Gray and Co., 1833).

110. Adams, *Relation*, pp. 17, 18 [49, 50].

111. Ibid., p. 23 [54].

112. Ibid., p. 20 [52].

113. Ibid., p. 17 [50].

114. William Waller Hening, ed., *The Statutes at Large; Being a Collection of All the Laws of Virginia, from the First Session of the Legislature, in the Year 1619*, vol. 12 (Richmond, Va.: J. and G. Cochran, 1823), p. 86. Jefferson's Bill for Establishing Religious Freedom is reprinted in Julian P. Boyd, ed., *The Papers of Thomas Jefferson*, vol. 2 (Princeton, N.J.: Princeton Univ. Press, 1950), pp. 545-47.

115. Letter from James Madison to Jasper Adams, Sept. 1833, Author's Notes, p. 14 [120]. See also the letter from James Madison to Edward Livingston, 10 July 1822, reprinted in Gaillard Hunt, ed., *The Writings of James Madison*, 9 vols. (New York: G.P. Putnam's Sons, 1900-1910), 9:101. In the letter to Livingston, Madison lamented "the old error, that without some sort of alliance or coalition between Govt. & Religion neither can be duly supported."

116. James Madison, "Memorial and Remonstrance against Religious Assessments," reprinted in Robert A. Rutland et al., eds., *The Papers of James Madison*, vol. 8 (Chicago: Univ. of Chicago Press, 1973), p. 301.

117. See generally Eva T.H. Brann, "Madison's 'Memorial and Remonstrance': A Model of American Eloquence," in *Rhetoric and American Statesmanship*, ed. Glen E. Thurow and Jeffrey D. Wallin (Durham, N.C.: Carolina Academic Press, 1984), pp. 28-31. See also the letter from James Madison to Edward Livingston, 10 July 1822, reprinted in Hunt, ed., *Writings of James Madison* 9:102-3: "[R]eligion & Govt. will both exist in greater purity, the less they are mixed together. . . . Religion flourishes in greater purity, without than with the aid of Govt."

118. Letter from Thomas Jefferson to Messrs. Nehemiah Dodge, Ephraim Robbins, and Stephen S. Nelson, a Committee of the Danbury Baptist Association, in the state of Connecticut, 1 Jan. 1802, reprinted in *Writings of Jefferson* 16:281-82.

119. Adams, *Relation*, pp. 15, 16 [48, 49]. Adams recognized the definitional

problems raised by the term *establishment* and carefully noted that the word was used here "in its usual and not in its legal or technical sense" (p. 16, n. † [49, n. 27]).

120. Letter from John Marshall to Jasper Adams, 9 May 1833, Author's Notes, pp. 2-3 [113].

121. Ibid., p. 3 [113-14].

122. Letter from Joseph Story to Jasper Adams, 14 May 1833, Author's Notes, p. 4 [115].

123. Ibid.; emphasis in the original. In his influential *Commentaries,* Justice Story offered an interpretation of the First Amendment religion provisions:

"[§ 1865.] . . . the right of a society or government to interfere in matters of religion will hardly be contested by any persons, who believe that piety, religion, and morality are intimately connected with the well being of the state, and indispensable to the administration of civil justice. The promulgation of the great doctrines of religion, the being, and attributes, and providence of one Almighty God; the responsibility to him for all our actions, founded upon moral freedom and accountability; a future state of rewards and punishments; the cultivation of all the personal, social, and benevolent virtues;—these never can be a matter of indifference in any well ordered community. It is, indeed, difficult to conceive, how any civilized society can well exist without them. And at all events, it is impossible for those, who believe in the truth of Christianity, as a divine revelation, to doubt, that it is the especial duty of government to foster, and encourage it among all the citizens and subjects. This is a point wholly distinct from that of the right of private judgment in matters of religion, and of the freedom of public worship according to the dictates of one's conscience. . . .

"§ 1867. Now, there will probably be found few persons in this, or any other Christian country, who would deliberately contend, that it was unreasonable, or unjust to foster and encourage the Christian religion generally, as a matter of sound policy, as well as of revealed truth. In fact, every American colony, from its foundation down to the revolution, with the exception of Rhode Island, (if, indeed, that state be an exception,) did openly, by the whole course of its laws and institutions, support and sustain, in some form, the Christian religion; and almost invariably gave a peculiar sanction to some of its fundamental doctrines. And this has continued to be the case in some of the states down to the present period, without the slightest suspicion, that it was against the principles of public law, or republican liberty. Indeed, in a republic, there would seem to be a peculiar propriety in viewing the Christian religion, as the great basis, on which it must rest for its support and permanence, if it be, what it has ever been deemed by its truest friends to be, the religion of liberty. . . .

"§ 1868. Probably at the time of the adoption of the constitution, and of the [first] amendment to it, now under consideration, the general, if not the universal, sentiment in America was, that Christianity ought to receive encouragement from the state, so far as was not incompatible with the private rights of conscience, and the freedom of religious worship. An attempt to level all religions, and to make it a matter of state policy to hold all in utter indifference, would have created universal disapprobation, if not universal indignation. . . .

"§ 1871. The real object of the amendment was, not to countenance, much less to advance Mahometanism, or Judaism, or infidelity, by prostrating Christianity; but to exclude all rivalry among Christian sects, and to prevent any national ecclesiastical establishment, which should give to an hierarchy the exclusive patronage of the national government." Story, *Commentaries* 3:722-28; footnotes omitted.

124. Letter from Joseph Story to Jasper Adams, 14 May 1833, Author's Notes, p. 5 [116-17].

125. Ibid., p. 6 [117]. See also R. Kent Newmyer's brief commentary on Story's letter in Newmyer, *Supreme Court Justice Joseph Story: Statesman of the Old Republic* (Chapel Hill: Univ. of North Carolina Press, 1985), pp. 183-84.

126. Letter from James Madison to Jasper Adams, Sept. 1833, Author's Notes, p. 15 [121]. A rough draft of Madison's letter, which differs in some respects from Adams's version, was reprinted in Gaillard Hunt's edition of the collected papers of James Madison. See Hunt, ed., *Writings of James Madison* 9:484-88. Hunt's version, however, was misdated as written in "1832," and the recipient was identified only as "Rev. ——— Adams." Hunt was apparently unaware of the context in which the letter was written.

Hunt identified the source of this manuscript as the Chicago Historical Society. The society's Archives and Manuscript Department, however, has no record that the letter was ever in its collection. The Library of Congress has a rough draft of the letter in its Madison Papers that corresponds with Hunt's version and may have been purchased from the Chicago Historical Society. See James Madison Papers, Manuscript Division, Library of Congress.

127. Letter from James Madison to Jasper Adams, Sept. 1833, Author's Notes, p. 12 [117]; Koch, *Madison's "Advice,"* p. 38.

128. Letter from James Madison to Jasper Adams, Sept. 1833, Author's Notes, p. 12 [117].

129. Ibid.

130. Ibid., p. 14 [120]; emphasis in the original. The content and themes of this letter are strikingly similar to those of Madison's earlier letters to Robert Walsh, 2 March 1819; to Edward Livingston, 10 July 1822; and to Edward Everett, 19 March 1823, reprinted in Hunt, ed., *Writings of James Madison* 8:425-33, 9:98-103, and 9:124-30 respectively.

131. Letter from James Madison to Jasper Adams, Sept. 1833, Author's Notes, p. 12 [117]. This analysis borrows from Koch, *Madison's "Advice,"* pp. 38-42.

132. Letter from James Madison to Jasper Adams, Sept. 1833, Author's Notes, pp. 14-15 [120]. These lines were quoted by Justice Rutledge in his dissenting *Everson* opinion. *Everson v. Board of Education,* 330 U.S. 1, 40 n. 28 (1947) (Rutledge, J., dissenting).

133. Letter from James Madison to Jasper Adams, Sept. 1833, Author's Notes, p. 14 [120]; emphasis added.

134. Sidney E. Mead, "Neither Church nor State: Reflections on James Madison's 'Line of Separation,'" *Journal of Church and State* 10 (1968): 350.

135. Richard P. McBrien, *Caesar's Coin: Religion and Politics in America* (New York: Macmillan, 1987), p. 66. See Terry Eastland, "In Defense of Religious America," *Commentary* 71, no. 6 (June 1981): 39: "[I]n today's usage the idea of a wall connotes antagonism and suspicion between the two sides thus separated."

136. Cf. *McCollum v. Board of Education,* 333 U.S. 203, 231 (1948): "Separation means separation, not something less. Jefferson's metaphor in describing the relation between Church and State speaks of a 'wall of separation,' not of a fine line easily overstepped."

137. Letter from James Madison to Jasper Adams, Sept. 1833, Author's Notes, p. 14 [120]. McBrien noted that "theoretical appeals to the 'wall of separation' notwithstanding, the Court has adopted, in practice, the Madisonian rather than the Jeffersonian metaphor." For a discussion of the Supreme Court's references to the metaphor of the "line," see McBrien, *Caesar's Coin,* pp. 66-67.

138. Research for this essay has revealed only two independent examinations of Adams's sermon and the exchange it provoked. Both accounts are modest in scope and detail. See Koch, *Madison's "Advice,"* pp. 36-44; and McClellan, *Joseph Story,* pp. 136-42. Other scholars have drawn on these accounts. See, for example, Rodney K. Smith, *Public Prayer and the Constitution: A Case Study in Constitutional Interpretation* (Wilmington, Del.: Scholarly Resources, 1987), pp. 113-15; and Arlin M. Adams and Charles J. Emmerich, "A Heritage of Religious Liberty," *University of Pennsylvania Law Review* 137 (1989): 1590 and n. 135. Other writers have discussed Madison's letter to Adams without reference to or elaboration on the context in which it was written.

139. McClellan, *Joseph Story,* p. 136.

140. Koch, *Madison's "Advice,"* p. 46; emphasis in the original.

PART ONE

SERMON

THE RELATION OF CHRISTIANITY TO CIVIL GOVERNMENT IN THE UNITED STATES:

SERMON,

Preached in St. Michael's Church, Charleston,

FEBRUARY 13th, 1833,

BEFORE

THE CONVENTION

OF THE

PROTESTANT EPISCOPAL CHURCH

OF THE

DIOCESE OF SOUTH-CAROLINA:

By Rev. J. ADAMS,

PRESIDENT OF THE COLLEGE OF CHARLESTON, S. CAROLINA;
AND (EX-OFFICIO) HORRY PROFESSOR OF MORAL AND POLITICAL PHILOSOPHY.

SECOND EDITION.

Published at the request of the Bishop and Clergy of the Protestant Episcopal Church of the Diocese of South-Carolina.

CHARLESTON:
PRINTED BY A. E. MILLER,
No. 4 Broad-street.

1833.

The Relation of Christianity
to Civil Government
in the United States

Jasper Adams

Be ready always to give an answer to every man that
asketh you a reason of the hope that is in you,
with meekness and fear.—*I. Peter,* iii. 15.

Righteousness exalteth a nation, but sin is a reproach
to any people.—*Proverbs* xiv. 34.

The kingdoms of this world are become the kingdoms
of our Lord and of his Christ; and he shall reign
for ever and ever.—*Revelation* xi. 15.

As Christianity was designed by its Divine Author to subsist until the
end of time, it was indispensable, that it should be capable of adapting
itself to all states of society, and to every condition of mankind. We have the
Divine assurance that it shall eventually become universal, but without such
flexibility in accommodating itself to all the situations in which men can be
placed, this must have been impracticable. There is no possible form of individual or social life, which it is not fitted to meliorate and adorn. It not
only extends to the more transient connexions to which the business of life
gives rise, but embraces and prescribes the duties springing from the great
and more permanent relations of rulers and subjects, husbands and wives,
parents and children, masters and servants; and enforces the obligation of
these high classes of our duties by the sanctions of a judgment to come. We
find by examining its history, that, in rude ages, its influence has softened
the savage and civilized the barbarian; while in polished ages and communities, it has accomplished the no less important end, of communicating
and preserving the moral and religious principle, which, among a cultivated
people, is in peculiar danger of being extinguished amid the refinements,
the gaiety, and the frivolous amusements incident to such a state of society.

The relation which the prevailing system of religion in various countries and in successive ages, has sustained to civil government, is one of the
most interesting branches of the history of mankind. According to the structure of the Hebrew Polity, the religious and political systems were most in-

timately, if not indissolubly combined: and in the Mosaic Law, we find religious observances, political ordinances, rules of medicine, prescriptions of agriculture, and even precepts of domestic economy, brought into the most intimate association. The Hebrew Hierarchy was a literary and political, as well as a religious order of men. In the Grecian States and in the Roman Empire, the same individual united in his own person, the emblems of priest of their divinities and the ensigns of civil and political authority. Christianity, while it was undermining, and until it had overthrown the ancient Polity of the Jews on the one hand; and the Polytheism of the Roman Empire on the other; was extended by the zeal and enterprize of its early preachers, sustained by the presence of its Divine Author[1] and accompanied by the evidence of the miracles which they were commissioned to perform. It is not strange, therefore, that when, under the Emperor Constantine, Christianity came into the place of the ancient superstition, it should have been taken under the protection, and made a part of the constitution of the Imperial government. It was the prediction of ancient prophecy, that, in the last days, kings should become nursing fathers and queens nursing mothers to the Church;[2]—and what was more natural than to understand this prophecy as meaning a strict and intimate union of the Church, with the civil government of the Empire. Ancient usage, with all the influence which a reverence for antiquity is accustomed to inspire, was on the side of such a union. We may well believe, then, that Christianity was first associated with civil government, without any intention on the part of civil governors to make it the odious engine of the State which it afterwards became. And if the Roman Emperors had been satisfied to receive and to continue the new religion without distinction of sects, as the broad ground of all the great institutions of the Empire, it is impossible to shew or to believe, that such a measure would not have been both wise and salutary. The misfortune was, that there soon came to be a legal preference of *one form* of Christianity over *all others*. Mankind are not easily inclined to change any institution which has taken deep root in the structure of society, and the principle of the union of *one form* of Christianity with the imperial authority under the Roman Emperors, had acquired too many titles to veneration to be relinquished, when the new kingdoms were founded which rose upon the ruins of the Roman Empire. This principle has always pervaded and still pervades the structure of European society, and the necessity of retaining it is still deeply seated in the convictions of the inhabitants of the Eastern continent.

---

1. Matthew xxviii. 20.

2. Isaiah xlix. 23. [Bishop of London, Robert] Lowth says of this prophecy: "It was remarkably fulfilled, when Constantine and other Christian princes and princesses, showed favour to the Church."

The same principle was transferred to these shores when they were settled by European colonists. In Massachusetts and some other Northern colonies, no man could be a citizen of the Commonwealth, unless he were a member of the Church as there established by authority of law.[3] In Virginia and some of the more Southern colonies, the Church of England was established by law.[4] In this State [South Carolina], legal provision was made for the establishment of religious worship according to the Church of England, for the erecting of churches and the maintenance of clergymen; and it was declared, that "in a well grounded Commonwealth, matters concerning religion and the honour of God, ought in the first place, (i.e. in preference to all others,) to be taken into consideration."[5]

It is the testimony of history, however, that ever since the time of Constantine, *such* an union of the ecclesiastical with the civil authority, has given rise to flagrant abuses and gross corruptions. By a series of gradual, but well contrived usurpations, a Bishop of the Church claiming to be the successor of the Chief of the Apostles and the Vicar of Christ, had been seen for centuries, to rule the nations of Christendom with the sceptre of despotism. The argument against the use of an institution arising from its abuse, is not valid, unless, when, after sufficient experience, there is the best reason to conclude, that we cannot enjoy the use without the accompanying evils flowing from the abuse of it. Such perhaps is the case in regard to the union between any particular form of Christianity and civil government. It is an historical truth established by the experience of many centuries, that whenever Christianity has *in this way* been incorporated with the civil power, the lustre of her brightness has been dimmed by the alliance.

The settlers of this country were familiar with these facts, and they gradually came to a sound practical conclusion on the subject. No nation on earth, perhaps, ever had opportunities so favorable to introduce changes in their institutions as the American people; and by the time of the Revolution, a conviction of the impolicy of a further union of Church and State *according to the ancient mode,* had so far prevailed, that nearly all the States in framing their new constitutions of government, either silently or by direct enactment, discontinued the ancient connexion.

---

3. In 1631, the General Court of Massachusetts Bay passed an order, "that for the time to come, none should be admitted to the freedom of the body politic, but such as were Church-members."—1 *Story's Commentaries,* 39, 73.

4. 1 Tucker's Blackstone, p. 376.—Under the crowns of France and Spain, Roman Catholicism was the religion of Louisiana exclusive of all others. As late as 1797, the instructions of Governor Gayoso to the commandants for the regulation of the province, speak thus:— "Art. 8. The commandants will take particular care, that no Protestant Preacher, or one of any sect other than the Catholic, shall introduce himself into the province. The least neglect in this respect, will be a subject of great reprehension."—*Documents annexed to Judge Peck's trial,* p. 585.

5. Act of November 30, 1706.

A question of great interest here comes up for discussion. In thus discontinuing the connexion between Church and Commonwealth;—did the people of these States intend to renounce all connexion with the Christian religion? Or did they only intend to disclaim all preference of one sect of Christians over another, as far as civil government was concerned; while they still retained the Christian religion as the foundation of all their social, civil and political institutions? Did Massachusetts and Connecticut, when they declared, that the legal preference which had heretofore been given to Puritanism, should continue no longer, intend to abolish Christianity itself within their jurisdictions? Did Virginia and S. Carolina when they discontinued all legal preference of the Church of England as by law established, intend to discontinue their observance of Christianity and their regard for its Divine authority? Did the people of the United States, when in adopting the Federal Constitution they declared, that "Congress shall make no law respecting an establishment of religion or prohibiting the free exercise thereof," expect to be understood as abolishing the national religion, which had been professed, respected and cherished from the first settlement of the country, and which it was the great object of our fathers in settling this then wilderness to enjoy according to the dictates of their own consciences?

The rightful solution of these questions has become important to the religion, the morals, the peace, the intelligence, and in fact, to all the highest interests of this country. It has been asserted by men distinguished for talents, learning and station,[6] and it may well be presumed that the assertion is gradually gaining belief among us, that Christianity has no connexion with the law of the land, or with our civil and political institutions. Attempts are making, to impress this sentiment on the public mind. The sentiment is considered by me, to be in contradiction to the whole tenor of our history, to be false in fact, and in the highest degree pernicious in its tendency, to all our most valuable institutions, whether social, legal, civil or political. It is moreover, not known to the preacher, that any serious effort has been made to investigate the relation which Christianity sustains to our institutions, or to enlighten the public understanding on the subject. Under these circumstances, I have thought it a theme suitable for discussion on an occasion, when the clergy of the diocese and some of the most influential laymen of our parishes, are assembled in convention. I may well expect to prove inadequate to the full discussion, and still more to the ultimate settlement of the principles involved in the inquiry. But I may be permitted to presume, that when it is once brought to the notice of this Convention, any deficiency of mine in treating the subject will not long remain to be satisfactorily supplied.

---

6. 4 Jefferson's Works, p. 397.

The relation of Christianity to the civil institutions of this country cannot be investigated with any good prospect of success, without briefly reviewing our history both before and since the Revolution, and making an examination of such authorities as are entitled to our respect and deference. It is an historical question, and to arrive at a sound conclusion, recurrence must be had to the ordinary means which are employed for the adjustment of inquiries of this kind.

I. The originators and early promoters of the discovery and settlement of this continent, had the propagation of Christianity before their eyes, as one of the principal objects of their undertaking. This is shewn by examining the charters and other similar documents of that period, in which this chief aim of their novel and perilous enterprize, is declared with a frequency and fulness which are equally satisfactory and gratifying. In the Charter of Massachusetts Bay, granted in 1644 by Charles I., the colonists are exhorted by "theire good life and orderly conversation, to winne and invite the natives of that country to the knowledge and obedience of the onely true God and Saviour of mankind and the Christian faith, which in our royall intention and the adventurers' free profession, (i.e. the unconstrained acknowledgment of the colonists,) is the principal end of this plantation."[7] In the Virginia Charter of 1606, the enterprize of planting the country is commended as "a noble work, which may, by the providence of Almighty God, hereafter tend to the glory of his Divine Majesty, in propagating of Christian religion to such people as yet live in darkness and miserable ignorance of the true knowledge and worship of God;"—and the Pennsylvania Charter of 1682, declares it to have been one object of William Penn, "to reduce the savage nations, by gentle and just manners, to the love of civil society and Christian religion."[8] In the Charter of Rhode Island, granted by Charles II. in 1682-3, it is declared to be the object of the colonists to pursue "with peace, and loyal minds, their sober, serious and religious intentions of godly edifying themselves and one another, in the holy Christian faith and worship, together with the gaining over and conversion of the poor ignorant Indian natives to the sincere profession and obedience of the same faith and worship."[9] The preceding quotations furnish a specimen of the sentiments and declarations with which the colonial Charters and other ancient documents abound.[10] I make no apology for citing the passages without abridgment. They are authentic memorials of an age long since gone by. They make known the intentions and breathe the feelings of our pious forefa-

---

7. Almon's Collection of Charters, p. 63.

8. Almon, pp. 68, 104.

9. Idem, p. 34.

10. See Note A.

thers; a race of men who, in all the qualities which render men respectable and venerable, have never been surpassed; and who ought to be held by us their offspring, in grateful remembrance. We very much mistake, if we suppose ourselves so much advanced before them, that we cannot be benefited by becoming acquainted with their sentiments, their characters and their labours. The Christian religion was intended by them to be the corner stone of the social and political structures which they were founding. Their aim was as pure and exalted, as their undertaking was great and noble.

II. We shall be further instructed in the religious character of our origin as a nation, if we advert for a moment to the rise and progress of our colonial growth. As the colonists desired both to enjoy the Christian religion themselves, and to make the natives acquainted with its divine blessings, they were accompanied by a learned and pious Ministry; and wherever a settlement was commenced, a Church was founded. As the settlements were extended, new Churches were established. Viewing education as indispensable to Freedom, as well as the handmaid of Religion, every neighbourhood had its school. After a brief interval, Colleges were instituted; and these institutions were originally designed for the education of Christian Ministers.[11] Six days of the week they spent in the labours of the field; but on the seventh, they rested according to the commandment, and employed the day in the duties of public worship, and in the religious instruction of their children and servants. Thus our colonization proceeded on the grand but simple plan of civil and religious freedom, of universal industry, and of universal literary and religious education.

The Colonies, then, from which these United States have sprung, were originally planted and nourished by our pious forefathers, in the exercise of

---

11. Scarcely had the Massachusetts' colonists arrived at their new scene of labour, when their thoughts were turned to the establishment of a College; and in 1636, Harvard University was founded. Dr. C. Mather says:—"The ends for which our fathers chiefly erected a College were, that so scholars might there be educated for the service of Christ and his Churches in the work of the Ministry, and that they might be seasoned in their tender years, with such principles as brought their blessed progenitors into this wilderness. There is no one thing of greater concernment to these Churches in present and after-times, than the prosperity of that society. They cannot subsist without a College."—*Magnalia, B.V.* The inscription, "Christo et Ecclesiæ," on the seal of the University, is at once emphatic evidence, and a perpetual memorial of the great purpose for which it was established. In the year 1662, the Assembly of Virginia passed an Act to make permanent provision for the establishment of a College. The preamble of the Act establishing it recites, "that the want of able and faithful Ministers in this country, deprives us of those great blessings and mercies that always attend upon the service of God;"— and the Act itself declares, "that for the advancement of learning, education of youth, supply of the ministry, and promotion of piety, there be land taken up and purchased for a College and Free School; and that with all convenient speed, there be buildings erected upon it for the entertainment of students and scholars. In 1693, the College of William and Mary was founded."—*Quar. Register.* vol. iii. p. 268. Quotations of similar import might be made pertaining to Yale, Nassau Hall and in fact, to all the Colleges first established in this country.

a strong and vigorous Christian faith. They were designed to be Christian communities. Christianity was wrought into the minutest ramifications of their social, civil and political institutions. And it has before been said, that according to the views which had prevailed in Europe since the days of Constantine, *a legal preference of some one denomination over all others,* prevailed in almost all the colonies. We are, therefore, now prepared:

III. To examine with a good prospect of success, the nature and extent of the *changes* in regard to Religion, which have been introduced by the people of the United States in forming their State Constitutions, and also in the adoption of the Constitution of the United States.

In perusing the twenty-four Constitutions of the United States with this object in view, we find all of them[12] recognising Christianity as the well known and well established religion of the communities, whose legal, civil and political foundations, these Constitutions are. The terms of this recognition are more or less distinct in the Constitutions of the different States; but they exist in all of them. The reason why any degree of indistinctness exists in any of them unquestionably is, that at their formation, it never came into the minds of the framers to suppose, that the existence of Christianity as the religion of their communities, could ever admit of a question. Nearly all these Constitutions recognise the customary observance of Sunday, and a suitable observance of this day, includes a performance of all the peculiar duties of the Christian faith.[13] The Constitution of Vermont declares, that "every sect or denomination of Christians, ought to observe the Sabbath or Lord's Day, and keep up some sort of religious worship, which to them shall seem most agreeable to the revealed will of God."[14] The Constitutions of Massachusetts and Maryland, are among those which do not prescribe the observance of Sunday: yet the former declares it to be "the right, as well as the duty of all men in society, publicly and at stated seasons, to worship the Supreme Being, the great Creator and Preserver of the Universe;["][15]—and the latter requires every person appointed to any office of profit or trust, to "subscribe a declaration of his belief in the Christian religion."[16] Two of them concur in the sentiment, that "morality and piety, rightly grounded on Evangelical principles, will be the best and greatest security to government; and that the knowledge of these is most likely to be propagated through a society, by the institution of the public worship of the

---

12. The author has not seen the *new* Constitution of Mississippi, and, therefore, this assertion may possibly not apply to that document.

13. See Note C.

14. Art. 3.

15. Part 1. Art. 2.

16. Art. 55.

Deity, and of public instruction in morality and religion."[17] Only a small part of what the Constitutions of the States contain in regard to the Christian religion, is here cited; but my limits do not permit me to cite more.[18] At the same time, they all grant the free exercise and enjoyment of religious profession and worship, with some slight discriminations, to all mankind. The principle obtained by the foregoing inductive examination of our State Constitutions, is this:—THE PEOPLE OF THE UNITED STATES HAVE RETAINED THE CHRISTIAN RELIGION AS THE FOUNDATION OF THEIR CIVIL, LEGAL AND POLITICAL INSTITUTIONS; WHILE THEY HAVE REFUSED TO CONTINUE A LEGAL PREFERENCE TO ANY ONE OF ITS FORMS OVER THE OTHER. In the same spirit of practical wisdom, moreover, they have consented to tolerate all other religions.

The Constitution of the United States contains a grant of specific powers, of the general nature of a trust. As might be expected from its nature, it contains but slight references of a religious kind. In one of these, the people of the United States profess themselves to be a Christian nation. In another, they express their expectation, that the President of the United States will maintain the customary observance of Sunday; and by parity of reasoning, that such observance will be respected by all who may be employed in subordinate stations in the service of the United States.[19] The first amendment declares, that "Congress shall make no law respecting an establishment of religion, or prohibiting the free exercise thereof."[20] This leaves the entire subject in the same situation in which it found it; and such was precisely the most suitable course. The people of the United States having, in this most solemn of all their enactments, professed themselves to be a Christian nation; and having expressed their confidence, that all employed in their service will practice the duties of the Christian faith;—and having, moreover, granted to all others the free exercise of their religion, have emphatically declared, that Congress shall make no change in the religion of the country. This was too delicate and too important a subject to be entrusted

---

17. The quotation here is from the Constitution of New-Hampshire; (*Part* i. *Art.* 6.) and the concurrence is substantial, not verbal. The parallel passage in the Constitution of Massachusetts runs thus:—"The happiness of a people, and the good order and preservation of civil government, essentially depend upon piety, religion and morality, and these cannot be generally diffused through the community but by the institution of a public worship of God, and of public institutions, (instructions) in piety, religion and morality."—*Part* i. *Art.* 3.

18. See Note B.

19. See Note C.

20. The meaning of the term "establishment" in this amendment unquestionably is, the preference and establishment given by law to one sect of Christians over every other. This is the customary use of the term in English history and in English law, and in our colonial history and law. See 3 Story's Comm. 722-731, where the author has commented on this amendment with his usual learning and candour.

to their guardianship. It is the duty of Congress, then, to permit the Christian religion to remain in the same state in which it was, at the time when the Constitution was adopted. They have no commission to destroy or injure the religion of the country. Their laws ought to be consistent with its principles and usages. They may not rightfully enact any measure or sanction any practice calculated to diminish its moral influence, or to impair the respect in which it is held among the people.[21]

If a question could be raised, in regard to the soundness of the view, which has now been taken, of the relation in which our Constitutions of government stand to the Christian religion, it must be settled by referring to the practice which has existed under them from their first formation. The public authorities both in our State and National Governments, have always felt it to be required of them, to respect the peculiar institutions of Christianity, and whenever they have ventured to act otherwise, they have never failed to be reminded of their error by the displeasure and rebuke of the nation. From the first settlement of this country up to the present time, particular days have been set apart by public authority, to acknowledge the favour, to implore the blessing, or to deprecate the wrath of Almighty God. In our Conventions and Legislative Assemblies, daily Christian worship has been customarily observed. All business proceedings in our Legislative halls

---

21. It has sometimes been concluded, that Christianity cannot have any direct connexion with the Constitution of the United States, on the ground, that the instrument contains no express declaration to this effect. But the error of such a conclusion becomes manifest, when we reflect, that the case is the same with regard to several other truths, which are notwithstanding, fundamental in our constitutional system. The Declaration of Independence says, that "governments are instituted among men, to secure the rights of life, liberty and the pursuit of happiness;" and that "whenever any form of government becomes destructive of these ends, it is the right of the people to alter or to abolish it, and to institute a new government." These principles lie at the foundation of the Constitution of the United States. No principles known to the Constitution are more fundamental than these. But the instrument contains no declaration to this effect; these principles are no where mentioned in it; and the references to them are equally slight and indirect with those which are made to the Christian religion. The same may be said, of the great republican truth, that political sovereignty resides in the people of the United States. If then, any one may rightfully conclude, that Christianity has no connexion with the Constitution of the United States, because this is nowhere expressly declared in the instrument; he ought, in reason, to be equally convinced, that the same Constitution is not built upon and does not recognize the sovereignty of the people, and the great republican truths above quoted from the Declaration of Independence. This argument receives additional strength, when we consider that the Constitution of the United States was formed directly for political, and not for religious objects. The truth is, they are all equally fundamental, though neither of them is expressly mentioned in the Constitution.

Besides, the Constitution of the United States contemplates, and is fitted for such a state of society as Christianity alone can form. It contemplates a state of society, in which strict integrity, simplicity and purity of manners, wide diffusion of knowledge, well disciplined passions, and wise moderation, are the general characteristics of the people. These virtues, in our nation, are the offspring of Christianity, and without the continued general belief of its doctrines, and practice of its precepts, they will gradually decline and eventually perish. See Note D.

and Courts of justice, have been suspended by universal consent on Sunday. Christian Ministers have customarily been employed to perform stated religious services in the Army and Navy of the United States. In administering oaths, the Bible, the standard of Christian truth is used, to give additional weight and solemnity to the transaction. A respectful observance of Sunday, which is peculiarly a Christian institution, is required by the laws of nearly all, perhaps of all the respective States.[22] My conclusion, then, is sustained by the documents which gave rise to our colonial settlements, by the records of our colonial history, by our Constitutions of government made during and since the Revolution, by the laws of the respective States, and finally by the uniform practice which has existed under them.[23] Manifold more authorities and illustrations might have been given, if such a course had been consistent with the limits which it was necessary to prescribe to myself on this occasion. But the subject is too important to be brought to a close without some further observations.

1st. We cannot too much admire the wisdom displayed by the American people in establishing such a relation between the Christian religion and their political institutions. To have abolished Christianity, or to have shewn indifference to its sacred nature and claims in framing their political institutions, would have been committing a great national sin. It would have been, also, to forget the Divine warning, that "except the Lord build the house, they labour in vain that build it."[24] To have given a legal preference to any one form of Christianity over another, would have been to depart from the usage of primitive times, and to sanction abuses to which it was no longer necessary to adhere. To have refused to others the free exercise of their religion, whatever this might be, would have been illiberal and at variance with the spirit of the age.[25] They wisely chose the middle course;—the

---

22. "All the States of the Union, I believe, (twenty-three of them certainly,) by explicit legislative enactments, acknowledge and declare the religious authority of Sunday."—*Speech of Mr. Frelinghuysen of New-Jersey, in the Senate of the United States, 8th May,* 1830.

23. See Note E.

24. Psalm 127.1.

25. The Constitution of S. Carolina, contains this provision; "The free exercise and enjoyment of religious profession and worship, without discrimination or preference, shall, forever hereafter, be allowed within this State to all mankind: *Provided,* that the liberty of conscience thereby declared, shall not be so construed as to excuse acts of licentiousness, or justify practices inconsistent with the peace or safety of this State." The Constitutions of New-York, of the dates both of 1777 and 1821 contain this same provision, and as it appears to be frequently misunderstood, the author adds Ch. J. [James] Kent's exposition of it, contained in 8 Johnson, 296. He speaks of it thus:—"This declaration (noble and magnanimous as it is, when duly understood) never meant to withdraw religion in general, and with it the best sanctions of moral and social obligation, from all consideration and notice of the law. It will be fully satisfied by a free and universal toleration, without any of the tests, disabilities or discriminations, incident to a religious establishment. To construe it as breaking down the

only course in fact warranted by Scripture, by experience and by primitive usage. They rightly considered their religion as the highest of all their interests,[26] and refused to render it in any way or in any degree, subject to governmental interference or regulations. Thus, while all others enjoy full protection in the profession of their opinions and practice, Christianity is the established[27] religion of the nation, its institutions and usages are sustained by legal sanctions, and many of them are incorporated with the fundamental law of the country.[28]

2. The doctrine against which I am contending; to wit, that Christianity has no connexion with our civil Constitutions of government, is one of those which admit of being tested by the absurd and dangerous consequences to which they lead. It cannot be disguised, that a general belief, that Christianity is to receive no regard and no countenance from our civil institutions, must tend to degrade it and to destroy its influence among the community. It has hitherto been believed, that Christian morals, Christian sentiments, and Christian principles ought to form the basis of the education of our youth; but this belief cannot continue to prevail, if the opinion in question shall once become general. It has hitherto been supposed, that our judges, our legislators, and our statesmen ought to be influenced by the spirit, and bound by the sanctions of Christianity, both in their public and private conduct; but no censure can be rightfully attached to them for re-

---

common law barriers against licentious, wanton and impious attacks upon Christianity itself, would be an enormous perversion of its meaning." The proviso, continues he, guards the article from such dangerous latitude of construction when it declares, that "'*the liberty of conscience hereby granted,* (declared) shall not be so construed as to excuse acts of licentiousness, or justify practices inconsistent with the peace or safety of this State.'" "The proviso is a species of commentary upon the meaning of the article. The framers of the Constitution intended only to banish test oaths, disabilities and the burthens and sometimes the oppressions of Church establishments; and to secure to the people of this State, freedom from coercion, and an equality of right on the subject of religion. This was no doubt the consummation of their wishes. It was all that reasonable minds could require and it had long been a favourite object, on both sides of the Atlantic, with some of the most enlightened friends to the rights of mankind, whose indignation had been roused by infringements of the liberty of conscience, and whose zeal was inflamed in the pursuit of its enjoyment."

26. The great interests of a country may be ranked thus:—1. Its religious and moral interests. 2. The peace of the country both in regard to foreign enemies and internal convulsions. 3. The intellectual interests, or the interests of education. 4. The pecuniary interests.

27. The term "established" is here used as well as at p. 11 [45], in its usual and not in its legal or technical sense, see p. 13 [46].

28. "Let us not forget the religious character of our origin. Our fathers were brought hither by their high veneration for the Christian religion. They journeyed by its light and laboured in its hope. *They sought to incorporate its principles with the elements of their society, and to diffuse its influence through all their institutions, civil, political or literary.* Let us cherish these sentiments, and extend this influence still more widely; in the full conviction, that that is the happiest society, which partakes in the highest degree of the mild and peaceable spirit of Christianity."—*Webster's Discourse at Plymouth,* p. 54. See Note F.

fusing to comply, if nothing of this kind is required by the commissions under which they act, and from which their authority is derived. If the community shall ever become convinced, that Christianity is not entitled to the sustaining aid of the civil Constitutions and law of the country, the outposts of the citadel will have been taken, and its adversaries may successfully proceed in their work of undermining and destroying it. In this country, where the authority of law is comparatively feeble, every enterprise must be accomplished by influencing public opinion; and the strength of public opinion is irresistible and overwhelming. In fact, under a belief, that such a conviction has been wrought in the public mind, the adversaries of Christianity have begun to break new ground against it; and this too with renewed confidence of ultimate success. It is announced from stations usually supposed to be entitled to respect and confidence, that the Scriptures of the New Testament expressly forbid all praying in public;—that the Christian Clergy are an unnecessary and useless order of men;—and that the setting apart of Sunday, is not authorized in any part of the Christian dispensation. These are novel and sweeping assertions, and they have already been repeated so often, that they sound less harsh than they once did, in the ears of our community. Those who attempt to impose such assertions upon us, must calculate with much confidence, either on our willingness to be deceived, or on our having too little acquaintance with the subject to detect their mistakes, or on our feeling too much indifference to our religion to take an interest in refuting them. Who believes, that without an order of men to administer the sacraments, to illustrate the doctrines and enforce the duties of Christianity, without public worship, and without the general and respectful observance of Sunday, there would be the least vestige of religion among us at the end of half a century[?] As well might we expect the preservation of public order and civil obedience in the community, if our laws were permitted to remain in the statute-book, without a Judiciary to explain their import, or an Executive to enforce their observance.

3. Let us not forget what is historically true, that Christianity has been the chief instrument by which the nations of Christendom have risen superior to all other nations;—but if its influence is once destroyed or impaired, society instead of advancing, must infallibly retrograde. This superiority of the nations of Christendom is a fact, and as such can only be accounted for by assigning an adequate cause. "With whatever justice other lands and nations may be estimated," says [Arnold] Heeren,[29] "it cannot be denied that the noblest and best of every thing, which man has produced, sprung up or at least ripened, on European soil. In the multitude, variety, and beauty of their natural productions, Asia and Africa far surpass Europe; but in every

---

29. Politics of Ancient Greece, translated by Mr. [George] Bancroft, p. 1.

thing which is the work of man, the nations of Europe stand far above those of the other continents. It was among them," continues he, "that by making marriage the union of but two individuals, domestic society obtained that form without which so many parts of our nature could never have been ennobled;—and it was chiefly and almost exclusively among them, that such constitutions were framed, as are suited to nations who have become conscious of their rights. If Asia, during all the changes of its extensive empires, does but shew the continued reproduction of despotism, it was on European soil that the germ of political freedom unfolded itself, and under the most various forms, in so many parts of the same, bore the noblest fruits; which again were transplanted from thence to other parts of the world." These remarks, though applied by the author to Europe only, have respect equally to the descendants of Europeans on this side of the Atlantic. They are true of all Christian nations. These golden fruits are what Christianity has produced, and they have been produced by no other religion. If, then, we permit this chief cause of all our choicest blessings to be destroyed or counteracted in its effects; what can we expect from the dealings of a righteous Providence, but the destiny of a people who have rejected the counsel of God against themselves?[30] If we refuse to be instructed by the Divine assurance, we shall be made to feel by the intensity of our sufferings, "that righteousness exalteth a nation, and that sin is a reproach to any people."

4. No nation on earth, is more dependent than our own, for its welfare, on the preservation and general belief and influence of Christianity among us. Perhaps there has never been a nation composed of men whose spirit is more high, whose aspirations after distinction are more keen, and whose passions are more strong than those which reign in the breasts of the American people. These are encouraged and strengthened by our systems of education, by the unlimited field of enterprise which is open to all; and more especially by the great inheritance of civil and religious freedom, which has descended to us from our ancestors. It is too manifest, therefore, to require illustration, that in a great nation thus high spirited, enterprising and free, public order must be maintained by some principle of very peculiar energy and strength;—by some principle which will touch the springs of human sentiment and action. Now there are two ways, and two ways only by which men can be governed in society; the one by physical force; the other by religious and moral principles pervading the community, guiding the conscience, enlightening the reason, softening the prejudices, and calming the passions of the multitude. Physical force is the chief instrument by which mankind have heretofore been governed; but this always

---

30. Luke vii. 30.

has been, and I trust will always continue to be inapplicable in our case. My
trust, however, in this respect, springs entirely from a confidence, that the
Christian religion will continue as heretofore to exert upon us, its tranquilizing, purifying, elevating and controlling efficacy. No power less efficacious
than Christianity, can permanently maintain the public tranquillity of the
country, and the authority of law.[31] We must be a Christian nation, if we
wish to continue a free nation. We must make our election:—to be swayed
by the gentle reign of moral and Christian principle, or ultimately, if not
soon, by the iron rod of arbitrary sway.

Nor will it be sufficient for any of us to say, that we have not been
active participators in undermining and destroying our religion;—we cannot escape crime, if it shall be destroyed by our neglect or indifference. The
guilt of nations which have never been evangelized, for not rendering to
Jehovah the glory due to his name, must be very much palliated by their
ignorance; which is, in some respects, and in a considerable degree, invin-
cible. But how can we escape, if we neglect, or abuse, or fail to improve the
Christian inheritance which has come down to us from our fathers, and
which it cost them such sacrifices to acquire. Have we forgotten the saying
of our Saviour, that the damnation of Sodom, in the day of judgment, will
be tolerable when compared with the sufferings which will, on that day, be
inflicted upon Capernaum, which had been exalted to heaven by being made
the scene of his miracles, but which still persisted in its impenitence?[32] In
the Divine administration, then, the principle applies to nations, as well as
to individuals, that their punishment will be severe in proportion to the
advantages which they have neglected to improve, and the blessings which
they have undervalued and despised. If, therefore, Christianity is permitted
to decline among us, we cannot fold our arms in silence and be free from all
personal responsibility. As a citizen of our community, no man can escape
criminality, if he believes in the truth of Christianity, and still, without making resistance, sees its influence undermined and destroyed.

We are accustomed to rejoice in the ancestry from which we are descended, and well we may, for our ancestors were illustrious men. One of
the colonial governors said in 1692, "God sifted a whole nation, that he might
send choice grain over into this wilderness."[33] And the present Lord Chan-
cellor of Great Britain has thus spoken of them:—"The first settlers of all
the colonies, says he, were men of irreproachable characters. Many of them
fled from persecution; others on account of an honorable poverty; and all
of them with their expectations limited to the prospect of a bare subsistence

31. See Note G.
32. Matthew xi. 23.
33. Am. Q. R. No. xviii. p. 128.

in freedom and peace. All idea of wealth or pleasure was out of the question. The greater part of them viewed their emigration as a taking up of the cross, and bounded their hopes of riches to the gifts of the spirit, and their ambition to the desire of a kingdom beyond the grave. A set of men more conscientious in their doings, or simple in their manners, never founded any Commonwealth. It is, indeed, continues he, the peculiar glory of North America, that with very few exceptions, its empire was originally founded in charity and peace."[34] They were, in truth, men who feared God and knew no other fear.[35]

    In no respect, therefore, were these illustrious men so peculiar, for no trait of character were they so distinguished, as for the strength of their religious principles. The perilous enterprise in which they were engaged, was chiefly a religious enterprise. To enjoy their religion according to the dictates of their own consciences, and to effect the conversion of the native Indians,[36] we have seen, were the great objects of their toils and sufferings. The principles which supplied them with the high motives from which they acted, were perseveringly taught to their children, and aided by their own bright example, became the vital sentiment of the new communities which they founded. What must have been the strength of the conviction of Christian Truth in the American mind, when the popular names of [Benjamin] Franklin[37] and of [Thomas] Jefferson among its adversaries, have not been able *much* to impair its influence. May Christianity, clear and convincing as she is in her evidences, pure in her doctrines, conservative in her moral influences, imperishable in her destiny, the last consolation of those who have outlived all earthly hopes, and the last restraint of those who are above all earthly fear, continue, with her benign reign, to bless our country, to the end of time, the crowning glory of the American name.[38]

    The conspiracy formed in Europe to destroy Christianity in the last century, has been overthrown and put to shame on that continent, by the overwhelming convulsions, distress and ruin brought upon its guilty nations, through the dissemination of its destructive principles.[39] In the whirlwind and storm of this mighty moral tempest, its seeds were wafted to our shores. They have taken root in our land, and we are threatened with their pestilential fruit in disastrous plenty. Infidelity advanced at first in this coun-

---

34. Brougham's Col. Pol. vol. i. p. 59.
35. Je crains Dieu, cher Abner, et n'ai point d'autre crainte.—*Racine.* [I fear God, dear Abner, and have no other fear.]
36. Note H.
37. Note I.
38. Note K.
39. Mr. Macaulay's Speech in House of Commons, April 17th, 1833.

try with cautious steps, and put on the decorous garb of rational and philosophical enquiry; until at length, having examined its ground and prepared
its way, it has assumed the attitude of open and uncompromising hostility
to every form and every degree of the Christian faith.

Our regard for the civil inheritance bequeathed us by our fathers, leads
us to guard it with the most jealous vigilance. And shall we permit our religious inheritance, which in their estimation was of still higher value and is
of infinitely more enduring interest, to be taken from us without a struggle?
Are we not convinced, that if our religion is once undermined, it will be
succeeded by a decline of public and private morals, and by the destruction
of those high and noble qualities of character, for which as a community we
have been so much distinguished?[40] Christianity, in its integrity, will never
perish; the gates of Hell, shall never prevail against the Church of God.[41]
But it has perished and may perish again in particular districts of [the] country. Are we accustomed to reflect on the consequences of a decline of the
influence of Christianity among us, and along with it, of public and private
morals? And on the other hand, are we sensible of the consequences which
must attend the introduction and general belief of the infidel system in our
land? The Christian and infidel systems have been long known in the world,
and their opposite moral effects on mankind, have been manifested by the
most ample experience. A tree is not more unequivocally known by its fruit,
than are these two systems by the results which they have respectively produced. What has Christianity done for the nations which have embraced it?
It has done much, very much. It has diminished the horrors of war. The
spirit of ancient war, was a relentless and sanguinary vengeance, which knew
not how to be satisfied but by the destruction of its victim. This fell spirit
has in a goodly measure, been softened in the conduct of modern warfare.
It has meliorated the calamitous lot of captives. Anciently, death, slavery, or
an enormous ransom, was their customary doom every where; and this still
continues to be the case in all countries not Christian. And when Christian
principles, motives and feelings shall have become universal, "glory to God
in the highest, and on earth peace, good will towards men," will universally
prevail.[42] In arbitrary governments, it has relaxed the stern rigour of des-
potic sway. It has suppressed infanticide. It has secured the life and limbs of
the slave against the caprice or passion of a tyrannical master. The frequent
periodical recurrence of a Day of Rest, has elevated the character and meliorated the state of the labouring classes of every Christian country. It has

---

40. Note L.

41. Matthew xvi. 18.

42. Milton says;—"He shall ascend / The throne hereditary, and bound his reign / With earth's
wide bounds, his glory with the heavens."

restored the wife from a condition of humiliation and servitude, to be the companion, the associate, the confidential adviser and friend of the husband. It has restored marriage to the standard ordained "at the beginning,"[43] the indissoluble union of two individuals, called by St. Paul a great mystery symbolical of the spiritual union between Christ and his Church; and has thus furnished the only reasonable security for domestic tranquillity, and the suitable nurture and education of children. Under its influence, the combats of gladiators, the impurities of superstitious rites, and unnatural vices, are no longer tolerated. The poor, the sick and the forsaken, are relieved by the numerous hospitals and asylums which are provided in all countries in which its authority is acknowledged. Moreover, it has been chiefly instrumental in rendering the nations of Christendom superior in virtue, intelligence and power, to all the other nations of the earth. Nor are we to estimate its principal benefits by what is visible. "The Kingdom of God cometh not with observation;" it does not consist in external splendour; its chief influence is unseen, renewing and sanctifying the hearts of the multitude who throng the obscure and humble walks of life. Again, what has Christianity done for our own nation? The answer is once more; much, very much. It was the moving cause which led our ancestors to transfer themselves to these shores, and to procure for us the fair inheritance which we now enjoy. It was an intimate and practical acquaintance with the doctrines, history and spirit of Christianity, which imparted to them that entire dependence on God, that unhesitating confidence in the protection of his Providence, that deep conviction of his favour, and those commanding moral virtues which shone in their lives with so resplendent a lustre. Especially it is to Christianity, that we are indebted for the steady self-control, and power of habitually subjecting our passions to the sway of reason and conscience, which have preserved us to this day, a free and a united people. May the future historian never record of us, that becoming wise above what is written, and forsaking the paths of our pious forefathers, we brought the judgments of Heaven upon our guilty land, and were made to drink to the dregs of the cup of national humiliation and shame. And what has Christianity done for us personally? The answer is not only much, very much, but every thing. In infancy it may very possibly have saved us from death by exposure; no uncommon fate wherever Christianity has not prevailed. Born, as we were by nature, children of wrath, she received us by baptism into the fold of Christ, and made us heirs of the promises, the hopes and the consolations of the Gospel. Sensibly alive to the transitory nature of all human connexions, and the instability of all earthly prospects, she provided sureties, who, in case of the demise or default of our natural guardians, might feel

---

43. Matthew xix. 4-6.

themselves responsible for fitting us to receive the Christian inheritance, to which we were admitted in prospect, by baptism. On arriving at years of discretion, she confirmed us in the privileges of our high estate; and as we journey onward in the thorny path of life, she feeds us with "that bread which came down from Heaven," rescues us from temptation, strengthens us amid our infirmities, and animates our weary steps by the kind voice of encouragement. Aided and animated by her divine guidance, when we shall come to the end of our path, we shall not be overwhelmed with fearful apprehensions. We shall contemplate the solitude of the grave without dismay. She will not leave us within its narrow and lonely precincts. She will guide and sustain us through the dark valley of the shadow of death, and will bring us to mansions of immortality and glory. And what has the infidel system to give us in exchange for the Christian promises, hopes, virtues, consolations and final inheritance which it destroys? What has it done for those who have embraced it? And in case we embrace it, what effects may it be expected to produce on our national destinies, on our domestic tranquillity, on ourselves personally, and "on all estates and orders of men?" We can have no difficulty in answering these questions;—we have the oracular voice of the experience of the last half century. These will be the burthen of its teachings, the fruit of its instructions. By excluding a Supreme Being, a superintending Providence, and a future state of rewards and punishments, as much as possible, from the minds of men, it will destroy all sense of moral responsibility; for, the lively impression of an omnipresent Ruler of the Universe and a strong sense of moral obligation, have, in the history of mankind, always accompanied each other; and whenever the former has been weakened, it has never failed to be followed by a corresponding moral declension. Now what is to preserve an habitual reverence for Almighty God in the public mind, if the institution of public worship ever comes to be disregarded, if the Christian Ministry shall be rendered odious in the eyes of the community, if the observance of Sunday shall be generally neglected, and if the Scriptures shall be brought into general discredit? Yet with just such a state of things we are threatened. Let us not refuse to look at the real nature of the case. The fact is, that a man's sense of duty, his moral sensibility, is the conservative element of his character; and no man can receive so great an injury himself, or inflict so great a calamity on another, as the impairing or the destruction of this grand principle. Of all unpromising indications in a youth, is not insensibility to moral considerations, the most decisive and unequivocal? When the sense of duty is extinguished in an individual, he becomes a burthen to himself and a nuisance to others, the sport of every wind of caprice and passion. From infecting individuals, a moral taint soon comes to infect a nation, which now becomes, in the natural order of a descending course, the theatre of every crime which can degrade individuals, disturb society and brutalize mankind. In such a community, all the virtues which procure respect and esteem, and still more, those which elevate and adorn society, must decline and perish. The security of society depends on the conviction which we habitually feel, that those among whom we dwell, are governed in their conduct by humanity, justice, moderation, kindness, integrity and good faith. When these main pillars of moral and social order are overthrown, general confidence between man and man must be exchanged for universal suspicion, every individual will be seized with apprehension and terror, the mild authority of law must cease its reign, and the dark and fearful passions of selfishness, lust and revenge break forth with unbridled violence and fury. During the last half century, where are the achievements of the infidel system to be seen, but in the ruin of hundreds of thousands of estimable families, unexampled distress of nations, general anarchy and convulsions, and in the devastation of much of the fairest portion of the earth. Encouragement of the infidel system among us, will dissolve all the moral ties which unite men in the bonds of society. Circumvention and fraud will come to be esteemed wisdom, the sacred mystery of "plighted troth" will be laughed to scorn, wise forbearance will be accounted pusillanimity, an enlightened practical benevolence will be supplanted by a supreme regard to self-gratification and an insensibility to the welfare of other men, the disregard of Almighty God will be equalled only by a corresponding contempt of mankind, personal aggrandizement will be substituted for love of country, social order and public security will be subverted by treason and violence;—these, and all these have been, and may again be the fruits of the infidel system.[44]

---

44. Gouverneur Morris resided in France during the first part of the Revolution, and in a letter to President Washington, dated Paris, April 29, 1789, he thus speaks of the state of morals.

"Every one agrees that there is an utter prostration of morals; but this general position can never convey to an American mind the degree of depravity. It is not by any figure of rhetoric, or force of language, that the idea can be communicated. A hundred anecdotes and a hundred thousand examples, are required to shew the extreme rottenness of every member. There are men and women who are greatly and eminently virtuous. I have the pleasure to number many in my acquaintance; but they stand forward from a back ground deeply and darkly shaded. It is, however, from such crumbling matter, that the great edifice of freedom is to be erected here. Perhaps, like the stratum of rock, which is spread under the whole surface of their country, it may harden when exposed to the air, but it seems quite as likely that it will fall and crush the builders. I own to you that I am not without such apprehensions, for there is one fatal principle which pervades all ranks. It is, perfect indifference to the violation of engagements. Inconsistency is so mingled in the blood, marrow and very essence of this people, that when a man of high rank and importance laughs to-day at what he seriously asserted yesterday, it is considered as in the natural order of things. Consistency is a phenomenon."— *Life by Sparks,* vol. ii. p. 68.

Again, p. 255, under date December 21, 1792, "the morals, or rather the want of morals, in this country, places every one at his ease. He may be virtuous if he pleases, but there is no

Finally, let us in the strength of Almighty God, cling with fresh ear-
nestness and new resolution to our religion, as to the last anchor of our
hope and safety. "It is not a vain thing for us, it is our life." It is our only
imperishable treasure. In it are comprised, at once, the great causes of peace,
of virtue, of intelligence, of freedom, of good government and of human
happiness.

necessity either to be or to appear so. The open contempt of religion, also, cannot but be
offensive to all sober minded men."
    For the best expositions of the character of modern infidelity, see Dr. [Timothy] Dwight's
Sermons on Infidelity.—[Edmund]Burke's Reflections on the Revolution in France, works,
vol. iii.—Letters on France and England, published in the American Review, 1811 and 1812.—
Rev. R[obert] Hall's Sermon on Ephesians, ii. 12.

ADAMS'S SERMON NOTES

<hr />

A.—*Page* 9 [43].

As the documents here referred to are not easily obtained, it may be useful to subjoin further quotations.

The aim of the crown and of the Colonists in planting Connecticut, is still more strongly expressed than in the case of Massachusetts. The General Assembly of the colony are instructed to govern the people, "so as their good life and orderly conversation may win and invite the natives of the country to the knowledge and obedience of the only true God and Saviour of mankind and the Christian faith: which in our royal intentions and the adventurers' free profession, is the *only* and principal end of this plantation." (*Almon.* p. 30.) The same declaration under considerable variations, is contained in nearly all the colonial charters. In the Rhode Island charter, at p. 39 of Almon,—Virginia, p. 93.—Maryland, pp. 115. 125.—For the Carolina charters, see Trott's Laws, vol. i. pp. xxi. xxxiii. In the Virginia Charter of 1609, it is said, moreover, that "it shall be necessary for all such as shall inhabit within the precincts of Virginia, to determine to live together in the fear and true worship of Almighty God, Christian peace and civil quietness:"—and that "the principal effect which we (the crown) can desire or expect of this action, (i.e. the granting of this charter) is the conversion and reduction of the people in those parts unto the true worship of God and Christian religion." (*Almon.* pp. 91. 92.)

The preamble to the celebrated articles of confederation between the colonies of Massachusetts, New-Plymouth, Connecticut and New-Haven, dated 1643, declares, that "wee all came into these parts of America with one and the same end and ayme, namely, to advaunce the kingdome of our Lord Jesus Christ, and to enjoy the liberties of the Gospell in puritie with peace;"—and Art. 2d. assigns one object of the league to be, "for preserueing and propagateing the truth and liberties of the Gospell" (2 *Hazard,* p. 1). A passage from the instructions of the N.E. Company in England, to John Endicott, dated April 1629, speaks thus:—"and for that the propagating of the Gosple is the thinge wee do profess *aboue all* to be our ayme in setling this Plantacon, wee haue bin carefull to make plentifull provision of Godly Ministers, by whose faithfull preachinge, Godly conversacon and exemplary Lyfe, wee trust not only those of our owne Nation, will be built vp in the Knowledge of God, but *also the Indians* may, in God's appointed tyme, be reduced to the obedyence of the Gosple of Christ," &c. After mentioning their names and some particulars respecting them, the instructions proceed thus:—"For the manner of the exercising their Ministrie, and teaching both our owne People *and the Indians,* wee leave that to themselves, hoping they will make God's Word the Rule of their Accons, and mutually agree in the discharge of their duties; and because *their* doctrine will hardly bee well esteemed whose persons are not reverenced, we desire that both by your owne example, and by commanding all others to doe the like, our Ministers may receive due Honor."—1 *Hazard,* pp. 256. 257.—Further illustrations on the subject of this note may be seen in 1 Hazard, 46. 82. 103. 117. 134. 148. 151. 155. 160. 184. 203. 259. 300.—For the Commissions of Columbus, John Cabot and his sons, Jacques Quartier, &c. see 1 Hazard, 1 9. 19. &c.

The value of this note cannot fail to be enhanced, if the author subjoins the sentiments and views of Columbus when he entered upon his adventurous enterprise. The materials are prepared to his hands.

Mr. [Washington] Irving says, "one of the great objects held out by Columbus in his undertaking, was the propagation of the Christian faith. He expected to arrive at the extremity of Asia, at the vast and magnificent empire of the Grand Khan. He contemplated that, by means of his discovery, an immediate intercourse might be opened with this immense empire, that the whole might speedily be brought into subjection to the Church; and thus, as had been foretold in Holy Writ, the light of revelation might be extended to the remotest ends of the earth." The Queen, also, was filled with pious zeal at the idea of effecting such a great work of salvation. He opens the journal of his first voyage by saying, that their Majesties of Spain (Ferdinand and Isabella) determined to send him to the parts of India, to see the princes, people and lands, and to discover the nature and disposition of them all, and the means to be taken for the conversion of them to the Holy Faith. In his will, moreover, Columbus enjoined on his son Diego, or whoever might inherit after him, "to spare no pains in having and maintaining in the Island of Hispaniola, four good professors of theology, to the end and aim of their studying and labouring to convert to our Holy Faith the inhabitants of the Indias;—and, continues he, in proportion as by God's will, the revenue of the estate shall increase, in the same degree, shall the number of teachers and devout persons increase, who are to strive to make Christians of the natives; in attaining which no expense should be thought too great.["] —*Life of Columbus,* vol. i. pp. 103. 104. 118.—vol. iii. p. 418.

B.—PAGE 12 [46].

Some further quotations are made for the benefit of those who may not have a copy of the American Constitutions at hand.

Constitution of Massachusetts, Part i. *Art.* 3.—"As the happiness of a people, and the good order and preservation of civil government, essentially depend upon piety, religion and morality; and as these cannot be generally diffused through the community, but by the institution of a public worship of God, and of public institutions (instructions) in piety, religion and morality; therefore, to promote their happiness, and to secure the good order and preservation of their government, the people of this Commonwealth have a right to invest their Legislature with power to authorize and require, and the Legislature shall, from time to time, authorize and require the several towns, parishes, precincts, and other bodies politic, or religious societies, to make suitable provision at their own expense, for the institution of the public worship of God, and for the support and maintenance of public Protestant teachers of piety, religion and morality, in all cases, where such provision shall not be made voluntarily.

["]And the people of the Commonwealth have also a right to, and do, invest their Legislature with authority to enjoin upon all the subjects, an attendance upon the instructions of the public teachers, as aforesaid, at stated times and seasons, if their be any one whose instructions they can conscientiously and conveniently attend. All moneys paid by the subject to the support of public worship, and of the public teachers aforesaid, shall, if he require it, be uniformly applied to the support of the public teacher or teachers of his own religious sect or denomination, provided there be any, on whose instructions he attends; otherwise, it may be paid towards the support of the teacher or teachers of the parish or precinct in which the said moneys are raised. And every denomination of Christians, demeaning themselves peaceably, and as good subjects of the Commonwealth, shall be equally under the protection of the law; and no subordination of any sect or denomination to another, shall ever be established by law." *Part* ii. *Ch.* v. *Sec.* i. *Art.* 1.—"Whereas our wise and pious ancestors so early as the year 1636, laid the foundation of Harvard College, in which University many persons of great eminence have, by the blessing of God, been initiated into those arts and sciences which qualified them for public employments, both in Church and State; and whereas the encouragement of arts and sciences, and all good literature, *tends to the honor of God, the advantage of the Christian religion,* and the great benefit of this and the other United States of America, it is declared that the President and fellows of Harvard College," &c.

New Hampshire.—The Constitution of this State contains provisions, in regard to the Christian Religion, substantially the same with those just quoted from the Constitution of Massachusetts, except so far as these relate to Harvard University. *See* p. 12 [45-46]. The Constitutions of Vermont and Rhode Island have been sufficiently quoted. *See* pp. 9. 11 [43, 45].

Connecticut, Art. 7 *Sec.* 1.—"It being the duty of all men to worship the Supreme Being, the great Creator and Preserver of the universe, and their right to render that worship in the mode most consistent with the dictates of their consciences; no person shall, by law, be compelled to join or support, nor be classed with, or associated to, any congregation, church, or religious association. But every person now belonging to such congregation, church, or religious association, shall remain a member thereof, until he shall have separated himself therefrom, in the manner hereinafter provided. And each and every society or denomination of Christians in this State, shall have and enjoy the same and equal powers, rights, and privileges; and shall have power and authority to support and maintain the ministers or teachers of their respective denominations, and to build and repair houses for public worship, by a tax on the members of any such society only, to be laid by a major vote of the legal voters assembled at any society meeting, warned and held according to law, or in any other manner."

New-Jersey.—The Constitution of this State declares, (*Art.* xix.) "that there shall be no establishment of any one religious sect in this province (this constitution was formed in 1776,) in preference to another, and that no protestant inhabitant of this colony shall be denied the enjoyment of any civil right, merely on account of his religious principles; but that all persons professing a belief in the faith of any protestant sect who shall demean themselves peaceably under the government, as hereby established, shall be capable of being elected into any office of profit or trust, or being a member of either branch of the Legislature, and shall fully and freely enjoy every privilege and immunity enjoyed by others their fellow subjects."

Maryland.—The declaration of rights says, (*Art.* xxxiii.) "that as it is the duty of every man to worship God in such manner as he thinks most acceptable to him, all persons professing the Christian religion are equally entitled to protection in their religious liberty." And again, (*Art.* xxxv.) "that no other test or qualification ought to be required, on admission to any office of trust or profit than such oath of support and fidelity to this State, and such oath of office, as shall be directed by this Convention or the Legislature of this State, *and a declaration of belief in the Christian religion.*" *See also* p. 12 [45].

North-Carolina in her Constitution (*Art.* xxxii.) says, "that no person who shall deny the being of a God, or the truth of the Protestant religion, or the divine authority of either the Old or New Testament, or shall hold religious principles incompatible with the freedom and safety of the State, shall be capable of holding any office, or place of trust or profit, in the civil department within this State."

So far as these quotations make any distinction between denominations of Christians, the author does not concur with them, but they conclusively shew, that the constitutions from which they are taken, unequivocally sustain the Christian religion.

C.—PAGE 11, 13 [45, 46].

In Art. 7th of the Constitution of the United States, that instrument is said to have been framed, "by the unanimous consent of the States present, the seventeenth day of September, *in the year of our Lord,* 1787, and of the independence of the United States of America, the twelfth." In the clause printed in Italic letters, the word *Lord* means the Lord Jesus Christ, and the word *our* preceding it, refers back to the commencing words of the Constitution; to wit, "We the people of the United States." The phrase, then, *our Lord,* making a part of the dating of the Constitution when compared with the commencing clause, contains a distinct recognition of the authority of Christ, and of course, of his religion by the people of the United States. This conclusion is sound, whatever theory we may embrace in regard to the Constitution;—whether we consider it as having been ratified by the people of the United States in the aggregate, or by States, and whether we look upon the Union in the nature of a government, a compact or a league. The date of the Constitution is twofold;—it is first dated by the birth of our Lord Jesus Christ; and then by the Independence of the United States of America. Any argument which should be supposed to prove, that the authority of Christianity is not recognised by the people of the United States in the first mode, would equally prove that the Independence of the United States is not recognised by them in the second mode. The fact is, that the Advent of Christ and the Independence of the country, are the two events in which of all others, we are most interested; the former in common with all mankind, and the latter as the Birth of our Nation. This twofold mode, therefore, of dating so solemn an instrument, was singularly appropriate and becoming. The Articles of Confederation are dated in the same twofold way.

Again, in Art. 1, Sec. 7, c. 2 of the Constitution of the United States, provision is made, that, "if any bill shall not be returned by the President within ten days (Sundays excepted) after it shall have been presented to him, the same shall be a law in like manner as if he had signed it, unless the Congress by their adjournment prevent its return; in which case it shall not be a law." In adopting this provision, it was clearly presumed by the people, that the President of the United States would not employ himself in public business on Sunday. There is no other way of explaining the fact, that in the case contemplated, they have given him ten business days, during which he may consider a bill and prepare his objections to it. The people had been accustomed to pay special respect to Sunday from the first settlement of the country. They assumed, that the President also would wish to respect the day. They did not think it suitable or becoming to require him, by a constitutional provision, to respect the day;—they assumed that he would adhere to the customary observance without a requirement. To have enacted a constitutional provision, would have left him no choice, and would have been placing no confidence in him. They have placed the highest possible confidence in him, by assuming without requiring it, that his conduct in this respect would be according to their wishes. Every man who is capable of being influenced by the higher and more delicate motives of duty, cannot fail to perceive, that the obligation on the President to respect the observance of Sunday, is greatly superior to any which could have been created by a constitutional enactment. It is said in the text, that this obligation extends by parity of reasoning to all persons employed in stations subordinate to the Presidency in the service of the United States. This is certainly true, but it is perhaps not putting the argument in its strongest light. The reasoning is quite as much *a fortiori* as *a pari*. The people in adopting the Constitution, must have been convinced, that the public business entrusted to the President, would be greater in importance and variety, than that which would fall to the share of any functionary employed in a subordinate station. The expectation and confidence, then, manifested by the people of the United States, that their President will respect their Sunday, by abstaining from public business on that day, must extend *a fortiori* to all employed in subordinate stations.★

The recognitions of Christianity in the State Constitutions are of three kinds. 1. These instruments are usually dated in the *year of our Lord,* and the same observations which were made on this phrase in the case of the Constitution of the United States, are no less applicable, *mutatis mutandis,* to the Constitutions of the respective States. 2. Nearly all of them refer to the ob-

---

★The author is happy to sustain his views by the authority of Mr. [Theodore] Frelinghuysen, United States Senator from New-Jersey.

   "Our predecessors have acted upon a true republican principle, that the feelings and opinions of the majority were to be consulted. And when a collision might arise, inasmuch as only one day could be thus appropriated, they wisely determined, in accordance with the sentiments of at least nine-tenths of our people, that the first day of the week should be the Sabbath of our government. This public recognition is accorded to the Sabbath in our Federal Constitution. The President of the United States, in the discharge of the high functions of his Legislative Department, is expressly relieved from all embarrassment on Sunday. Both Houses of Congress, the Offices of the State, Treasury, War, and Navy Departments, are all closed on Sunday." Speech in the Senate 8th May, 1830.

servance of Sunday by the Chief Executive Magistrate, in the same way in which such observance is referred to, in the Constitution of the United States; and, therefore, in regard to them, no further observations are required. 3. Definite constitutional provisions not only recognising the Christian religion, but affording it countenance, encouragement and protection; the principal of which are quoted in the text p. 12 [45-46], and in Note B. pp. 30, 31 [61, 62]. See also p. 13 [46].

D.—Page 14 [47].

This appears to the author the most convincing ground upon which to rest the argument against Sunday mails. The observance of Sunday, and its appropriation to the duties of religion, had been established from the first settlement of the country. Laws were in force and had long been in force, requiring its respectful observance, in all the thirteen States which were originally parties to the Constitution of the United States. No authority over the Christian religion, or its institutions, has been given to the National Legislature by this Constitution. All their measures ought to be consistent with its institutions, and none of them ought to be in violation of them. And until within a few years, our national legislation was, in this respect, suitable and highly commendable. It is not known to the author, that until very lately there existed any Act of Congress requiring a violation of any Christian institution. (*Mr. Frelinghuysen's Speech in Senate*, p. 5.) The Act of 3d March, 1825 section 11th, makes it the duty of every postmaster to deliver letters, papers, &c. *on every day of the week*, at all reasonable hours. (*Gordon's Digest*, 427.) This is the first statute enacted by Congress, authorizing and requiring a violation of the religion of the country. Congress can rightfully make no change in the religion of the nation; but in this instance, they have enacted, that as far as the mail department of the public business is concerned, there shall no longer exist the established (by law) observance of Sunday. This Act does not leave Christianity in the same situation in which it was, before it was passed. It employs some thousands in desecrating and destroying an institution peculiar to Christianity. It is, therefore, in the judgment of the author, unconstitutional, and ought to be rescinded. Nor is the argument from the alleged necessity of Sunday mails, any better than the constitutional argument. London is the first city on earth for wealth, business and enterprise; but no mail is opened or closed in it on Sunday. And notwithstanding the immense intercourse between London and Liverpool, no mail leaves the Metropolis for Liverpool, between Saturday evening and Monday morning. (*Mr. Frelinghuysen's Speech in the United States' Senate*, 8th May, 1830.)

It is mentioned above by the author, that a very suitable concern has, in general, been manifested by the Federal Government, to prevent the desecration of Sunday. The rules and regulations of the Army of the United States, present an instance in point. By Art. 2d of these rules and regulations, which every officer, before he enters on the duties of his office, is required to subscribe: "it is earnestly recommended to all officers and soldiers diligently to attend divine service; and all officers who shall behave indecently or irreverently at any place of divine worship, shall, if commissioned officers, be brought before a general court-martial, there to be publicly and severely reprimanded by the President; if non-commissioned officers or soldiers, every person so offending, shall for his first offence, forfeit one-sixth of a dollar, to be deducted out of his next pay; for the second offence, he shall not only forfeit a like sum, but be confined twenty-four hours; and for every like offence, shall suffer and pay in like manner." (Act of April 10th, 1806, Sec. 1.) (*Gordon's Digest,* Art. 3269.) This Art. is taken almost verbatim from the "rules and orders" enacted by the Old Congress on the same subject. (See Journal of 30th June, 1775.) Will it be arrogating too much, if the author respectfully asks any military commander into whose hands these pages may come, candidly to examine the bearing which the above regulation may rightfully have upon military reviews held on Sunday, and upon marching on Sunday, when the exigencies of the service do not require it? He is under a belief, that military reviews are quite as common on Sunday as upon any other day of the week. He also within a few weeks observed, with regret, a statement in the newspapers, that certain of our citizens went from the city to a neighbouring island, for the purpose of attending a military review on Sunday.

E.—*Page* 15 [48].

An examination of the journals of the Old Congress has given results on this subject highly satisfactory which for the sake of method may be thus classed:—

1. Days of humiliation, fasting and prayer. June 7th, 1775, "Resolved, that Thursday the 20th of July next, be observed throughout the twelve United Colonies, as a day of humiliation, fasting and prayer." At the same time, a committee was appointed on the subject. June 12th, this committee brought in their report, or proclamation. It occupies an entire page of the journals and concludes thus:—"And it is recommended to *Christians of all denominations* to assemble for public worship, and to abstain from servile labour and recreation on said day." July 19th.—"Agreed, that the Congress meet at this place to-morrow, and from this place, go in a body to attend

Divine service."—March 16th, 1776, Mr. W[illiam] Livingston brought in are solution for appointing a fast in the colonies, on Friday 17th of May. A part of it runs thus:—"That we may with united hearts, confess and bewail our manifold sins and transgressions, and by a sincere repentance and amendment of life, appease his righteous displeasure, and *through the merits and mediation of Jesus Christ,* obtain his pardon and forgiveness." As one motive for recommending this day of fasting &c. Congress say, they are "desirous to have people of all ranks and degrees duly impressed with a solemn sense of God's superintending Providence, and of their duty, devoutly to rely, in all their lawful enterprises, on his aid and direction." December 9th, 1776, a committee was appointed to prepare a recommendation to the several States, to appoint a similar day. This committee reported on the 11th and on this occasion;—"the Congress in the most earnest manner, recommend to all the members of the United States, and particularly the officers civil and military under them, the exercise of repentance and reformation; and further require of them the strict observation of the articles of war, and particularly that part of the said articles which forbids profane swearing and all immorality, of which all such officers are desired to take notice." *See Journals for June 30th,* 1775.—February 27th, and March 7th, 1778;—a similar day, (22d April,) is recommended. A part of the recommendation runs thus:—"that at one time and with one voice, the inhabitants may acknowledge the righteous dispensations of Divine Providence, and confess their iniquities and transgressions for which the land mourneth; that they may implore the mercy and forgiveness of God; and beseech him that vice, profaneness, extortion and every evil may be done away; and that we may be a reformed and happy people; that it may please him to bless our schools and seminaries of learning, and make them nurseries of true piety, virtue and useful knowledge."—March 20th, 1779, a similar recommendation, a part of which is thus:—"that Almighty God will be pleased to avert those impending calamities which we have but too well deserved; *that he will grant us his grace to repent of our sins, and amend our lives according to his holy word;* that he will grant us patience in suffering and fortitude in adversity; that he will inspire us with humility, moderation and gratitude in prosperous circumstances; that he will diffuse useful knowledge, *extend the influence of true religion,* and give us that peace of mind, which the world cannot give."—March 11th, 1780, is a proclamation for another fast, which in part is thus:—"that we may with one heart and one voice, implore the Sovereign Lord of heaven and earth to remember mercy in his judgments; to make us sincerely penitent for our transgressions; to banish vice and irreligion from among us, and establish virtue and piety by his Divine grace," &c.—March 20th, 1781, another recommendation of the same kind running in part thus:—"that we may, with united hearts, confess and bewail our manifold sins and transgressions, and by sincere repentance and amendment of life, appease his righteous displeasure, and *through the merits of our blessed Saviour,* obtain pardon and forgiveness; that it may please him to inspire our rulers with incorruptible integrity, and to direct and prosper their councils; that it may please him to bless all schools and seminaries of learning, and to grant, that truth, justice and benevolence, and pure and undefiled religion may universally prevail."—March 19th, 1782, another similar proclamation; a part is thus:— "The United States in Congress assembled, think it their indispensable duty to call upon the several States, to set apart the last Thursday in April next as a day of fasting, humiliation and prayer, that our joint supplications may then ascend to the Throne of the Ruler of the Universe, beseeching Him to diffuse a spirit of universal reformation among all ranks and degrees of our citizens; and make us a holy, so that we may be a happy people; that it would please him to impart wisdom, integrity and unanimity to our counsellors; that he would protect the health and life of our Commander in Chief; that he would take under his guardianship all schools and seminaries of learning, and make them nurseries of virtue and piety; that he would incline the hearts of all men to peace, and fill them with universal charity and benevolence, and *that the religion of our Divine Redeemer,* with all its benign influences, may cover the earth as the waters cover the seas."

2. Days of thanksgiving, gratitude and praise. Journals, Oct. 31st, and Nov. 1st, 1777; it is recommended "to the several States, to set apart a day for thanksgiving, for the signal success lately obtained over the enemies of these United States." After saying that "it is the indispensable duty of all men to adore the superintending Providence of Almighty God; to acknowledge with gratitude their obligation to him for benefits received,["] &c. the document "sets apart the 18th of December, for solemn thanksgiving and praise," and proceeds thus:—"that with one heart and one voice, the good people may express the grateful feelings of their hearts, and consecrate themselves to the service of their Divine Benefactor; and that together with their sincere acknowledgments and offerings, they may join the penitent confession of their manifold sins, whereby they had forfeited every favor, and their humble and earnest supplication that it may please God, *through the merits of Jesus Christ,* mercifully to forgive and blot them out of remembrance; to take schools and seminaries of education, so necessary for cultivating the principles of true liberty, virtue and piety, under his nurturing hand, and to prosper the means of religion for the promotion and enlargement of *that kingdom which consisteth in righteousness, peace and joy in the Holy Ghost.*" See also Journals of Nov. 7th, 1777.—Nov. 7th, and 17th, 1778, a similar recommendation—Oct. 14th and 20th, 1779, a similar recommendation. The preamble of which after enumerating various causes of national thankful-

ness, says; "and above all, that he hath diffused the glorious *light of the Gospel,* whereby, *through the merits of our gracious Redeemer, we may become the heirs of his eternal glory."* The resolution, after appointing the 9th of December as "a day of public and solemn thanksgiving to Almighty God for his mercies, and of prayer for the continuance of his favor and protection to these United States," proceeds:—"that he would grant *to his church the plentiful effusions of Divine grace, and pour out his Holy Spirit on all Ministers of the Gospel;* that he would bless and prosper the means of education, and *spread the light of Christian knowledge through the remotest corners of the earth;* that he would in mercy look down upon us, pardon our sins and receive us into his favour, and finally, that he would establish the independence of these United States upon the basis of *religion* and virtue."—Oct. 18th, 1780, another document of similar import. The last of the petitions to Almighty God recommended, is, that he will "cherish all schools and seminaries of education, and cause *the knowledge of Christianity to spread over all the earth."*—Sept. 13th, 1781, on motion of Mr. [Roger] Sherman, a committee was appointed to prepare a proclamation for a day of thanksgiving throughout the United States. Oct. 26th, a proclamation was reported and agreed to. Oct. 11th, 1782, a similar recommendation. Oct. 18th, 1783, a proclamation was prepared and agreed to. This was at the close of the war, and after enumerating the chief causes of national thankfulness connected with the successful result of the revolutionary contest, the document continues:—"And above all, that he hath been pleased to continue to us *the light of the blessed Gospel, and secured to us in the fullest extent the rights of conscience in faith and worship.* And while our hearts overflow, and our lips set forth the praises of our great Creator, that we also offer up fervent supplications, that it may please him to pardon all our offences, to give wisdom and unanimity to our public councils, to cement all our citizens in the bonds of affection, and to inspire them with an earnest regard for the national honor and interest; to enable them to improve the days of prosperity by every good work, and to be lovers of peace and tranquillity; that he may be pleased to bless us in our husbandry, our commerce and navigation; to smile upon our seminaries and means of education, to cause *pure religion* and virtue to flourish, to give peace to all nations and *to fill the world with his glory."* These sentiments are worthy of our revolutionary Congress at the close of a contest, "on which," as they well say in the same document, "the most essential rights of human nature depended."

The following members of Congress, were, at different times, on the committees which prepared the proclamations just reviewed;—Messrs. [William] Hooper, J[ohn] Adams, [Robert Treat] Paine, [John] Witherspoon, R[ichard] H[enry] Lee, [Daniel] Roberdeau, [Samuel] Huntington, [Nathaniel] Scudder, G[ouverneur] Morris, [William Henry] Drayton,

[William] Paca, [James] Duane, [Jesse] Root, [James] Madison, [Joseph] Montgomery, [Oliver] Wolcott, [John Morin] Scott, S[amuel] Adams, [Samuel] Holten, [Frederick] Muhlenberg, Morris, [James] Varnum, [Roger] Sherman, [and] [Hugh] Williamson. Several of these gentlemen served two and three times on this business. The following gentlemen were Chairmen of the Committees:—Messrs. Hooper, Witherspoon, Roberdeau, G. Morris, Duane, Montgomery, S. Adams, [and] Root. Mr. Duane appears to have written two of the proclamations, Mr. Root two, and Mr. Witherspoon three. It does not appear from the Journals who were on the Committee which prepared the proclamation of Oct. 18th, 1780. In *one* instance, the Chaplains of Congress prepared the proclamation according to instructions from Congress; Journals, Nov. 7th and 17th, 1778. Mr. Witherspoon was the *only* clerical member of the old Congress. Of the three proclamations, of which, being Chairman of the Committee, he may be presumed to have been the author, *no part* is quoted in the above extracts. The same is true of the proclamation prepared by the Chaplains. The above extracts, therefore, contain the religious sentiments, and make us acquainted in some measure with the religious feelings of the lay-members of Congress. The above review warrants some further remarks. 1. The old Congress paid respect to religion by system and on principle. If they were ever without a Chaplain performing daily religious services, it was for a very short time; and it may well be presumed, that Mr. Witherspoon *then* performed the stated divine service. 2. The proclamations do not merely contain general references to a superintending Providence, and a Supreme Creator and Governor of the world, but they usually contain sentiments unequivocally *Christian.* 3. The journals disclose various circumstances which indicate the personal interest taken by the members in the stated and occasional religious services. The proclamations are among the very best specimens of the kind of writing to which they belong, with which the author is acquainted. It is a noble and sublime spectacle, to see an assembly of such men, making use of all the rightful means in their power to accomplish a transcendently great object, but still depending on the God of Heaven for the ultimate issue.

3. Appointment of Chaplains, their qualifications, duties, &c. The first revolutionary Congress assembled Sept. 5th, 1774, and in an entry on the journal of the 6th, we read, "*Resolved,* That Rev. Mr. [Jacob] Duché be desired to open the Congress to-morrow morning with prayers." Sept. 7th, 1774, "the meeting was opened with prayers by the Rev. Mr. Duché." "Voted, that the thanks of the Congress be given to Mr. Duché for performing divine service." Congress adjourned October 26th, but reassembled 10th May 1775, on the journals of which day, there is this entry;—"Agreed that the Rev. Mr. Duché be requested to open the Congress with prayers to-morrow morning." May 11th, "Agreeable to the order of yesterday, the Con-

gress was opened with prayers by the Rev. Mr. Duché." October 23, 1775, on occasion of the sudden demise of Peyton Randolph, Congress resolved to attend his funeral as mourners, and among other things appointed a Committee "to wait on the Rev. Mr. Duché, and request him to prepare a proper discourse to be delivered at the funeral." July 9th, 1776, "*Resolved,* that the Rev. Mr. Duché be appointed Chaplain to Congress, and that he be desired to attend every morning at 9 o'clock." October 17, 1776, "Mr. Duché having by letter informed the President, that the state of his health, and his parochial duties, were such, as obliged him to decline the honour of continuing Chaplain to Congress;—*Resolved,* that the President return the thanks of this house to the Rev. Mr. Duché for the devout and acceptable manner in which he discharged his duty during the time he officiated as Chaplain to it; and that 150 dollars be presented to him, as an acknowledgement from the house of his services." October 30th, 1776, Mr. Duché writes to Congress and requests that, as he became their Chaplain from motives perfectly disinterested, the 150 dollars voted to him, may be applied to the relief of the widows and children of such of the Pennsylvania officers, as have fallen in battle in the service of their country. In consequence, Congress orders the money to be deposited with the Council of safety of Pennsylvania, to be applied agreeably to his request. December 23, 1776, "agreeable to the order of the day, Congress elected the Rev. Mr. P[atrick] Allison, and the Rev. Mr. W[illiam] White, Chaplains.["] May 27th, 1777, "*Resolved,* that for the future, that there be only one Chaplain allowed in each brigade of the army, and that such Chaplain be appointed by Congress; that each brigade Chaplain be allowed the same pay, rations, and forage allowed to a Colonel in the said corps; that each Brigadier-General be requested to nominate and recommend to Congress a proper person for Chaplain to his brigade; and that *they recommend none but such as are clergymen of experience, and established public character for piety, virtue and learning.*" September 18th, 1777, "*Resolved,* that Chaplains be appointed to the Hospitals in the several departments, and that their pay be each 60 dollars a month, and three rations a day, and forage for one horse. The Rev. Mr. Noah Cook was elected Chaplain of the Hospitals in the Eastern department." Other appointments of Chaplains appear on the Journals for Oct. 1st, 1777.—Jan. 22d, 1784.—Aug. 5th, 1785.—Feb. 2d, 1787.—Feb. 29th, 1788.

4. *Miscellaneous.*—Saturday July 15th, 1775, "on motion, *Resolved,* that the Congress will, on Thursday next, attend divine service in a body, both morning and afternoon.["] September 12th, 1782, a Committee of which Mr. [James] Duane is Chairman, report on a memorial of R[obert] Aitken respecting an edition of the Holy Scriptures, "that Mr. Aitken has at a great expense now finished an American edition of the Holy Scriptures in English; that the Committee have, from time to time attended to his progress

in the work," &c. "Whereupon, *Resolved,* that the United States in Congress assembled, highly approve the pious and laudable undertaking of Mr. Aitken, as subservient to the interest of religion," &c. Also, "they recommend this edition of the Bible to the inhabitants of the United States, and hereby authorize him to publish this recommendation in the manner he shall think proper." Also, Journals Sept. 3, 1788.

The above result is from a careful examination of the Journals of the Revolutionary Congress. A review of the Journals of the new Congress must necessarily be brief and imperfect.

President Washington was inaugurated and took the oath of office, April 30th, 1789, and on the Journal of the preceding day is this entry; ["]*Resolved,* that after the oath shall have been administered the President; the Vice-President and Members of the Senate, the Speaker and Members of the House of Representatives, will accompany him to St. Paul's Chapel, to hear divine service, performed by the Chaplain of Congress." See also Journal of 27th April.

1. *Days of public Humiliation and Prayer.*—May 1st, 1782, "on motion, *Resolved,* that a joint Committee of both Houses be directed to wait on the President of the United States, to request that he would recommend to the people of the United States a day of public Humiliation and Prayer to be observed by supplicating Almighty God for the safety, peace and welfare of these States." June 4th, 1794, is a similar entry. On the same subject are entries, July 19th, 20th, and 23d, 1813.—Oct. 29th, Nov. 1st, 4th and 8th, 1814.

2. *Days of Thanksgiving and Prayer.*—Sept. 25th, 1789, "*Resolved,* that a Joint Committee of both houses be directed to wait upon the President of the United States, to request that he would recommend to the people of the United States, a day of public Thanksgiving and Prayer, to be observed by acknowledging with grateful hearts, the many signal favours of Almighty God, especially by affording them an opportunity peaceably to establish a constitution of government for their safety and happiness." See also Journal of Feb. 18th, 21st, and March 2d, 1815.

3. *Appointment, &c. of Chaplains.*—The House of Representatives met 4th of March, 1789, but a quorum was not formed until 1st April. April 9th, a joint movement of the House and the Senate was made, "to regulate the appointment of Chaplains." May 1st, the very day of the inauguration of the President, a Chaplain was elected for the House. Other entries to the same effect are found, Jan. 8th, 1790.—Dec. 8th, 1790, "*Resolved,* that two Chaplains of different denominations, be appointed to Congress for the present session, one by each House, who shall interchange weekly." See Dec. 10th, 1790. Oct. 14th, 1791.—Nov. 5th, 1792. The Journals abound with notices of the appointment of Chaplains too numerous to be quoted up to

March, 1815, beyond which the author has not the means of examining any of the subjects of this note. It may be stated, however, on the ground of general notoriety, that both Houses of Congress have always appointed Chaplains, that days of national humiliation and prayer, and of national thanksgiving, have been occasionally appointed, and that public worship has been customarily celebrated, during the sessions of Congress, in the Hall of the House of Representatives.

F.—PAGE 17 [49].

The author proposes briefly to review the legislation of S. Carolina, so far as this subject is concerned, and to extend his enquiries, to the Federal Government, and to the other States, as far as circumstances permit.

The Carolina Charter of 1662-3, granted to the Lords Proprietors "the patronage of all the Churches which might be built in the Province, and the administration of all other things pertaining to Religion, according to the Ecclesiastical Laws of England, together with all and as ample rights, jurisdictions, privileges, prerogatives," &c. A new charter was granted in 1665, by which the former was confirmed and enlarged in some particulars, though not in respect to Religion. By reason of the remote distance of the Province, it was permitted by the Charter to the Lords Proprietors, "to grant at their discretion, fit and reasonable indulgences to all such as really in their judgments and for conscience sake could not confirm to the Liturgy and ceremonies of the established Church." This the Charter hopes, considering the distance, will be no breach of the unity and uniformity established in England. Such indulgence was to be granted, however, on condition, that the persons to whom it might be given, "should not disturb the peace and safety of the Province, or scandalize or reproach the Liturgy, forms and ceremonies of the Church of England, or any thing thereunto relating." (*Trott's Laws of S. Carolina,* vol. i. p. 21, &c.) Such was the original fundamental Law of South-Carolina in regard to religion. The Constitutions of Mr. Locke, expanded the provisions just quoted into details; but as they were never adopted in the Province, it is not necessary further to notice them. (*Dalcho's History of the P. E. Church of S. Carolina,* p. 7.—2 *Ramsay,* p. 123.) By comparing, however, the Constitutions from Art. 97 to 106, it seems probable that they were used in compiling Art. 38 of our Constitution of 1778. See 2 *Ramsay,* 136.

The Statute of December 12th, 1712, in adopting the Common Law of England as the Law of S. Carolina, (*Grimké's Laws of S. Carolina,* p. 99,) made Christianity (if it was not so before) a part of our fundamental Law, it being a well established principle that Christianity is a part of the Common Law of England.*

But besides this Statute, incorporating Christianity with our law, we have many others bearing immediately on the subject. The Act of 1712, for securing the observance of Sunday, (*Grimké's Laws,* p. 19,) after reciting that "nothing is more acceptable to God than the true and sincere service and worship of him, according to his holy will, and that the holy keeping of the Lord's Day is a principal part of the true service of God," requires that "all persons shall observe this day, by exercising the duties of piety publicly and privately, and shall resort to their parish Church, or some meeting or assembly for religious worship." The same Act further provides, that "no person shall exercise any worldly labour, or work of their ordinary callings on the Lord's Day, works of necessity and charity excepted;"—and that "persons exposing for sale, on the Lord's Day, any goods, wares, fruits, &c. shall

---

*See 11 Sergeant & Rawle, pp. 400, 401, where the Supreme Court of Pennsylvania says, that "from the time of [Henry de] Bracton, Christianity has been received as part of the Common Law of England." To this effect, the opinions of Lord Chief Justice Hale, Lord Chief Justice Raymond, and Lord Mansfield, are quoted. The Court refer to the King vs. Taylor, 1 Ventris, 293.—3 Keble, 607.—The King vs. Woolston, 2 Strange, 834.—Fitzgibbons, 64.—3 Burns' Ecclesiastical Law, 201.

Also, 8 Johnson, 292, where the Supreme Court of New-York quote the same authorities, and add Tremaine's Pleas of the Crown, 226, S. C.—4 Blackstone's Com. 54.—1 Easts' Pleas of the Crown, 3.—1 Hawkins B. 1. C. 5.—The King vs. Williams, tried before Lord Kenyon 1797, 26 Howell's State Trials, 653. Wood's Institute, 391.—The King vs. Waddington, 1 Barnewell & Cresswell 26, K. B. 1822.

In the late debate in the House of Commons on Jewish disabilities, April 17th, 1833;—Mr. R[obert] Grant said "Christianity, as now professed, was so recognised by law that no man was permitted to outrage its ordinances, or to trample on its great maxims." Mr. Grant introduced the motion for removing the Jewish disabilities. In opposing this motion, Sir R[obert] Inglis said, "it had been a maxim of the legislature, as well as of our Courts of Justice, that religion was part and parcel of the law of the land." Such language as this, appears to be regarded as a matter of course, in the House of Commons. The author does not perceive, that the sentiment of Mr. Grant and Sir R. Inglis, was contradicted or opposed during the debate. (See [Robert] Walsh's National Gazette, 8th June, 1833.)

In addition to the authorities on this point quoted above, the author subjoins the opinion of Mr. Justice [Joseph] Story of the Supreme Court of the United States, contained at p. 20 of his Dane and inaugural Discourse, "One of the beautiful boasts, says he, of our municipal jurisprudence is, that Christianity is a part of the common law, from which it seeks the sanction of its rights, and by which it endeavours to regulate its doctrines. And notwithstanding the specious objection of one of our distinguished statesmen, the boast is as true as it is beautiful. There never has been a period, in which the common law did not recognise Christianity as lying at its foundation. (See the remarks of Mr. Justice [James Alan] Park, in Smith vs. Sparrow, 4 Bing. R. 84, 88.) For many ages it was almost exclusively administered by those who held its ecclesiastical dignities. It now repudiates every act done in violation of its duties of perfect obligation. It pronounces illegal every contract offensive to its morals. It recognises with profound humility its holidays and festivals, and obeys them as dies non juridici [day not juridical (or, for legal proceedings)]. It still attaches to persons believing in its divine authority the highest degree of competency as witnesses.["]

See also the Jurist for April, 1833, No. 18, p. 347, in which there is an examination of Mr. Jefferson's letter to Major [John] Cartwright. (4 Jefferson's Works, 393.) The writer (J.S.) maintains that Christianity is a part of the common law, and reviews the principal authorities on the subject.

forfeit the articles so offered for sale." Travelling is also forbidden "by land
or water, except to some place of religious worship, or to visit and relieve
the sick, unless (a person is) belated the night before, or on some extraordinary occasion, to be allowed of by a justice of the peace." It permits no sports
or pastimes of any kind on Sundays, and prohibits innkeepers from entertaining any person in their houses excepting strangers. It requires the
Church-Wardens and Constables of Charleston, twice on each Sunday in
time of Divine Service, "to walk through the town and apprehend all offenders against this Act." All persons are commanded to aid the constables.
A penalty is inflicted on any master, mistress or overseer commanding or
encouraging any servant or slaves to work on Sunday. No writ, process,
warrant, order, judgment or decree can be served on Sunday, excepting in
case of treason, felony, or breach of the peace. The service of such writ is to
be void, and the party serving the same is to answer in damages to the persons aggrieved. In case any person shall be imprisoned or detained by any
writ served on Sunday, he shall be discharged. This entire act contains two
quarto pages closely printed, and of course, this sketch is very imperfect. It
is very minute in its specifications, and each offence is visited with its appropriate penalty. It is unquestionably at this day a part of the law of S. Carolina. (*Brevard's Digest,* ii. 272.—*Const. of S. Carolina, Art.* 7.) The Act of June
7, 1712 shews the solicitude of our fathers for the salvation of the slaves. It
says, "since Charity and the Christian religion which we profess, obliges us
to wish well to the souls of all men, and that religion may not be made a
pretence, to alter any man's property and right, and that no person may
neglect to baptize their negroes or slaves, or suffer them to be baptized, for
fear that thereby they should be manumitted and set free; *Be it therefore enacted,* that it shall be and is hereby declared lawful for any negro or Indian
slave, or any other slave or slaves whatsoever, to receive and profess the
Christian faith, and be thereunto baptized." The Act of 1740, inflicts a penalty of £5 on any person who shall on Sunday, employ any slave in any work
or labour, and excepts only "works of absolute necessity, and the necessary
occasions of the family.["] (*Grimké,* 168.) The Act of 29th July, 1769, for
establishing Courts, &c., after specifying particular days for holding courts,
says, "that if any of the days above appointed for holding the said courts,
shall happen to be on Sunday, the said courts shall begin on the day following.["] (*Idem.* p. 269.) The Act of 17th March, 1785, for establishing County
Courts, &c. says, that "it shall not be lawful for any sheriff or other officer
to execute any writ or other process on the Sabbath day; and all process so
executed shall be void, unless the same shall be issued against any person or
persons for treason, sedition, felony, riot, or breach of the peace, on behalf
of the State, or upon any escape out of prison or custody." (*Grimké's Laws,*
p. 376.) The Ordinances of the City Council of Charleston, forbid under a

penalty, all labour and all pastimes on Sunday. The Marshal is required to pass through the city twice on Sunday to see that order is preserved. It is his duty to seize goods offered for sale. For selling liquors of any sort on Sunday, a penalty is imposed of $100 for every offence. (*Digest of Ord.* p. 171. 218. 231.)

It has been mentioned, that during the Revolution, or soon afterwards, the greatest part of the States framed for themselves new constitutions of government, and our first Constitution under the new order of things, is dated 26th of March, 1776. This instrument, however, was designed to be "temporary only, looking forward to an accommodation with Great-Britain," and contained no special reference to the subject of religion. Our next Constitution is dated March 19th, 1778, and the 38th Section of this document, conveys to us with great distinctness, the sentiments of this community in regard to religion at that time, and continued to be our fundamental Law on the subject until the adoption of our present Constitution in 1790. The section is interesting in itself, and must be in a great measure unknown to the present generation. For this reason, the author feels justified in republishing it entire:—

"38th. That all persons and religious societies who acknowledge that there is one God, and a future state of rewards and punishments, and that God is publicly to be worshipped, shall be freely tolerated. The Christian Protestant Religion shall be deemed, and is hereby constituted and declared to be the established religion of this State. That all denominations of Christian Protestants in this State, demeaning themselves peaceably and faithfully, shall enjoy equal religious and civil privileges. To accomplish this desirable purpose without injury to the religious property of those societies of Christians, which are by law, already incorporated for the purpose of religious worship, and to put it fully into the power of every other society of Christian Protestants, either already formed or hereafter to be formed, to obtain the like incorporation, it is hereby constituted, appointed and declared, that the respective societies of the Church of England, that are already formed in this State, for the purpose of religious worship, shall still continue incorporate and hold the religious property now in their possession. And that whenever fifteen or more male persons, not under twenty-one years of age, professing the Christian Protestant Religion, and agreeing to unite themselves in a society for the purposes of religious worship, they shall, (on complying with the terms hereinafter mentioned,) be and be constituted a Church, and be esteemed and regarded in law as of the established religion of the State, and on a petition to the Legislature, shall be entitled to be incorporated and to enjoy equal privileges. That every society of Christians so formed, shall give themselves a name or denomination by which they shall be called and known in law, and all that associate with them for the purpose of worship, shall be esteemed as belonging to the society so called. But that previous to the establishment and incorporation of the respective societies of every denomination as aforesaid, and in order to entitle them thereto, each society so petitioning, shall have agreed to and subscribed in a book the following five articles; without which no agreement or union of men upon pretence of religion shall entitle them to be incorporated and esteemed as a Church of the established religion of this State. (*See Locke's Const. Art.* 97-100.)

["]I. That there is one Eternal God, a future state of rewards and punishments. II. That God is publicly to be worshipped. III. That the Christian Religion is the true religion. IV. That the Holy Scriptures of the Old and New-Testament are of divine inspiration, and are the rule of faith and practice. V. That it is lawful and the duty of every man being thereunto called by those that govern, to bear witness to truth. That every inhabitant of this State, when called to make an appeal to God as a witness to truth, shall be permitted to do it in that way which is most agreeable to the dictates of his own conscience. And that the people of this State may for ever enjoy the right of electing their own pastors or clergy, and at the same time, that the State may have sufficient security for the due discharge of the pastoral office by those who shall be admitted to be clergymen: No person shall officiate as minister of any established Church, who shall not have been chosen by a majority of the society to which he shall minister, or by persons appointed by the said majority to choose and procure a minister for them, nor until the minister so chosen and appointed, shall have made and subscribed the following declaration over and above the aforesaid five articles, viz: That he is determined by God's grace out of the Holy Scriptures, to instruct the people committed to his charge, and to teach nothing, (as required of necessity to eternal salvation,) but that which he shall be persuaded may be concluded and proved from the Scripture; that he will use both public and private admonitions, as well to the sick as to the whole within his cure, as need shall require and occasion shall be given, and that he will be diligent in prayers, and in reading of the Holy Scriptures, and in such studies as help to the knowledge of the same; that he will be diligent to frame and fashion his own self and his family according to the doctrine of Christ, and to make both himself and them, as much as in him lieth, wholesome examples and patterns to the flock of Christ; that he will maintain and set forwards as much as he can, quietness, peace and love among all people, and especially among those that are or shall be committed to his charge. No person shall disturb or molest any religious assembly; nor shall use any reproachful, reviling or abusive language against any Church, that being the certain way of disturbing the peace, and of hindering the conversion of any to the truth, by engaging them in quarrels and animosities, to the hatred of the professors, and that profession which otherwise they might be brought to assent to. No person whatsoever shall speak any thing in their religious assembly, irreverently or seditiously of the government of this State. No person shall by law, be obliged to pay towards the maintenance and support of a religious worship, that he does not freely join in or has not voluntarily engaged to support. But the Churches, chapels, parsonages, glebes and all other property now belonging to any societies of the Church of England, or any other religious societies, shall remain and be secured to them for ever."

This, then, was the state of things when the Constitution of 1790 became the principal branch of our fundamental Law. Now Art. 8th of this Constitution says, "the free exercise and enjoyment of religious profession and worship, without discrimination or preference, shall forever hereafter, be *allowed* within this State to all mankind: Provided, that the liberty of conscience thereby declared, shall not be so construed as to excuse acts of licentiousness, or justify practices inconsistent with the peace or safety of this State."* The word "allowed" in this provision is worthy of special notice, and is the key to the just construction of it. It is to be understood in reference to a *preceding state of things,* that is, chiefly in reference to the 38th Section of the Constitution of 1778. This section had said, that ["]the Christian Protestant Religion shall be deemed and is hereby constituted and declared to be the established religion of this State;" and the 3d Section of the same Constitution had required the Governor, Lieutenant-Governor and Privy Council, all to be of the Protestant Religion. But the Constitution of 1790, required that this state of things should continue no longer. Protestantism was no more to receive any preference. The free exercise and enjoyment of religious profession and worship, without discrimination or preference, was, forever hereafter, to "be allowed" within this State to all mankind. The Constitution of 1790, then, "alters and amends" (*Art. 8. Sec.* 2.) the former Constitution, so far as religion is concerned, chiefly in these particulars—1st. It discontinues all preference for Protestantism over any other form of Christianity. 2d. It "allows" the "free exercise of their religion," whatever this may be, to all mankind. It is too manifest to require argument, that these changes made by the Constitution of 1790, leave the substance of Christianity, that is, Christianity without distinction of sects, precisely as they found it established by the Constitution of 1778. Besides, the Constitution of 1790, contemplates a continuance of the public instruction of the people of the State in the truths of the Gospel; for it refers (*Art.* 1. *Sec.* 23.) to "Ministers of the Gospel" as a class of men "dedicated by their profession to the service of

---

*For Chief Justice [James] Kent's opinion of the meaning of this provision of our Constitution, which is also contained in the Constitution of New-York, see note at p. 16 [48–49, n. 25].

God and the care of souls," and considers "their functions as a great duty from which they ought not to be diverted."

It only remains to notice the Acts pertaining to this subject, which have been framed since the adoption of the Constitution of 1790. By the Act of 14th February, 1791, the Secretary of State, and various other officers, are required to keep their offices open every day in the year, Sundays, Christmas days, and the Anniversary of the Independence of America, excepted. (*Faust's Acts,* vol. i. p. 22.) By the Act of 19th February, 1791, for building a toll bridge across Edisto River, &c. "all Ministers of the Gospel, and all persons going to and from places of Divine worship, are exempted from any pontage or toll," (*Faust,* vol. i. 131.) and by the Act of 21st December 1792, the same classes of persons are exempted from payment of ferriage, toll or duty. (*Faust,* i. 282.) By the Act of 1807, persons exempted from such payments at public, are also exempted at private ferries. (*Brevard's Digest,* ii. 195.) The author finds the same exemption in the Act of 17th December, 1813, and presumes it exists in all the succeeding Acts pertaining to roads, bridges, ferries, &c. Such exemption is a distinct *legislative* encouragement to an attendance on the ordinances of the Gospel. In the case of Shaw vs. McCombs, in 1799, it was decided, all the Justices concurring, that "if a verdict be delivered in after 12 o'clock on *Saturday* night, and recorded on *Sunday* morning, it is void.["] (2 *Bay,* 232.) In Bell vs. Graham, it was decided in 1818, all the Justices concurring, that disturbing an assembly convened for religious worship on Sunday, during worship, is indictable. (1 *Nott & McCord,* 278.) A highly valuable legal friend informs the author, that until twenty-five or thirty years since, it was customary in Charleston to have a "session or assize sermon" at the opening of every Court of Common Pleas and Sessions; and on such occasions, the judge, jury, officers of court and prisoners, all went to St. Michael's Church to attend divine service and hear a sermon. The same custom still exists in the country. The Act of 27th March, 1787, assigns a fee of £3 sterling for every session sermon that shall be preached. (*Dalcho's Hist. of P. E. Church of S. Carolina,* p. 156.)

An annual appropriation of $2000 is made by the Legislature, for the support of a "Professor of Metaphysics, Moral Philosophy and the *Evidences of Christianity,*" in the South-Carolina College established at Columbia. (See the appropriation Acts from 1824 to 1832.) The facts, that such an appropriation is annually made, and that it is made a part of the duty of one of the Professors to teach the "Evidences of Christianity," must indicate the opinion of the Legislature, not only that Christianity is the well recognised religion of the State, but that the State College is a suitable instrument for advancing the interests of this religion in the community, by imparting that knowledge which is calculated to strengthen the foundations of the public belief in its Divine Authority. This could not be more effectually done than by requiring instruction to be given in its "Evidences," in a State Institution, organised on a liberal scale and sustained at the public expense.

Thus the author has reviewed a series of legislative acts and other documents from the first settlement of the State, by which it appears, that Christianity has been made a part of our law, that its peculiar institutions and usages have been legally protected, and uniformly aided and encouraged. Now the laws of any community are the most authentic and most authoritative mode by which the sentiments of that community can be made known. The voice of South-Carolina, then, has been, through her entire history, uniform, distinct, unequivocal in favor of the Christian religion.

Government of the United States.—A very partial examination of our federal legislation has given these results:—

The Act of April 30th, 1816, provides for the appointment of Chaplains to the two Houses of Congress, and assigns their compensation. The Act of April 14, 1818, Sec. 2, provides for the appointment of a Chaplain to the Military Academy at West-Point. By the Act of April 12, 1808, Sec. 7, a Chaplain is to be appointed to each brigade of the Army. The Act of April 23, 1800, Sec. 1, prescribes the rules and regulations for the government of the Navy of the United States. Art. 1. requires all commanders of vessels of war, to shew in themselves a good example of virtue, honor, patriotism and subordination, and to guard against and suppress all dissolute and immoral practices, and to correct all such as are guilty of them. The whole of the 2d Art. will bear quoting. It says: "The commanders of all vessels in the Navy, having Chaplains on board, shall take care that Divine service be performed in a solemn, orderly and reverent manner twice a-day, and a sermon preached on Sunday, unless bad weather, or other extraordinary accidents prevent it; and that they cause all, or as many of the ship's company as can be spared from duty, to attend every performance of the worship of Almighty God." Art. 3. visits with a severe penalty any officer or other person in the Navy who shall be guilty of fraud, profane swearing, drunkenness, or any other scandalous conduct, tending to the destruction of good morals. (*See Note D.* p. 34 [66].) The author has not found any statute to this effect: he, therefore, states on the authority of Mr. Frelinghuysen, that "the business of the Supreme Court, the highest judicial tribunal of the country, is *by law,* directed to suspend its session on Sunday."—*Senate Speech 8th May,* 1830, p. 5.

The author cannot doubt that an extensive search into the laws of the United States, the Reports of the Courts of the United States, and our immensely voluminous Congressional documents, would be rewarded with proofs equally numerous and gratifying, of regard, respect and aid manifested towards Christian institutions by the Federal Government. Such examination it is not in the author's power at this time to make;★ he will, therefore, content himself with copying a single instance which has fallen in his way without searching. The Secretary of War, (Mr. [Lewis] Cass,) in his report to the President of the United States, 25th November, 1832, speaking of the Military Academy at West-Point, says, "especially am I impressed with the importance of a proper place of public worship, where all the persons attached to the institution, amounting, with their families, to more than eight hundred individuals, can assemble and unite in the performance of religious duties. In a Christian community, the obligations upon this subject will not be questioned; and the expense of providing a suitable place of worship, especially as a Chaplain is maintained there, cannot be put in competition with the permanent advantages of a course of religious instruction to such a number of persons; a large portion of whom are at that critical period which determines whether the future course of life shall be for evil or for good."

Pennsylvania.—In the case of Updegraph vs. the Commonwealth, in 1824, (11 *Sergeant & Rawle,* 394.) the Supreme Court of Pennsylvania extensively reviewed the subject now under discussion, and the author presumes he shall be justified in quoting, with an unsparing hand, from so distinguished a source. The trial was on an indictment for blasphemy, founded on an Act of Assembly, passed in 1700.

The Court said, that "even if Christianity was not part of the law of the land, it is the popular religion of the country, an insult on which would be indictable, as directly tending to disturb the public peace. Christianity, general Christianity, is, and always has been a part of the common law of *Pennsylvania;* not Christianity founded on any particular religious tenets; not Christianity with an established Church, and tithes, and spiritual courts; but Christianity with liberty of conscience to all men.["] The first legislative act in the colony was the recognition of the Christian religion and establishment of liberty of conscience. It is called "the Great Law." And after quoting it at length, the Court further says, "Thus this wise Legislature framed this great body of laws for a Christian country and a Christian people. Infidelity was then rare, and no infidels were among the first colonists. They fled from religious intolerance, to a country where all were allowed to worship according to their own understanding. Every one had the right of adopting for himself whatever opinion appeared to be the most rational concerning all matters of religious belief; thus securing by law this inestimable freedom of conscience, one of the highest privileges and greatest interests of the human race. This is the Christianity of the common law, incorporated into the great law of Pennsylvania; and thus, it is irrefragably proved, that the laws

---

★Since the first edition was published, the author has made a partial examination of the documents above referred to. See Note E. p. 35 [66].

and institutions of this State are built on the foundation of reverence for Christianity. On this, the Constitution of the *United States* has made no alteration, nor in the great body of the laws which was an incorporation of the common law doctrine of Christianity, as suited to the condition of the colony, and without which no free government can long exist. Under the Constitution, penalties against cursing and swearing have been enacted. If Christianity was abolished, all false oaths, all tests by oath in the common form by the book, would cease to be indictable as perjury. The indictment must state the oath to be on the Holy Evangelists of Almighty God." After reviewing a series of decisions made in Pennsylvania and elsewhere, the Court continues thus; "It has long been firmly settled, that blasphemy against the Deity generally, or an attack on the Christian religion indirectly, for the purpose of exposing its doctrines to ridicule and contempt, is indictable and punishable as a temporal offence. The principles and actual decisions are, that the publication, whether written or oral, must be malicious, and designed for that end and purpose." After stating that the law gave free permission for the serious and conscientious discussion of all theological and religious topics; the Court said, that "a malicious and mischievous intention is, in such a case, the broad boundary between right and wrong, and that it is to be collected from the offensive levity, scurrilous and approbrious language, and other circumstances, whether the act of the party was malicious; and since the law has no means of distinguishing between different degrees of evil tendency, if the matter published contains any such evil tendency, it is a public wrong. An offence against the public peace, may consist either of an actual breach of the peace, or doing that which tends to provoke and excite others to do it. Within the latter description fall all acts and all attempts to produce disorder, by written, printed, or oral communications; for the purpose of generally weakening those religious and moral restraints, without the aid of which mere legislative provisions would prove ineffectual. No society can tolerate a wilful and despiteful attempt to subvert its religion, no more than it would to break down its laws;—a general, malicious, and deliberate intent to overthrow Christianity, general Christianity. This is the line of indication where crime commences, and the offence becomes the subject of penal visitation. The species of offence may be classed under the following heads. 1. Denying the Being and Providence of God. 2. Contumelious reproaches of Jesus Christ; profane and malevolent scoffing at the Scriptures, or exposing any part of them to contempt and ridicule. 3. Certain immoralities tending to subvert all religion and morality, which are the foundations of all governments. Without these restraints, no free government could long exist. It is liberty run mad, to declaim against the punishment of these offences, or to assert that the punishment is hostile to the spirit and genius of our government. They are far from being the friends to liberty who support this doctrine; and the promulgation of such opinions, and general receipt of them among the people, would be the sure forerunner of anarchy, and finally of despotism. No free government now exists in the world, unless where Christianity is acknowledged, and is the religion of the country. Christianity is part of the common law of this State. It is not proclaimed by the commanding voice of any human superior, but expressed in the calm and mild accents of customary law. Its foundations are broad, and strong, and deep; they are laid in the authority, the interest, the affections of the people. Waiving all questions of hereafter, it is the purest system of morality, the firmest auxiliary, and only stable support of all human laws. (*See* p. 20 [52].) It is impossible to administer the laws without taking the religion which the defendant in error has scoffed at, that Scripture which he has reviled, as their basis; to lay aside these is at least to weaken the confidence in human veracity so essential to the purposes of society, and without which no question of property could be decided, and no criminal brought to justice; an oath in the common form on a discredited book, would be a most idle ceremony. No preference is given by law to *any particular* religious persuasion. Protection is given to all by our laws. It is only the malicious reviler of Christianity who is punished. While our own free Constitution secures liberty of conscience and freedom of religious worship to all, it is not necessary to maintain that any man should have the right publicly to vilify the religion of his neighbours and of the country. These two privileges are directly opposed. It is open, public vilification of the religion of the country that is punished, not to force conscience by punishment, but to preserve the peace of the country by an outward respect to the religion of the country, and not as a restraint upon the liberty of conscience;—but licentiousness endangering the public peace, when tending to corrupt society, is considered as a breach of the peace, and punishable by indictment. Every immoral act is not indictable, but when it is destructive of morality generally, it is, because it weakens the bonds by which society is held together, and government is nothing more than public order.["] (*Guardians of the Poor vs. Greene,* 5 *Binn.* 555.)

"This is the Christianity which is the law of our land, and," continues the Court, "I do not think it will be an invasion of any man's right of private judgment, or, of the most extended privilege of propagating his sentiments with regard to religion, in the manner which he thinks most conclusive. If from a regard to decency, and the good order of society, profane swearing, breach of the Sabbath, and blasphemy, are punishable by civil magistrates, these are not punished as sins or offences against God, but crimes injurious to, and having a malignant influence on society; for it is certain, that by these practices no one pretends to prove any supposed truths, detect any supposed error, or advance any sentiment whatever."

New-York.—The subject to which this note pertains, was further discussed in the Supreme Court of New-York in 1811, in the case of the People vs. Ruggles. (8 *Johnson,* 290.) The trial was for blasphemy. In delivering the opinion of the Court, Chief Justice Kent said, "the authorities shew that blasphemy against God, and contumelious reproaches and profane ridicule of Christ, or the Holy Scriptures, (which are equally treated as blasphemy) are offences punishable at common law, whether uttered by words or writings. The consequences may be less extensively pernicious in the one case than in the other; but in both instances, the reviling is still an offence, because it tends to corrupt the morals of the people, and to destroy good order. Such offences have always been considered independent of any religious establishment or the rights of the Church. There is nothing in our manners and institutions which has prevented the application or the necessity of this point of the common law. We stand equally in need now as formerly, of all that moral discipline, and of those principles of virtue, which help to bind society together. The people of this State, in common with the people of this country, profess the general doctrines of Christianity, as the rule of their faith and practice; and to scandalize the author of these doctrines is not only, in a religious point of view extremely impious, but even in respect to the obligations due to society, is a gross violation of decency and good order. Nothing could be more offensive to the virtuous part of the community, or more injurious to the tender morals of the young, than to declare such profanity lawful. It would go to confound all distinction between things sacred and profane; for to use the words of one of the greatest oracles of human wisdom, 'profane scoffing doth by little and little deface the reverence for religion;' and who adds in another place, 'two principal causes have I ever known of Atheism;—curious controversies and profane scoffing.' (*Bacon's Works,* vol. ii. pp. 291. 503.) The very idea of jurisprudence with the ancient law-givers and philosophers, embraced the religion of the country. *Jurisprudentia est divinarum atque humanarum rerum notitia.* [Jurisprudence is the knowledge of things divine and human. (*Digest of Justinian* 1.10.2)] (*Dig.* b. 1. 10. 2. *Cic. De legibus* b. 2. *passim*)."

["]Though the Constitution has discarded religious establishments, it does not forbid judicial cognizance of those offences against religion and morality, which have no reference to any such establishment, or to any particular form of government, but are punishable, because they strike at the root of moral obligation, and weaken the security of the social ties. The legislative exposition of the Constitution is conformable to this view of it. Christianity in its enlarged sense, as a religion revealed and taught in the Bible, is not unknown to our law. *The statute for preventing immorality,* (*Laws* [*of the State of New-York*], vol. i. p. 224,) consecrates the first day of the week as holy time, and considers the violation of it immoral. *The Act concerning*

oaths, (Laws, vol. i. p. 405,) recognises the common law mode of administering an oath, 'by laying the hand on and kissing the gospels.' Surely, then,
we are bound to conclude, that wicked and malicious words, writings and
actions which go to vilify those gospels, continue as at common law, to be
an offence against the public peace and safety. They are inconsistent with
the reverence due to the administration of an oath, and among other evil
consequences, they tend to lessen in the public mind, its religious sanction." In this decision, all the justices concurred.

In the Convention of New-York, assembled in 1821, to revise the Constitution of that State, this decision of the Supreme Court was condemned
with unsparing severity by General [Erastus] Root, who said that he wished
for freedom of conscience, and that if judges undertake to support religion
by the arm of the law, it will be brought into abhorrence and contempt.
(*Debates,* p. 463.) In defending the decision of the Court, Ch. J. Kent said:
"such blasphemy was an outrage upon public decorum, and if sanctioned
by our tribunals would shock the moral sense of the country, and degrade
our character as a Christian people. The authors of our Constitution never
meant to extirpate Christianity, more than they meant to extirpate public
decency. It is in a degree recognised by the statute for the observance of the
Lord's Day, and for the mode of administering oaths. The Court never intended to interfere with any religious creeds or sects, or with religious discussions. They meant to preserve, so far as it came within their cognizance,
the morals of the country, which rested on Christianity as the foundation.
They meant to apply the principles of common law against blasphemy, which
they did not believe the Constitution ever meant to abolish. Are we not a
Christian people? Do not ninety-nine hundredths of our fellow-citizens hold
the general truths of the Bible to be dear and sacred? To attack them with
ribaldry and malice, in the presence of these very believers, must, and ought
to be a serious public offence. It disturbs, and annoys, and offends, and
shocks, and corrupts the public taste. The common law, as applied to correct such profanity, is the application of common reason and natural justice
to the security of the peace and good order of society."

Mr. [Daniel] Tompkins, (President of the Convention and Vice-President of the United States,) said; "the Court had never undertaken to uphold by the authority of law, any particular sect, but they had interposed,
and rightfully interposed, as the guardians of the public morals, to suppress
those outrages on public opinion and public feeling, which would otherwise reduce the community to a state of barbarism, corrupt its purity, and
debase the mind. He was not on the bench at the time the decision alluded
to took place, but he fully accorded in the opinions that were advanced; and
he could not hear the calumnies that had gone forth against the judiciary on
that subject, without regret and reprobation. No man of generous mind; no

man who regarded public sentiment, or that delicacy of feeling which lies at the foundation of moral purity, could defend such an outrage on public morals, or say that the decision was unmerited or unjust."

In this note, the author has reviewed with some care the legislation of South-Carolina in regard to the Christian religion. He has also quoted several statutes, &c. of the United States on the same subject. He has freely quoted a single decision of each of the Supreme Courts of Pennsylvania and New-York; and also a specimen of the discussion held in the Convention of New-York in 1821. The sentiments of Massachusetts, can be seen in her Constitution quoted above, (p. 30 [61].) and also in the extract from an opinion of the late Ch. J. [Theophilus] Parsons, given in Note G. To these it may be well to add the very recent authority of Judge [Peter Oxenbridge] Thacher of the Municipal Court of Boston, contained in a charge to the Grand Jury of the County of Suffolk, Dec. 1832, p. 6, "you are to present, says he, *all offences against religion, public decency, good morals, in profanation of the Sabbath, or in disturbance of those who are met for the public worship of God.* Who may not hail with pleasure the return of the Sabbath. The wisdom of the institution is proof of its divine origin. It is a day consecrated by heaven and by the laws of society, for the worship of the Supreme Being, for the rest of man and beast, for the study and contemplation of religious truth, for cultivating the purest moral and social qualities of our nature, and for indulging in the pleasures of devotion, and in the hopes of immortality." The author does not think it necessary or useful to continue his search in regard to other States. He has every reason to believe, that if search were made into the legislation and decisions of the other States, they would be found to speak as decisively on this subject as those whose records he has examined.★ Notwithstanding the fullness and distinctness which are found in the decisions of Pennsylvania and New-York, their Constitutions contain less in regard to Christianity, than is found in those of most of the other States. As Sunday is peculiarly a Christian institution, laws requiring its observance are a species of test in regard to this subject; and Mr. [Theodore] Frelinghuysen says, that twenty-three at least out of twenty-four States have such laws. (p. 15 [48, n. 22]) To them the author is able to add, upon the same authority, (Speech in 1830) the Territory of Michigan, which, by an Act of May, 1820, ordains, "that the first day of the week shall be kept and observed by the people of the Territory as a Sabbath, holy day, or day of rest, from all secular labour and employments." The preamble declares, "that in every community, some portion of time ought to be set apart for relaxation from worldly

---

★While revising this discourse, the author perceives it has been decided in Vermont, that "no action can be maintained on a contract made on Sunday, it being contrary to the obvious meaning of the statute relating to that day, as well as a violation of moral law."—Gospel Messenger for Aug. 1833.

care and employments, and devoted to the social worship of Almighty God, and the attainment of religious and moral instruction, which are in the highest degree promotive of the peace, happiness and prosperity of a people." The author now hopes and believes, that his readers will conclude with him, (See p. 16 [49],) that Christianity (without distinction of sects) is the established religion of the nation, that its institutions and usages are sustained by legal sanctions, and that many of them are incorporated with the fundamental law of the country.

G.—PAGE 20 [52].

With a view of illustrating this subject by uniting high authority with great clearness of argument, the author subjoins a part of the opinion of the late Chief Justice [Theophilus] Parsons, of Massachusetts, in the case of Barnes *vs.* First Parish in Falmouth, contained 6 Mass. Reports, p. 404, &c. In this case, the Court had occasion to vindicate Art. 3, Part i. of the Constitution of that State (p. 30 [61].) So far as the Massachusetts' Constitution and the argument vindicating it make a discrimination between Christian denominations, they do not meet the concurrence of the author, but he considers the main positions of the Chief Justice incontrovertible, and his course of reasoning highly instructive and convincing. To the members of the legal profession, it is not necessary to say any thing of this celebrated jurist; and to all others, it is sufficient to say, that in all the qualities which adorn the bench, he may fairly be placed by the side of Holt, Hale, Hardwicke, Mansfield, Scott, Marshall, Kent and Story.

"The object of a free civil government, (says the Chief Justice,) is the promotion and security of the happiness of the citizens. These effects cannot be produced, but by the knowledge and practice of our moral duties, which comprehend all the social and civil obligations of man to man, and the citizen to the State. If the civil magistrate in any State, could procure by his regulations an uniform practice of these duties, the government of that State would be perfect.

"To obtain that perfection, it is not enough for the magistrate to define the rights of the several citizens, as they are related to life, liberty, property and reputation, and to punish those by whom they may be invaded. Wise laws, made to this end, and faithfully executed, may leave the people strangers to many of the enjoyments of civil and social life, without which their happiness will be extremely imperfect. Human laws cannot oblige to the performance of the duties of imperfect obligation; as the duties of charity and hospitality, benevolence and good neighbourhood; as the duties resulting from the relation of husband and wife, parent and child; of man to man as children of a common parent; and of real patriotism, by influencing every citizen to love his country, and to obey all its laws. These are moral duties, flowing from the disposition of the heart, and not subject to the control of human legislation.

"Neither can the laws prevent by temporal punishment, secret offences committed without witness, to gratify malice, revenge, or any other passion, by assailing the most important and most estimable rights of others. For human tribunals cannot proceed against any crimes unless ascertained by evidence; and they are destitute of all power to prevent the commission of offences, unless by the feeble examples exhibited in the punishment of those who may be detected.

"Civil government, therefore, availing itself only of its own powers, is extremely defective; and unless it could derive assistance from some superior power, whose laws extend to the temper and disposition of the human heart, and before whom no offence is secret; wretched indeed would be the state of man under a civil constitution of any form.

"This most manifest truth has been felt by legislators in all ages; and as man is born not only a social but a religious being, so in the pagan world, false and absurd systems of religion were adopted and patronized by the magistrate, to remedy the defects necessarily existing in a government merely civil.

"On these principles tested by the experience of mankind, and by the reflections of reason, the people of Massachusetts, in the frame of their government, adopted and patronized a religion, which by its benign and energetic influences, might co-operate with human institutions, to promote and secure the happiness of the citizens, so far as might be consistent with the imperfections of man.

["]In selecting a religion, the people were not exposed to the hazard of choosing a false and defective religious system; Christianity had long been promulgated, its pretensions and excellencies well known, and its divine authority admitted. This religion was found to rest on the basis of immortal truth; to contain a system of morals adapted to man in all possible ranks and conditions, situations and circumstances, by conforming to which he would be ameliorated and improved in all the relations of human life; and to furnish the most efficacious sanctions, by bringing to light a future state of retribution. And this religion as understood by protestants, tending by its effects to make every man, submitting to its influences, a better husband, parent, child, neighbour, citizen and magistrate, was, by the people, established as a fundamental and essential part of their Constitution.

"The manner in which this establishment was made, is liberal, and consistent with the rights of conscience on religious subjects. As religious opinions, and the time and manner of expressing the homage due to the

Governor of the Universe, are points depending on the sincerity and belief of each individual, and do not concern the public interest, care is taken in the second article of the Declaration of Rights, to guard these points from the interference of the civil magistrate; and no man can be hurt, molested or restrained in his person, liberty or estate, for worshipping God in the manner and season most agreeable to the dictates of his own conscience, or for his religious profession or sentiment, provided he does not disturb the public peace, or obstruct others in their religious worship; in which case he is punished, not for his religious opinions or worship, but because he interrupts others in the enjoyment of the rights he claims for himself, or because he has broken the public peace.

"Having secured liberty of conscience, on the subject of religious opinion and worship for every man, whether Protestant or Catholic, Jew, Mahometan or Pagan, the Constitution then provides for the public teaching of the precepts and maxims of the religion of Protestant Christians to all the people. And for this purpose, it is made the right and duty of all corporate religious societies to elect and support a public Protestant teacher of piety, religion and morality; and the election and support of the teacher depend exclusively on the will of a majority of each society incorporated for those purposes. As public instruction requires persons who may be taught, every citizen may be enjoined to attend on some one of those teachers, at times and seasons stated by law, if there be any on whose instructions he can conscientiously attend.

"In the election and support of a teacher, every member of the corporation is bound by the will of the majority; but as the great object of this provision was to secure the election and support of public Protestant teachers by corporate societies, and some members of any corporation might be of a sect or denomination of Protestant Christians different from the majority of the members, and might choose to unite with other Protestant Christians of their own sect or denomination, in maintaining a public teacher, who by law was entitled to support, and on whose instruction they usually attended; indulgence was granted, that persons thus situated might have the money they contributed to the support of public worship, and of the public teachers aforesaid, appropriated to the support of the teacher, on whose instructions they should attend.

"Several objections have at times been made to this establishment, which may be reduced to three: that when a man disapproves of any religion, or of any supposed doctrine of any religion, to compel him by law to contribute money for public instruction in such religion, or doctrine, is an infraction of his liberty of conscience;—that to compel a man to pay for public religious instructions, on which he does not attend, and from which he can, therefore, derive no benefit is unreasonable and intolerant;—and that it is anti-christian for any State to avail itself of the precepts and maxims of Christianity to support civil government; because the founder of it has declared, that his kingdom is not of this world.

"These objections go to the authority of the people to make this Constitution, which is not proper nor competent for us to bring into question. And although we are not able, and have no inclination to assume the character of theologians, yet it may not be improper to make a few short observations, to defend our Constitution from the charges of persecution, intolerance and impiety.

"When it is remembered, that no man is compellable to attend on any religious instruction, which he conscientiously disapproves; and that he is absolutely protected in the most perfect freedom of conscience in his religious opinions and worship; the first objection seems to mistake a man's conscience for his money, and to deny the State a right of levying and of appropriating the money of the citizens, at the will of the Legislature, in which they are all represented. But as every citizen derives the security of his property, and the fruits of his industry from the power of the State; so, as the price of this protection, he is bound to contribute in common with his fellow-citizens for the public use, so much of his property and for such public uses, as the State shall direct. And if any individual can lawfully withhold his contribution, because he dislikes the appropriation, the authority of the State to levy taxes would be annihilated; and without money it would soon cease to have any authority. But all monies raised and appropriated for public uses by any corporation, pursuant to powers derived from the State, are raised and appropriated substantially by the authority of the State. And the people in their Constitution, instead of devolving the support of public teachers on the corporations by whom they should be elected, might have directed their support to be defrayed out of the public treasury, to be reimbursed by the levying and collection of state taxes. And against this mode of support, the objection of an individual disapproving of the object of the public taxes, would have the same weight it can have, against the mode of public support through the medium of corporate taxation. In either case, it can have no weight to maintain a charge of persecution for conscience sake. The great error lies in not distinguishing between liberty of conscience in religious opinions and worship, and the right of appropriating money by the State. The former is an unalienable right, the latter is surrendered to the State as the price of protection.

"The second objection is, that it is intolerant to compel a man to pay for religious instruction, from which, as he does not hear it, he can derive no benefit. This objection is founded wholly in mistake. The object of public religious instruction is, to teach and to enforce by suitable arguments, the practice of a system of correct morals among the people, and to form and cultivate reasonable and just habits and manners; by which every man's person and property are protected from outrage; and his personal and social enjoyments promoted and multiplied. From these effects every man derives the most important benefits, and whether he be or be not an auditor of any public teacher, he receives more solid and permanent advantages from this public instruction, than the administration of justice in courts of law can give him. The like objection may be made by any man to the support of public schools if he have no family who attend; and any man who has no law suit may object to the support of judges and jurors on the same ground; when if there were no courts of law, he would unfortunately find that causes for law suits would sufficiently abound.

"The last objection is founded upon the supposed anti-christian conduct of the State, in availing itself of the precepts and maxims of Christianity, for the purposes of a more excellent civil government. It is admitted that the founder of this religion did not intend to erect a temporal dominion, agreeably to the prejudices of his countrymen; but to reign in the hearts of men by subduing their irregular appetites and propensities, and by moulding their passions to the noblest purposes. And it is one great excellence of his religion, that not pretending to worldly pomp and power, it is calculated and accommodated to ameliorate the conduct and condition of man under any form of civil government.

"The objection goes further, and complains that Christianity is not left for its promulgation and support, to the means designed by its author, who requires not the assistance of man to effect his purposes and intentions. Our Constitution certainly provides for the punishment of many breaches of the laws of Christianity; not for the purpose of propping up the Christian religion, but because those breaches are offences against the laws of the State; and it is a civil, as well as religious duty of the magistrate, not to bear the sword in vain. But there are many precepts of Christianity, of which the violation cannot be punished by human laws; and as the obedience to them is beneficial to civil society, the State has wisely taken care that they should be taught and also enforced by explaining their moral and religious sanctions, as they cannot be enforced by temporal punishments. And from the genius and temper of this religion, and from the benevolent character of its author, we must conclude that it is his intention, that man should be benefited by it in his civil and political relations, as well as in his individual capacity. And it remains for the objector to prove, that the patronage of Christianity by the civil magistrate induced by the tendency of its precepts to form good citizens, is not one of the means, by which the knowledge of its doctrines was intended to be disseminated and preserved among the human race.

"The last branch of the objection rests on the very correct position, that the faith and precepts of the Christian religion are so interwoven that they must be taught together; whence it is inferred, that the State by enjoining instruction in its precepts, interferes with its doctrines, and assumes a power not entrusted to any human authority.

"If the State claimed the absurd power of directing or controlling the faith of the citizens, there might be some ground for the objection. But no such power is claimed. The authority derived from the Constitution extends no further than to submit to the understandings of the people, the evidence of truths deemed of public utility, leaving the weight of the evidence and the tendency of those truths, to the conscience of every man.

"Indeed this objection must come from a willing objector; for it extends in its consequences, to prohibit the State from providing for public instruction in many branches of useful knowledge which naturally tend to defeat the arguments of infidelity, to illustrate the doctrines of the Christian religion, and to confirm the faith of its professors.

"As Christianity has the promise not only of this, but of a future life; it cannot be denied that public instruction in piety, religion and morality by Protestant teachers, may have a beneficial effect beyond the present state of existence. And the people are to be applauded, as well for their benevolence as for their wisdom, that in selecting a religion, whose precepts and sanctions might supply the defects in civil government, necessarily limited in its power, and supported only by temporal penalties, they adopted a religion founded in truth; which in its tendency will protect our property here, and may secure to us an inheritance in another and a better country."

To illustrate and enforce his views further on this subject, the author reprints a part of a speech of Alexander H. Everett, late American Minister to Spain, delivered in the Senate of Massachusetts, last winter.

"Without going into general and merely speculative reasoning, I ask, gentlemen, to produce an instance of any considerable State, of ancient or modern times, in which public worship and public instruction in religion have been kept up without the aid of Government. The science of politics is eminently a practical one, and it is rarely safe to adopt any principle that has not been sanctioned by former experience. If gentlemen undertake to maintain, that religion will take care of itself;—that it will be properly supported, whether the Government provide for it or not, let them point out a community in which the experiment has been made and has succeeded. Sir, I apprehend that none will be found. I can say at least, with perfect truth, that in the limited range of my researches into history, I have never met with an account of such instance. In all the most distinguished States, whether of ancient or modern times; one of the principal, I may say indeed, the principal care of the community has been, to provide for the support of religion. In Egypt, Palestine, and the Oriental nations, religion has always been the main object of the Government. In Greece it was the only bond of union, that held together the several members of that illustrious Common-wealth of States. The Amphyctionic Council, which corresponded, as far as any part of the Greek Constitution can be said to correspond with it, with our General Government, was authorized to act upon no other subject. In the Constitution of ancient Rome, the same feature is not less apparent, and it is to this very fact that Cicero attributes the remarkable success of the State. 'However much we may be disposed to exalt our advantages,' says this illustrious orator, in one of his addresses to the Senate, 'it is neverthe-less certain, that we have been surpassed in population by the Spaniards, in physical force by the Gauls, in shrewdness and cunning by Carthage, in the fine arts by Greece, and in mere native talent by some of our Italian fellow-countrymen; but in the single point of attention to religion we have ex-ceeded other nations, and it is by the favourable influence of this circumstance upon the character of the people that I account for our suc-cess in acquiring the political and military ascendency that we now enjoy throughout the world.' It is needless to add, that in all the modern Euro-pean nations and their colonies, religion is amply and carefully provided for by the community, and is in fact one of the great objects of the care and attention of the Government.

"In this respect, the experience of the world is uniform and without exception. It is accordingly laid down in general terms, as an acknowledged principle, by one of the most judicious political writers, that no State, whether of ancient or modern times, has ever flourished, of which the foun-dation was not laid, in one way or another, on religion. The great Lord Chan-cellor Bacon, whose name alone is almost decisive authority on any one point of general philosophy, in enumerating what he calls the four pillars of Government, three of which are justice, counsel and treasure, places reli-gion as the first in order and importance at the head of the list. The reason why religion is universally and justly represented as essential to the pros-perity of States, is not less obvious than the fact. The object of Government is to enforce among individuals the observance of the moral law, and States are prosperous in proportion as this object is attained. But the only effec-tual sanction of this law is to be found in religion. Hence a Government, which neglects the care of religion, is guilty of the folly of promulgating laws unaccompanied with any adequate sanction, of requiring the commu-nity to obey without presenting to their minds the motives that generally induce to a prompt and cheerful obedience. Under these circumstances, the only resource left to the public authorities is mere physical force, and experience has abundantly shewn, that this is wholly ineffectual, excepting as an aid and supplement in particular cases, to the moral influences which alone can be depended on for the preservation of the tranquility and good order of society.

"I am aware, that some of our sister States may be regarded as exceptions to the remark, that in all civilized communities, religion has been a principal object of the attention of the Government. They have in fact been mentioned as such in the course of this debate. It has been said, I believe with truth, that Massachusetts is now the only one of the United States, in which the Legislature is authorized by the Constitution to make any public provision by law for the support of religion. Sir, I for one am proud of the distinction, such as it is. If the sacred guest whose influence has for two centuries, in the language of Burke, 'consecrated the Commonwealth,' is in future to be banished from our councils, I rejoice that the last lingering traces of her presence will be seen on the soil, which has been, from the beginning of our history, her favorite abode; in the midst of the places that have been rendered famous by the exploits which her influence inspired; on the heights of Dorchester and Charlestown, and the bloody plains of Lexington. But, Sir, the exception is only apparent, and I undertake to say, that there is no community on earth, of which the history illustrates more fully and pointedly than ours, the principle, that those States only have flourished, whose foundations were laid in religion.

"I confess that I have seen with regret and uneasiness an apparent disposition in a part of the community in this as well as in some other countries, to overlook these obvious truths. There are persons, and even parties, who at the very moment when the use of physical force as an engine of government is discredited and abandoned, seem to be laboring with a sort of frantic energy to destroy the influence of all the moral motives that can be substituted for it; more especially religion. The effort now making in this Commonwealth, apparently with a prospect of success, to amend or rather virtually to abolish Art. iii. of the Bill of Rights, is one of the symptoms of the spirit to which I now allude. Another may be seen in the growing inclination to exclude religion from our colleges and other institutions for education. We have seen within two or three years, in another State, a college founded and endowed with princely liberality, but on the scandalous condition, that no clergyman should even set foot within its walls. Such a condition, as being contrary to good morals, is, in my opinion, void, and the bequest might be made to take effect without it. But however this may be, the introduction of it into the will of the founder, and the acquiescence in it by the parties interested, are melancholy indications of the state of public feeling. Even in this section of the country, once, I may say still, the head quarters of good principles, in the selection of persons to be employed in the government and instruction of the principal colleges, a preference has of late years been almost avowedly given to persons of other professions over clergymen. I am aware, Sir, that some pretext is afforded for such a preference and for such an exclusion as the one to which I have alluded in the will of Mr. [Stephen] Girard, by the acrimony with which the different theological parties contend with each other about trivial points of doctrine and discipline; to the utter neglect of the real truths, and above all the deep and sincere religious feeling, which alone (chiefly?) are of any importance. But, Sir, whatever plausible pretext may be found for such a tendency, were it even justifiable under all circumstances, in the particular cases to which I allude, its practical results are not the less mischievous. I have said and I repeat, that if, while we abandon the use of physical force as an engine of maintaining order, we also discard the only valuable and effectual moral influences, and leave the individual to the unchecked guidance of his own selfish passions, our institutions will be found to be impracticable, and society will fall into a state of dissolution.

"The gentleman from Berkshire tells us that religion will exist; that it is independent of the aid of Government;—that it will take care of itself. Why, Sir, this is all true, but in what way? Religion takes care of herself by giving stability, permanence, vigour, health, life to the individuals, the families, the communities, that care for her. The individuals, the communities that are penetrated with a truly religious spirit, and exercise the moral qualities which flow from that source only, regularly prosper. They inherit the earth! Those that pursue a different course, as regularly dwindle into nothing and disappear. This, Sir, is the way in which religion takes care of itself. How then does the principle apply to the case in question? If we, Sir, as a community reject religion, we shall gradually decline from our present prosperous social condition, until the places that now know us, know us no more, and other communities, animated by a better spirit, come up and occupy them in our stead. This is the order of nature, or in other words, the will of Providence, and we can no more expect to escape from the operation of it, than an individual can expect to escape from the usual physical results of intemperance and vice."

H.—PAGE 22 [53].

Nor were the professions made by the colonists of a desire to convert the native tribes of this country to the Christian Faith, vain and unsubstantial. The labours of [John] Eliot, of [Daniel] Gookin, and of the five Mayhews, are a model of missionary zeal, enterprise, perseverance and self-devotion. In 1674, the single colony of Massachusetts contained not less than 3600 Christian Indians. In 1698, report was made to the commissioners of the Society for Propagating the Gospel, that within the same colony, there were thirty distinct assemblies of Indians, having 36 teachers, 5 schoolmasters and 20 rulers. The whole number of Indians under this arrangement, was

3080. All the rulers, teachers and schoolmasters were Indians; but the teachers were occasionally assisted by the neighboring clergy. A favorable report was given of the improvement and manners of the Indians, of their sobriety, decent dress, and proficiency in reading and writing. Mr. Eliot, often called the Apostle of the Indians, translated the entire Bible, Baxter's Call, &c. into the Indian language. He, moreover, composed and published Catechisms, Primers, Grammars, &c. for their use. Mr. Eliot declared to Mr. Gookin, that he considered himself pledged "to endeavour, so far as in him lay, the accomplishment and fulfilling the covenant and promise, which the people of New-England made to the King when he granted their charters; viz. that one great end of their emigration to the new world, was, to communicate the gospel to the native Indians."—*Quar. Reg.* vol. iv. pp. 199-204.

Endeavours for the conversion of the Indians were not confined to individuals. In 1619, twelve years after the first settlement of Virginia, we find this record:—"The King of England having formerly issued his letters to the several bishops of the kingdom, for collecting money to erect a college in Virginia, for the education of the Indian children, nearly £1,500 had been already paid towards this benevolent and pious design, and Henrico had been selected as a suitable place for the Seminary. The Virginia Company, on the recommendation of Sir Edwin Sandys, its treasurer, now granted 10,000 acres of land, to be laid off for the University at Henrico." "The first design," says Anderson, "was to erect and build a college in Virginia, for the training up and educating infidel (Indian) children in the true knowledge of God." (*Am. Qua. Reg.* vol. iv. p. 123.) One of the principal designs of the founders of the college of William and Mary in Virginia, was, to provide instruction for the Indians. The Hon. Robert Boyle, one of the Governors, gave large sums of money for this purpose. He was very zealous in this work, sending 400 miles to collect Indian children, "first establishing a school on the frontiers convenient to the Indians, that they might often see their children under the first management, where they learnt to read; paying £500 per annum out of his own pocket to the schoolmaster there; after which they were brought to the college." *Beverly's Hist. of Virginia, quoted in Amer. Quar. Reg.* vol. iii. p. 269.

The original of Dartmouth College in New-Hampshire, was an Indian Charity School, instituted about the year 1754, by the Rev. Dr. Eleazar Wheelock. For several years, with some assistance from others, he clothed, maintained and educated a number of Indian children, "with a view to their carrying the gospel in their own language, and spreading the knowledge of the Great Redeemer among their savage tribes." The charter of the college (granted by George III. in 1769,) also says, in addition to the preceding quotation, that Dr. Wheelock "actually employed a number of them (educated Indians) as missionaries and schoolmasters in the wilderness for that purpose; and that by the blessing of God upon his endeavours, the design became reputable among the Indians, insomuch that a larger number desired the education of their children in said school, and were also disposed to receive missionaries and schoolmasters in the wilderness, more than could be supplied by the charitable contributions in the American colonies." Accordingly contributions were sought and obtained in England. The charter further recites, "that we (the Crown) willing to encourage the laudable and charitable design of spreading Christian knowledge among the savages of our American wilderness, and also that the best means of education be established in our province of New-Hampshire, constitute a college by the name of Dartmouth College, for the education and instruction of youth, of the Indian tribes in this land, in reading, writing, and all parts of learning which shall appear necessary and expedient for civilizing and christianizing children of Pagans, as well as in all liberal arts and sciences; and also of English youth and any others." (4 *Wheaton's Reports,* pp. 519-524.) This college still has a fund appropriated to the education of Indian youths; and there has seldom, if ever, been a time, when there were not some Indian youths members of it, or attached to its preparatory school. Not less than fifteen or twenty Indian youths have received the degrees of this college, and many have passed through the earlier stages of a collegiate education. Occasionally an Indian youth has been graduated at other Northern colleges. Mr. Justice Story says:—(Centennial Discourse) "they (the colonists) were aided by higher considerations, by the desire to propagate Christianity among the Indians; a desire, which is breathed forth in their confidential papers, in their domestic letters, in their private prayers, and in their public devotions. In this object, they were not only sincere, but constant. So sincere and so constant, that one of the grave accusations against them has been, that in their religious zeal, they compelled the Indians, by penalties, to attend public worship, and allured them by presents, to abandon their infidelity. In truth, the propagation of Christianity was a leading motive with many of the early promoters of the settlement; and we need no better proof of it, than the establishment of an Indian school at Harvard College to teach them the rudiments of the Christian faith."

I.—*PAGE* 22 [53].

No one individual, perhaps, has contributed so much as Dr. [Benjamin] Franklin, towards forming the peculiar traits of the American character. His love of knowledge, his patient industry, his frugality, his moderation, his love of peace, his disciplined temper, his keen sagacity, and public spirit, have deeply impressed themselves on his countrymen. His influence has been unfavourable to religion, by causing many to believe, that morality without the sustaining aid of personal religion, is sufficient for this life, and adequate to secure happiness in the life to come. His early scepticism may be ascribed in some measure to his injudicious parental education and discipline. The most authentic memorials of his religious opinions, are his letters to the Rev. Mr. [George] Whitefield and President [Ezra] Stiles, the former written in 1753, and the latter in 1790. (*Franklin's Works*, vol. vi. pp. 34. 241.) In the latter, he speaks of Christianity as "the best system of religion and morals the world ever saw or is like to see." To some (unknown) person, who seems to have consulted him in regard to publishing a work against Christianity, he replies by putting the question; "if mankind are so wicked *with religion,* what would they be *without it?*" He advises the same person to burn his manuscript before it is seen by any one else, and to "think how great a portion of mankind consists of weak and ignorant men and women, and of inexperienced inconsiderate youth of both sexes, who have need of the motives of religion to restrain them from vice, to support their virtue, and to retain them in the practice of it till it becomes habitual, which (says he) is the great point for its security." (*Idem.* vi. 243.) He here distinctly admits the necessity of religion to support the morals of the community. In fact, his sound common sense and good feelings, always led him in his more mature years, to discourage all disrespect to religion, and to aid any thing which tended to enlarge its influence. (*Tudor's Life of James Otis,* pp. 386-391.) But the most remarkable proof of his increased sensibility to the value of religion, late in life, is contained in a speech delivered by him in the Convention assembled in 1787, to form the present Constitution of the United States. The Convention had fallen into great difficulties, and the business had come apparently to a stand. In justice to Dr. Franklin, as well as for the sake of its good tendency and intimate connection with this discussion, the speech is attached to this note.

"Mr. President, (says he) the small progress we have made after four or five weeks close attendance and continual reasoning with each other, our different sentiments on almost every question, several of the last producing as many Noes as Ayes, is, methinks, a melancholy proof of the imperfection of the human understanding. We, indeed, seem to feel our own want of political wisdom, since we have been running all about in search of it. We have gone back to ancient history, for models of government, and examined the different forms of those republics, which, having been originally formed with the seeds of their own dissolution, now no longer exist; and we have viewed modern states all round Europe, but find none of their constitutions suitable to our circumstances.

"In this situation of this assembly, groping as it were in the dark, to find political truth, and scarce able to distinguish it when presented to us, how has it happened, Sir, that we have not hitherto once thought of humbly applying to the Father of Lights to illuminate our understandings. In the beginning of the contest with Britain, when we were sensible of danger, we had daily prayers in this room for the divine protection. Our prayers, Sir, were heard;—and they were graciously answered. All of us, who were engaged in the struggle, must have observed frequent instances of a superintending Providence in our favour. To that kind Providence we owe this happy opportunity of consulting in peace on the means of establishing our future national felicity. And have we now forgotten that powerful friend?—or do we imagine we no longer need its assistance? I have lived, Sir, a long time; and the longer I live the more convincing proofs I see of this truth, that God governs in the affairs of men; and if a sparrow cannot fall to the ground without his notice, is it probable that an empire can rise without his aid? We have been assured, Sir, in the Sacred Writings, that 'except the Lord build the house, they labour in vain that build it.' I firmly believe this; and I also believe, that without his concurring aid, we shall succeed in this political building no better than the builders of Babel: we shall be divided by our little partial local interests: our projects will be confounded, and we ourselves shall become a reproach and a by-word down to future ages. And what is worse, mankind may hereafter, from this unfortunate instance, despair of establishing government by human wisdom, and leave it to chance, war, and conquest. I, therefore, beg leave to move, that henceforth prayers, imploring the assistance of Heaven, and its blessing on our deliberations, be held in this assembly every morning before we proceed to business: and that one or more of the clergy of this city, be requested to officiate in that service." (*Franklin's Works*, vol. i. 474.)

The opinion of George Washington in regard to the necessity of religion to sustain the morals of a nation, cannot be reprinted too often. In his Farewell Address, he says, "Of all the dispositions and habits, which lead to political prosperity, religion and morality are indispensable supports. In vain would that man claim the tribute of patriotism, who should labour to subvert these great pillars of human happiness, these firmest props of the duties of man and citizens. The mere politician equally with the pious man, ought to respect and to cherish them. A volume could not trace all their connexions with private and public felicity. Let it simply be asked, where is the security for property, for reputation, for life, if the sense of religious obligation desert the oaths which are the instruments of investigation in Courts of Justice? And let us with caution indulge the supposition, that morality can be maintained without religion. Whatever may be conceded to the influence of refined education on minds of peculiar structure, reason and experience both forbid us to expect, that national morality can prevail in exclusion of religious principle." See also 5 *Marshall's Washington*, pp. 44. 57.

K.—PAGE 22 [53].

Sir W[alter] Scott, speaking of this conspiracy to destroy Christianity in
Europe, and especially in France, says:—["]This work, the philosophers, as
they termed themselves, carried on with such an unlimited and eager zeal,
as plainly to show that infidelity, as well as divinity, has its fanaticism. An
envenomed fury against religion and all its doctrines; a promptitude to avail
themselves of every circumstance by which Christianity could be misrepresented; an ingenuity in mixing up their opinions in works, which seemed
the least fitting to involve such discussions; above all, a pertinacity in slan-
dering, ridiculing, and vilifying all who ventured to oppose their principles,
distinguished the correspondents in this celebrated conspiracy against a religion, which, however, it may be defaced by human inventions, breathes
only that peace on earth, and good will to the children of men, which was
proclaimed by Heaven at its divine origin.

["]If these prejudiced and envenomed opponents had possessed half
the desire of truth, or half the benevolence towards mankind, which were
eternally on their lips, they would have formed the true estimate of the spirit
of Christianity, not from the use which had been made of the mere name
by ambitious priests or enthusiastic fools, but by its vital effects upon mankind at large. They would have seen, that under its influence a thousand
brutal and sanguinary superstitions had died away; that polygamy had been
abolished, and with polygamy all the obstacles which it offers to domestic
happiness, as well as to the due education of youth, and the natural and
gradual civilization of society. They must then have owned, that slavery,
which they regarded or affected to regard with such horror, had first been
gradually ameliorated, and finally abolished by the influence of the Christian doctrines:—that there was no one virtue teaching to elevate mankind
or benefit society, which was not enjoined by the precepts they endeavoured
to misrepresent and weaken; no one vice by which humanity is degraded
and society endangered, upon which Christianity hath not imposed a solemn anathema. They might also, in their capacity of philosophers, have considered the peculiar aptitude of the Christian religion, not only to all ranks
and conditions of mankind, but to all climates and to all stages of society.

"Unhappily blinded by self-conceit, heated with the ardour of controversy, gratifying their literary pride by becoming members of a league, in
which kings and princes were included, and procuring followers by flatter-
ing the vanity of some, and stimulating the cupidity of others, the men of
the most distinguished parts in France became allied in a sort of anti-cru-
sade against Christianity, and indeed against religious principles of every
kind. How they succeeded is too universally known: and when it is considered that these men of letters, who ended by degrading the morals, and

destroying the religion of so many of the citizens of France, had been first called into public estimation by the patronage of the higher orders, it is impossible not to think of the Israelitish champion, who, brought into the house of Dagon to make sport for the festive assembly, ended by pulling it down upon the heads of the guests—and upon his own." *Life of Napoleon,* vol. i. pp. 36. 37.

It is understood, that within a few years, a society of professed infidels has been formed in New-York, (*See Gospel Messenger,* vol. v. p. 217.) and the author has observed by the newspapers, that within a few weeks, the birth day of Thomas Paine, has been celebrated in that city;—it is presumed by this society. If these humble pages shall by chance meet the eye of any one who has celebrated the birth day of Mr. Paine, he may, perhaps, be instructed by perusing the following passages from the correspondence of Gouverneur Morris.

Writing to Mr. Jefferson, under date of 21st January, 1794, Mr. Morris says, "I must mention, that Thomas Paine is in prison, where he amuses himself with publishing a pamphlet against Jesus Christ. I do not recollect whether I mentioned to you, that he would have been executed along with the rest of the Brissotines, if the adverse party had not viewed him with contempt. I incline to think, that if he is quiet in prison, he may have the good luck to be forgotten." (*Life by Sparks,* vol. ii. 393.) Again, under date of 6th March, 1794, Mr. Morris says, "in the best of times, he had a larger share of every other sense than of common sense, and lately the intemperate use of ardent spirits has, I am told, considerably impaired the small stock which he originally possessed." (vol. ii. 409.)

L.—Page 23 [54].

The 42d of the Letters on the Study of the Law, ascribed to the late Sir James Mackintosh, furnishes the most valuable illustrations of this subject. The gifted author was not only distinguished as a jurist and a statesman, but he was familiar with almost every walk of literature and philosophy.

"I am now to treat of religion, and of the claims which it has upon the acknowledgement and support of him, who sustains the character of an advocate in our courts of justice. The worship of a Supreme Cause and the belief of a future state, have not only, in general, been concomitant, but have so universally engaged the concurrence of mankind, that they who have pretended to teach the contrary, have been looked upon in every age and state of society, as men opposing the pure emotions of our nature. This Supreme Cause, it is true, has been prefigured to the imagination by symbols suited to the darkness and ignorance of unlettered ages; but the great and secret original has nevertheless been the same in the contemplation of the sim-

plest heathen and the most refined Christian. There must have been something exceedingly powerful in an idea that has made so prodigious a progress
in the mind of man. The opinions of men have experienced a thousand
changes; kingdoms that have been most powerful have been removed; the
form of the earth itself has undergone various alterations; but amidst these
grand and ruinous concussions, religion has remained unshaken; and a principle so consentaneous to the first formation of our nature must remain,
until by some power, of which, at present we have no conception, the laws
of that nature are universally dissolved. Powers thus singular must have their
foundation in truth; for men may rest in truth, but they can never rest in
error. To charm the human mind, and to maintain its monstrous empire,
error must, ere this, have chosen innumerable shapes, all, too, wearing, more
or less, the semblance of truth. And what is thus true must be also just; and
of course, to acknowledge its influence must be the spontaneous and natural effusion of a love of truth; and the love of truth either is really, or is
affected to be, the character of those who have dedicated themselves to the
study of our laws. Thus naturally, even upon the first glance, do the characters of the lawyer and the supporter of religion meet; the conclusion must
be, that he who affects to doubt of the fundamental truths of religion, much
more he who dares to deride them, is dissolving by fraud and violence, a tie
which all good men have agreed to hold in respect, and the violation of
which must render the violator unworthy the esteem and support of his
fellow creatures."—pp. 299-300.

"It is the nature of religion to preserve unbroken that secret chain by
which men are united, and, as it were, bound together; and as you are interested in common with the rest of your species in its preservation, particularly does it become you, as a professor of those laws which are one of its
instruments, to display an anxiety to guard it from violence or contempt.
Yet how do you do this, if you are either *forging doubts yourself, or listening to
them who forge doubts of the existence or authenticity of religion!* It is the great aim
of those who would overturn the peace and order of mankind to *undermine
the foundations of religion, by starting doubts and proposing questions,* which being
artfully calculated for every turn, are apt to dazzle and confound the common apprehension, like that famous question of the Elean philosopher;—
Can there be any such thing as motion, since a thing cannot move where it
is, nor where it is not? Yet, by the questions of an equally foolish and un-
manly nature, do many men, of no inferior learning or capcity, suffer their
time and their attention to be miserably wasted! But do you not perceive
the mischievous tendency of such questions? Do you not see that, by rendering every principle doubtful, they loosen all those sacred obligations by
which men are kept within the bounds of duty and subordination? And shall
you, who are continually in public to call out for the interposition of the
law against injustice and wrong, be forever in your private parties and con-

versations labouring to weaken every known and settled principle of justice and of right?

["]Give me leave to say, it is a weak pretence that is made use of by those who are thus unworthily engaged, *that they are searching after truth;* and indeed it is merely a pretence; for it is curious enough to observe, *that many of these searchers after truth are men who have been employed nearly half a century in this pretended pursuit, and yet have they not settled one single principle;* nay, they are more full than ever of doubts and conjectures; and as age and fatigue have exhausted their strength and robbed them of their wit, their questions gain in childishness and folly, what they loose in subtlety and invention; nor is this a single case; I never in my life met with *an old searcher after truth,* but I found him at once the most wretched and most contemptible of all earthly beings. The fact is, the men I mean, *are not searching after the truth;* for where is it to be found? or who is to be the judge of it, when every certain principle is shaken or overthrown by which the decision is to be made? They have robbed their own minds of a resting place, and they would reduce the minds of others to the same unhappy and unsettled condition. With this spirit they attack every sentiment whereon men have been accustomed to rely; and as words are the common medium through which ideas are delivered, they play upon the meanings of words, till they have thrown every thing into that confusion which, unfortunately for themselves and for others, is so congenial with their debased inclinations.

"The propagation of doubt, with respect to religion, is at all times an injudicious, and frequently becomes *an immoral act.* He who seeks to destroy a system by an adherence to the pure principles of which, mankind may be kept in peace and virtue, (how delusive soever he may esteem that system to be) without proposing a better for that important purpose, ought to be considered as an enemy to the public welfare. I am here naturally led to consider religion as peculiarly powerful in settling the mind. It is impossible for a great and expanded intellect to be untouched by considerations of so great importance as those which religion presents to the contemplation; it will therefore either decide in certainty, or it will wander in doubt; for, to a thinking mind, what intermediate state can there be? And he that is in doubt, as I have before observed, cannot be at rest; and he who is not at rest cannot be happy. Now if this be true of doubt, the reverse must be true of certainty, which is a contrary influence. And need I point out to you the necessity of such a state to a mind engaged in the pursuit of a science so various and profound as the law? Or, on the contrary, how utterly impossible it is for a mind entangled in scepticism, according to the modern idea of that term, to attend with regularity and happiness to an object so important? Let me advise you to rest satisfied with those clear and fundamental truths upon which so many great and wise men have rested before you: and that, not merely because they have thus rested, for that would not be to be like them, but because they are sustained by your uncorrupted sentiments, and produce clear ideas of the various virtues that adorn and elevate the mind, and also, which is of still greater importance, that stimulate you to the continual practice of them."—pp. 304-307.

"Why then not be content to argue in this respect from the effect to the cause, and rest satisfied with that as a matter of faith which the reason of man has never yet been able to explain? Reflect upon the thousands who are now in their graves, whose lives were spent in endeavours to ascertain that power which mocked all their efforts and baffled all their ingenuity; learn from them to confide in that first Great Cause, which, though it be hidden from your sight, you most sensibly feel, and against which your feeble arm is raised in vain. What is the grand aim and end of knowledge, but to regulate our practice? And whence is this knowledge primarily to be acquired? from books? from men? No; by contemplation of these, it is true our knowledge may be enriched and augmented; but it must first spring from the secret source of our own bosoms; these let us search with impartiality, and we shall need the assistance of no fine-spun theories, no finesse, no subtlety, to discover the truth; truth is of a certain simple nature, and accordingly all will be certainty and simplicity here."—pp. 307-308.

"Do you wish to obtain the rare and valuable faculty of solving difficulties and obviating doubts, by the exercise of which obscurity is in a moment rendered clear, and darkness changed into light? It is to be acquired only by industrious reading and profound contemplation. Do you desire to know upon what subject this power can be most worthily exercised? I answer, Religion in all its varieties; of its purity as it came forth from the hand of its Omnipotent Founder, and of its degeneracy under the operation of human influences.["]—p. 311.

Since this form was set up, the author has seen the opinion of Judge William D. Martin in the case of the Town Council of Columbia vs. C.O. Duke and Alexander Marks.

By an Ordinance of Council of 18th July 1833, Duke and Marks were fined each $12 for opening their shops and selling on Sunday. The relators complained of the ordinance as unconstitutional, and relied for protection against its enforcement, on the first amendment to the Constitution of the United States;—and more especially on Art. 8. Sec. 1. of the Constitution of this State. (See p. 15 [48, n. 25].) Judge Martin decided that the ordinance of the Council was constitutional, and accompanied his decision with a luminous and highly convincing argument. (See the Southern Times and State Gazette printed at Columbia, S.C. for Oct. 11, 1833.—Charleston Observer of November 2d, 1833.)

THE END.

WORKS CITED BY ADAMS

Adams drew on an extraordinarily diverse body of literature. His use of
sources reveals a familiarity with leading legal and political treatises of
the day. He cited, for example, St. George Tucker's five-volume edition of
Blackstone's Commentaries (1803), which was specially annotated for an American
audience. He also recognized the importance of Joseph Story's recently
published *Commentaries on the Constitution of the United States* (1833). Only
the commentaries of Chancellor James Kent rivaled those of Justice Story
in influence and popularity in nineteenth-century America. (See generally
Elizabeth Kelley Bauer, *Commentaries on the Constitution, 1790-1860* [New
York: Columbia Univ. Press, 1952]). Adams was also knowledgeable about
South Carolina legal sources. He cited, for example, John Faucheraud
Grimké's *Public Laws of the State of South-Carolina* (1790), which reported
the legal reforms in South Carolina following independence and remained
the definitive treatise on South Carolina law until Thomas Cooper published
his five-volume *Statutes at Large of South Carolina* (1836-39).

Adams demonstrated a familiarity with historical scholarship and great
works of classical and English literature. He made frequent reference to the
Bible and quoted from the literary works of Racine, Milton, and others. He
cited Cotton Mather's *Magnalia Christi Americana* (1702), Edmund Burke's
Reflections on the Revolution in France (1790), and David Ramsay's *The History
of South-Carolina* (1809). He also drew on a number of leading biographies
and the collected works of such figures as Christopher Columbus, Francis
Bacon, Napoleon Bonaparte, George Washington, Benjamin Franklin, Thomas
Jefferson, Gouverneur Morris, and James Otis.

This bibliography of the works cited in Adams's sermon and notes
was compiled with reference to Joseph Sabin, Wilberforce Eames, and R.W.G.
Vail, *Bibliotheca Americana: A Dictionary of Books Relating to America, from Its
Discovery to the Present Time*, 29 vols. (New York, 1868-1936); Charles Evans,
Clifford K. Shipton, and Roger Pattrell Bristol, *The American Bibliography: A
Chronological Dictionary of All Books, Pamphlets and Periodical Publications Printed
in the United States of America from the Genesis of Printing in 1639 Down to and
Including the Year 1820, with Bibliographical and Biographical Notes*, 14 vols. (New

York, 1903-59); and *The National Union Catalog, Pre-1956 Imprints,* 754 vols. (London: Mansell, 1968-81).

Three useful compilations of many of the colonial charters and state constitutions mentioned in the sermon are Benjamin Perley Poore, ed., *The Federal and State Constitutions, Colonial Charters, and Other Organic Laws of the United States,* 2 vols. (Washington, D.C.: GPO, 1877); Francis Newton Thorpe, ed., *The Federal and State Constitutions, Colonial Charters, Other Organic Laws of the States, Territories, and Colonies Now or Heretofore Forming the United States of America,* 7 vols. (Washington, D.C.: GPO, 1909); and William Finley Swindler, ed., *Sources and Documents of United States Constitutions,* 11 vols. (Dobbs Ferry, N.Y.: Oceana, 1988).

Not every work or authority cited in the sermon and notes is listed. In several instances Adams did not provide sufficient bibliographical detail to identify the work cited. If a work has more than one published edition, an effort was made to identify the precise edition on which Adams relied. It is not always clear from the information supplied by Adams, however, which edition he used. In any case, this bibliography includes only editions that would have been available to Adams. Finally, this bibliography does not address Adams's many references to the Bible, state constitutions, and legislative journals. These are generally accessible sources familiar to the modern scholar.

BOOKS, PAMPHLETS, AND ARTICLES

Acts of the General Assembly of the State of South-Carolina, from February, 1791, to December, 1794, Both Inclusive. Vol. 1. Columbia, S.C.: [Printed by D. and J.J. Faust, State Printers], 1808.

Bacon, Francis. *The Works of Francis Bacon, Baron of Verulam, Viscount St. Alban, Lord High Chancellor of England.* 10 vols. London, 1803.

Baxter, Richard. *A Call to the Unconverted.* London, 1658.

Beverly, Robert. *The History of Virginia, In Four Parts.* 2d ed. London, 1722.

Blackstone, William. *Commentaries on the Laws of England.* 4 vols. Oxford, 1765-69.

Brevard, Joseph. *An Alphabetical Digest of the Public Statute Law of South-Carolina.* 3 vols. Charleston, 1814.

"British House of Commons—Jewish Disabilities. April 17, 1833." *National Gazette and Literary Register* (triweekly ed.), 8 June 1833.

Brougham, Henry. *An Inquiry into the Colonial Policy of the European Powers.* 2 vols. Edinburgh, 1803.

Burke, Edmund. *Reflections on the Revolution in France, and on the Proceedings of*

Certain Societies in London Relative to That Event. In *The Works of the Right Honourable Edmund Burke.* First American ed. 4 vols. Boston, 1806-7.

Burn, Richard. *Ecclesiastical Law.* 2d ed. 4 vols. London, 1767.

The Charters of the British Colonies in America. London: [Printed for J. Almon], 1777.

Cicero, Marcus Tullius. *De Legibus* 2.

Dalcho, Frederick. *An Historical Account of the Protestant Episcopal Church, in South-Carolina, from the First Settlement of the Province, to the War of the Revolution.* Charleston, S.C., 1820.

Digest of Justinian 1.10.2.

Digest of the Ordinances of the City Council of Charleston, from the Year 1783 to July 1818. Charleston, S.C., 1818.

East, Edward Hyde. *A Treatise of the Pleas of the Crown.* 2 vols. London, 1803.

Edwards, B.B. "History of American Colleges." *Quarterly Register of the American Education Society* 3, no. 4 (May 1831): 263-76.

Everett, Alexander H. "Claims of Religion upon Government." *Gospel Messenger, and Southern Episcopal Register* 10, no. 115 (July 1833): 206-9. [Excerpt of speech in Massachusetts Senate.]

Franklin, Benjamin. *Memoirs of the Life and Writings of Benjamin Franklin. . . . Now First Published from the Original Manuscript Comprising the Private Correspondence & Public Negotiations of Dr. Franklin: Together with the Whole of His Political, Philosophical & Miscellaneous Works.* 6 vols. Philadelphia, 1818.

Frelinghuysen, Theodore. "Speech of Mr. Frelinghuysen, on the Subject of Sunday Mails." U.S. Congress, Senate, 21st Cong., 1st sess. *Register of Debates in Congress* (8 May 1830), vol. 6. Washington, D.C.: Gales and Seaton, 1830.

Gordon, Thomas F. *A Digest of the Laws of the United States, Including an Abstract of the Judicial Decisions Relating to the Constitutional and Statutory Law.* Philadelphia, 1827.

Grimké, John Faucheraud. *The Public Laws of the State of South-Carolina, from Its First Establishment as a British Province Down to the Year 1790.* Philadelphia, 1790.

Hall, Robert. "Modern Infidelity Considered, with Respect to Its Influence on Society: In a Sermon, Preached at the Baptist Meeting, Cambridge, England. A Sermon. Ephes. Chap. 2, Verse 12. 'Without God in the World.'" In *Sermons on Various Subjects.* New York, 1814.

Hawkins, William. *A Treatise of the Pleas of the Crown; or, A System of the Principal Matters Relating to That Subject, Digested under Their Proper Heads.* 2 vols. London, 1716-21.

Hazard, Ebenezer. *Historical Collections; Consisting of State Papers, and Other Authentic Documents; Intended as Materials for an History of the United States of America.* 2 vols. Philadelphia, 1792-94.

Heeren, Arnold Hermann Ludwig. *Reflections on the Politics of Ancient Greece.* Translated by George Bancroft. Boston, 1824.

"History of Revivals of Religion, from the Settlement of the Country to the Present Time." *American Quarterly Register* 4, no. 2 (Nov. 1831): 122-35, no. 3 (Feb. 1832): 198-213.

Irving, Washington. *A History of the Life and Voyages of Christopher Columbus.* 3 vols. New York, 1828.

Jefferson, Thomas. *Memoir, Correspondence, and Miscellanies, from the Papers of Thomas Jefferson.* Edited by Thomas Jefferson Randolph. 4 vols. Charlottesville, Va., 1829.

Laws of the State of New-York. 2 vols. Albany, N.Y.: [Printed by Charles R. and George Webster], 1802.

"Letters on France and England." In *The American Review of History and Politics and General Repository of Literature and State Papers,* edited by Robert Walsh. 4 vols. Philadelphia, 1811-12.

Locke, John. *Fundamental Constitutions of Carolina of 1669.*

Macaulay, Thomas Babington. Speech to the House of Commons, 17 April 1833. *Hansard's Parliamentary Debates* (Commons). 3d ser., vol. 17 (1833), cols. 227-38.

Mackintosh, James. "Letter XLII: On the Connection between the Study of Religion and the Law." In *The Study and Practice of the Law, Considered in Their Various Relations to Society. In a Series of Letters.* First American ed. Portland, 1806.

Marshall, John. *The Life of George Washington, Commander in Chief of the American Forces, during the War Which Established the Independence of His Country, and First President of the United States.* 5 vols. Philadelphia, 1804-7.

Mather, Cotton. *Magnalia Christi Americana; or, The Ecclesiastical History of New-England.* London, 1702.

Milton, John. *Paradise Lost* 12.369-71.

"Opinion of Judge Martin." *Charleston (S.C.) Observer.* 2 Nov. 1833.

"Opinion of Judge Martin." *(Columbia, S.C.) Southern Times and State Gazette.* 11 Oct. 1833.

Racine, Jean. *Athalie* 1.1.64.

Ramsay, David. *The History of South-Carolina, from Its First Settlement in 1670, to the Year 1808.* 2 vols. Charleston, S.C., 1809.

"Religious Intelligence." *Gospel Messenger, and Southern Episcopal Register* 5, no. 55 (July 1828): 217.

Reports of the Proceedings and Debates of the Convention of 1821, Assembled for the Purpose of Amending the Constitution of the State of New York. Albany, N.Y., 1821. [Nathaniel H. Carter and William L. Stone, reporters; and Marcus T.C. Gould, stenographer].

Scott, Walter. *The Life of Napoleon Buonaparte, Emperor of the French. With a Preliminary View of the French Revolution.* 3 vols. Philadelphia, 1827.

"Signs of the Times." *Gospel Messenger, and Southern Episcopal Register* 10, no. 116 (Aug. 1833): 253.

Sparks, Jared. *The Life of Gouverneur Morris, with Selections from His Correspondence and Miscellaneous Papers; Detailing Events in the American Revolution, the French Revolution, and in the Political History of the United States.* 3 vols. Boston, 1832.

Stansbury, Arthur J. *Report of the Trial of James H. Peck, Judge of the United States District Court for the District of Missouri, before the Senate of the United States, on an Impeachment Preferred by the House of Representatives against Him for High Misdemeanors in Office.* Boston, 1833. [Appendix 2 is "Spanish Regulations of Grants."]

Story, Joseph. "Christianity a Part of the Common Law." *American Jurist and Law Magazine* 9 (April 1833): 346-48.

———. *Commentaries on the Constitution of the United States.* 3 vols. Boston, 1833.

———. *A Discourse Pronounced at the Request of the Essex Historical Society, on the 18th of September, 1828, in Commemoration of the First Settlement of Salem, in the State of Massachusetts.* Boston, 1828. Reprinted in *The Miscellaneous Writings, Literary, Critical, Juridical, and Political, of Joseph Story.* Boston, 1835.

———. *A Discourse Pronounced upon the Inauguration of the Author, as Dane Professor of Law in Harvard University, on the Twenty-fifth day of August, 1829.* Boston, 1829. Reprinted in *The Miscellaneous Writings, Literary, Critical, Juridical, and Political, of Joseph Story.* Boston, 1835.

Thacher, Peter Oxenbridge. *A Charge to the Grand Jury of the County of Suffolk, for the Commonwealth of Massachusetts, at the Opening of the Municipal Court of the City of Boston, on the First Monday of December, A.D. 1832.* Boston, 1832.

Tremaine, John. *Pleas of the Crown in Matters Criminal and Civil.* London, 1723.

Trott, Nicholas. *The Laws of the Province of South-Carolina, in Two Parts.* 2 vols. Charles-Town, S.C., 1736.

Tucker, St. George. *Blackstone's Commentaries: With Notes of Reference, to the Constitution and Laws, of the Federal Government of the United States; and of the Commonwealth of Virginia.* 5 vols. Philadelphia, 1803.

Tudor, William. *The Life of James Otis of Massachusetts.* Boston, 1823.

Webster, Daniel. *A Discourse, Delivered at Plymouth, December 22, 1820. In Commemoration of the First Settlement of New-England.* 2d ed. Boston, 1821.

Wood, Thomas. *An Institute of the Laws of England; or, The Laws of England in Their Natural Order, According to Common Use. In Four Books.* 10th ed. London, 1772.

Legal Cases

Barnes v. First Parish in Falmouth, 6 Mass. 400 (1810).

Bell v. Graham, 1 Nott & M'Cord 278 (S.C. 1818).

Dartmouth College v. Woodward, 17 U.S. (4 Wheaton) 517 (1819).

The Guardians of the Poor v. Greene, 5 Binney 554 (Pa. 1813).

The King v. Taylor, 1 Ventris 293; 3 Keble 607, 621; 86 English Reports 189 (King's Bench, 1676).

The King v. Waddington, 1 Barnewall & Cresswell 26; 1 State Trials (N.S.) 1339; 1 Law Journal (O.S.) 37; 107 English Reports 11 (King's Bench, 1822).

The King v. Williams, 26 Howell's State Trials 653 (King's Bench, 1797).

The King v. Woolston, Fitz-Gibbon 64; 2 Strange 834; 1 Barnardiston 162; 94 English Reports 112, 655 (King's Bench, 1729).

People v. Ruggles, 8 Johnson 290 (N.Y. 1811).

Shaw v. M'Combs, 2 Bay 232 (S.C. 1799).

Smith v. Sparrow, 4 Bingham 84; 12 Moore 266; 5 Law Journal (O.S.) 80; 130 English Reports 700 (Common Pleas, 1827).

Town Council of Columbia v. C.O. Duke and Alexander Marks, 2 Strobhart 530 (S.C. 1833).

Updegraph v. Commonwealth, 11 Sergeant & Rawle 394 (Pa. 1824).

Vidal v. Girard's Executors, 43 U.S. (2 Howard) 127 (1844).

PART TWO

RESPONSE

LETTERS TO THE
REVEREND JASPER ADAMS

Eager to confirm his views, Jasper Adams sent copies of the printed sermon to numerous influential Americans, requesting that they respond to his arguments and offer their own opinions on the subject of his sermon. The following letters are reprinted from copies of the original letters sent to Adams, which he personally transcribed and attached to his own copy of the first printed edition of the sermon.

FROM JOHN MARSHALL

Richmond May 9th 1833.

Reverend Sir,

I am much indebted to you for the copy of your valuable sermon on the relation of Christianity to civil government preached before the convention of the Protestant Episcopal Church in Charleston, on the 13th of Feby. last. I have read it with great attention & advantage.

The documents annexed to the sermon certainly go far in sustaining the proposition which it is your purpose to establish. One great object of the colonial charters was avowedly the propagation of the Christian faith. Means have been employed to accomplish this object, & those means have been used by government.

No person, I believe, questions the importance of religion to the happiness of man even during his existence in this world. It has at all times employed his most serious meditation, & had a decided influence on his conduct. The American population is entirely Christian, & with us, Christianity & Religion are identified. It would be strange, indeed, if with such a people, our institutions did not presuppose Christianity, & did not often refer to it, & exhibit relations with

John Marshall. Engraving by Asher B. Durand, 1833.
Collection of the Supreme Court of the United States.

it. Legislation on the subject is admitted to require great delicacy, because fredom [*sic*] of conscience & respect for our religion both claim
our most serious regard. You have allowed their full influence to both.

With very great respect,
I am Sir, your Obedt.,

J. Marshall.

From Joseph Story

Cambridge May 14th 1833.

Dear Sir,

I am greatly obliged to you for the copy of your convention sermon, which you have been pleased to send me. I have read it with uncommon satisfaction, & think its tone & spirit excellent. My own private judgement has long been, (& every day's experience more & more confirms me in it,) that government can not long exist without an alliance with religion *to some extent;* & that Christianity is indispensable to the true interests & solid foundations of all free governments. I distinguish, as you do, between the establishment of a particular sect, as the Religion of the State, & the Establishment of Christianity itself, without any preference of any particular form of it. I know not, indeed, how any deep sense of moral obligation or accountableness can be expected to prevail in the community without a firm persuasion of the great Christian Truths promulgated in your South Carolina constitution of 1778. I look with no small dismay upon the rashness & indifference with which the American People seem in our day to be disposed to cut adrift from old principles, & to trust themselves to the theories of every wild projector in to [?] religion & politics.

Upon the point, how far the constitution of 1790 has, on the subject of religion, superseded that of 1778, it is somewhat difficult for me to form a decisive opinion without some additional documents, showing the authority of the convention, which framed it, & the effect given to it. If (as I suppose was the case) the object of the constitution of 1790 was, to supersede that of 1778, & to stand as a substitute, (which has been the general construction in like cases of a *general new*[?] constitution) then, it seems to me, that the constitution of 1778 is by necessary implication repealed, except so far as any of its provisions are expressly retained. It does not strike me that the 2^d section of the 8th article of 1790 retains any thing of the religious articles of that of 1778, but only provides that the *existing rights* &c. of religious societies & corporate bodies shall remain unaffected by the change of the constitution. The rights &c., here provided for, are the more private rights of those bodies, such as the rights of property, & corporate immunities; but not any rights as Christians or as Protestants to be entitled to the superior protection of the State. The first section of the 8th article seems to me intended to abolish all distinctions & preferences, as to the state, between all religious persuasions, whether Christian or other wise. But I doubt exceedingly, if it ought to be construed

Joseph Story. Engraving by J. Cheney from a crayon drawing by
William Wetmore Story. Collection of the Supreme Court of the United States.

so as to abolish Christianity as a part of the antecedent Law of the
Land, to the extent of withdrawing from it all recognition of it as a
revealed religion. The 23^d section of art. 1st seems to me manifestly to
point to a different conclusion.

Mr Jefferson has, with his accustomed boldness, denied that
Christianity is a part of the common Law, & D^r [Thomas] Cooper
has with even more dogmatism, maintained the same opinion. I am
persuaded, that a more egregious error never was uttered by able men.
And I have long desired to find leisure to write a dissertation to establish this conclusion. Both of them rely on authorities & expositions
which are wholly inadmissible. And I am surprised, that no one has as
yet exposed the shallowness of their enquiries. Both of them have

probably been easily drawn into the maintenance of such a doctrine by their own skepticism. It is due to truth, & to the purity of the Law, to unmask their fallacies.

I am gratified by your favourable opinion of my Commentaries on the constitution. If I shall be thought to have done anything to aid in perpetuating the true exposition of its rights & powers, & duties, I shall reap all the reward I desire. The Abridgment for colleges & schools will be published next week. I hope it may be found a useful manual.

I cannot conclude this letter without thanking you again for your sermon. These are times in which the friends of Christianity are required to sound the alarm, & to inculcate sound principles. I fear that infidelity is make [sic] rapid progress under the delusive guise of the freedom of religious opinion & liberty of conscience.

Believe me with great respect,
Your obliged servant,

Joseph Story.

From James Madison

Montpelier September 1833. *private*

Dear Sir,

I received in due time, the printed copy of your convention sermon on the relation of Christianity to civil government, with a manuscript request of my opinion on the subject.

There appears to be in the nature of man, what ensures his belief in an invisible cause of his present existence, & an anticipation of his future existence. Hence the propensities & susceptibilities, in the case of religion, which, with a few doubtful or individual exceptions, have prevailed throughout the world.

Waiving the rights of conscience, not included in the surrender implied by the social state, & more or less invaded by all Religious establishments, the simple question to be decided, is whether a support of the best & purest religion, the Christian Religion itself, ought not, so far at least as pecuniary means are involved, to be provided for by the Government, rather than be left to the voluntary provisions of those who profess it. And on this question, experience will be an admitted umpire the more adequate as the connexion between government & Religion, has existed in such various degrees & forms, & now can be compared with examples where the connexion has been entirely dissolved.

In the papal system, Government & Religion are in a manner consolidated; & that is found to be the worst of Governments.

In most of the governments of the old world, the legal establishment of a particular religion without any, or with very little toleration of others, makes a part [pact?] of the political & civil organization; & there are few of the most enlightened judges who will maintain that the system has been favourable either to Religion or to government.

Until Holland ventured on the experiment of combining a liberal toleration, with the establishment of a particular creed, it was taken for granted that an exclusive establishment was essential, and notwithstanding the light thrown on the subject by that experiment, the prevailing opinion in Europe, England not excepted, has been, that Religion could not be preserved without the support of Government, nor Government be supported without an established Religion, that there must be at least an alliance of some sort between them.

It remained for North America to bring the great & interesting subject to a fair, & finally, to a decisive test.

In the colonial state of this country, there were five examples, Rhode Island, New Jersey, Pennsylvania & Delaware, & the greater part of New York, where there were no religious establishments, the support of Religion being left to the voluntary associations & contributions of individuals; & certainly the religious condition of those colonies, will well bear a comparison, with that where establishments existed.

As it may be suggested, that experiments made in colonies more or less under the controul of a foreign government had not the full scope necessary to display their tendency, it is fortunate that the appeal can now be made to their effects, under a compleat exemption from any such controul.

It is true that the New England States have not discontinued establishments of Religion formed under very peculiar circumstances; but they have by successive relaxations, advanced towards the prevailing example; & without any evidence of disadvantage, either to Religion or to good government.

And if we turn to the Southern States where there was previous to the Declaration of Independence, a legal provision for the support of Religion; & since that event, a surrender of it to a spontaneous support of the people, it may be said that the difference amounts nearly to a contrast, in the greater purity & industry of the pastors & in the

James Madison. Oil portrait by Asher B. Durand, 1833.
Collection of the New-York Historical Society.

greater devotion of their flocks, in the latter period than in the former. In Virginia, the contrast is particularly striking to those whose memories can make the comparison.

It will not be denied that causes other than the abolition of the legal establishment of Religion are to be taken into view, in accounting for the change in the religious character of the community. But the existing character, distinguished as it is by its religious features, & the lapse of time, now more than fifty years, since the legal support of Religion was withdrawn, sufficiently prove, that it does not need the support of Government. And it will scarcely be contended that government has suffered by the exemption of Religion from its cognizance, or its pecuniary aid.

The apprehension of some seems to be, that Religion left entirely to itself, may run into extravagances injurious both to Religion & social order; but besides the question whether the interference of Government *in any form,* would not be more likely to increase than controul the tendency, it is a safe calculation that in this, as in other cases of excessive excitement, reason will gradually regain its ascendency. Great excitements are less apt to be permanent than to vibrate to the opposite extreme.

Under another aspect of the subject, there may be less danger that Religion, if left to itself, will suffer from a failure of the pecuniary support applicable to it, than that an omission of the public authorities, to limit the duration of the charters to Religious corporations, & the amount of property acquirable by them, may lead to an injurious accumulation of wealth from the lavish donations & bequests prompted by a pious zeal or by an atoning remorse. Some monitory examples have already appeared.

Whilst I thus frankly express my view of the subject presented in your sermon, I must do you the justice to observe, that you have very ably maintained yours. I must admit, moreover, that it may not be easy, in every possible case, to trace the line of separation, between the rights of Religion & the Civil authority, with such distinctness, as to avoid collisions & doubts on unessential points. The tendency to a usurpation on one side, or the other, or to a corrupting coalition or alliance between them, will be best guarded against by an entire abstinence of the Government from interference, in any way whatever, beyond the necessity of preserving public order, & protecting each sect against trespasses on its legal rights by others.

I owe you, Sir, an apology for the delay in complying with the request of my opinion on the subject discussed in your sermon, if not also for the brevity, & it may be thought, crudeness of the opinion itself. I must rest the apology on my great age now in its 83$^{d.}$ year, with more than the ordinary infirmities, & especially on the effect of a chronic rheumatism, combined with both, which makes my hands & fingers, as averse to the pen as they are awkward in the use of it.

Be pleased to accept, Sir, a tender of my cordial & respectful salutations.

James Madison.

At the end of his copy of the Madison letter, Adams made the following note: "The 'manuscript request' mentioned at the beginning of this letter, was an endorsement on the cover of the copy sent to M$^{r.}$ Madison in these words:—'If it suits the much respected patriot & statesman to whom this is sent, to write the author a few lines expressive of his opinion of the validity of the argument herein contained, it will be received as a distinguished favour.' The same endorsement was put upon the copy sent to Ch. J. Marshall."

From John Smythe Richardson, a South Carolina Jurist

21st March 1833.

My Dear Sir,

I have just read your sermon "on the relation of Christianity to civil government." The moral induction from our constitutions & laws, that Christianity forms the basis of our civil polity is rational, clear, & convincing; & is so well timed, that I cannot but think the friends of order & our government as well as your personal well wishers will be disposed to have an argument so useful & statesmanlike widely disseminated. It is distinctly the best antidote to the threatening spread of infidelity that I have seen; & pains should be taken to give it full effect. Taking it for granted that something will be done towards that end, I beg you to contribute for me, twenty dollars which I will repay in May on my visit to Charleston. Believe me, much good may be done & honour derived. I recommend & urge the effort for the general good.

With sincere respect & regard,
Yours Truly,

J.S. Richardson

Adams reported: "Soon after this sermon was published, [Charleston attorney] M^r [Thomas S.] Grimké insisted, that I had taken a very mistaken view of the relation of our constitution of 1790 to that of 1778. I requested Judge Richardson's opinion on this point, & the following letter is in answer to my request for his opinion. I proposed the same enquiry to Mr Justice Story, & a part of his letter is in answer to my enquiry." (Despite Grimké's disagreement with Adams's interpretation of the South Carolina constitution of 1790, he asked Adams to supply him with additional copies of the sermon. "When you contract for the reprinting of your Sermon," Grimké wrote Adams on 9 July 1833, "pray bespeak 100 extra copies for me besides my contribution of $20.") Judge Richardson responded to Adams's legal query in the following letter:

26th August 1833.

My Dear Sir,

Your query (upon the constitution of So. Ca.) of the 20th March, to wit:—"whether the constitution of 1778, be still of force, wherein it stands unaltered by the consti. of '90," remains unanswered by me. I percieve [*sic*] no sufficient reason, for differing from your opinion in ps. 37 & 38.. That opinion has been heretofore my own; that is to say, the consti. of '78 remains a *Law* of the State, except wherein it has been repealed, by the constitution of '90, or *some Law*. You perceive, I do not view that of '78 as a *constitution;* but as a *Law,* or Legislative compact, & of course, subject to Legislative control. I have it not at hand, but I think you will find, that it was enacted by no higher power than the *Legislature*. There was no convention called to enact it; but it stands as a law. It may be added, that for many years after the constitution of '90, it regulated the tenure of many offices; perhaps it governs some of them now which have not been altered; & may be important in reference to jury trials, &c. &c. "preserved" &c. "as heretofore in this State," under Art. 9. Sec. 6 of the const. of 1790. You & I differ very little, therefore, & perhaps not at all, on this subject.

Yours very respectfully
& Truly,

J.S. Richardson

REVIEW ESSAY:
"IMMUNITY OF RELIGION"

INTRODUCTION

"Immunity of Religion" is a review of Adams's sermon that was published in an 1835 edition of the *American Quarterly Review*.[1] Edited by Robert Walsh, a lawyer, prolific journalist, and accomplished scholar, the *Review* was an independent publication devoted to critical treatments of political, scientific, historic, and literary concerns.[2] The review essay offered a biting critique of Adams's interpretation of the appropriate relationship between Christianity and civil government. The author embraced the separationist view frequently attributed to Thomas Jefferson and consistent with the policies of the Jackson Administration on issues such as fast day proclamations and the Sunday mails. The review bristles with sarcasm and allusions to partisan church-state controversies of the day.

The review essay was noticed in the infamous blasphemy case of *State v. Chandler* (1837). Counsel for Thomas Jefferson Chandler, the defendant, specifically cited the *American Quarterly Review* essay, along with Thomas Jefferson's letter to Major Cartwright, "to prove that christianity was no part of the law of the land."[3]

This essay reviewed the first edition of Adams's sermon. Accordingly, a few references (including page references) to the sermon do not correspond with the contents of the second edition reproduced in this volume. The fact that some criticisms of the first edition were addressed in the second edition suggests the possibility that Adams was familiar with this review when he made revisions for the second edition in 1833. In other words, Adams may have perused a draft of the review in 1833, two years before its publication in 1835.

Although the essay was unsigned, as were most articles in the *Review,* there are a few clues to the identity of the author.[4] First, the writer was familiar with Adams and his standing in South Carolina, leading one to conclude that the author was either a South Carolinian or had substantial contact with the state. Second, given the writer's facility with the law and legal sources, it is likely that the review was authored by a lawyer.[5] Additionally, the writer's familiarity with South Carolina law in particular supports the conclusion that the reviewer was a South Carolina attorney. The detailed knowledge of state and national constitutions revealed in the review further suggests that the author had expertise in constitutional law.

It is conceivable that Thomas Cooper, who fits this profile and was a target of Adams's criticism, penned the essay. Furthermore, Cooper was a longtime resident of Pennsylvania and had extensive contacts with the literati of Philadelphia, where the *Review* was published. Cooper's *Treatise on the Law of Libel* (1830), however, is favorably cited in the review essay for its content but sharply criticized for its form, thus pointing away from Cooper as the author.[6]

A more plausible source is Randell Hunt (1807–92), a native of South Carolina and one of Cooper's students at South Carolina College.[7] As a young man, Hunt gained a statewide reputation as a gifted lawyer, orator, and Unionist partisan. A decline in family fortunes, however, prompted him to leave the state in 1832. He eventually settled in New Orleans, where he quickly established himself as a prominent lawyer and political figure. Although appointed to the U.S. Senate in 1866, he was never seated, as a result of the political turmoil of Reconstruction. For more than four decades (1847–88) he was a professor of constitutional law at the University of Louisiana (now Tulane University), and for a decade and a half (1867–84) he served as university president.[8] Adams reported that he received from Hunt "for my inspection, a letter containing 29 pages of letter paper, closely written, controverting the chief positions of the sermon." Adams dismissed the missive as "a specimen of the style of the Jefferson & Cooper school."[9] Unfortunately, Adams did not preserve Hunt's letter together with the correspondence from Madison, Marshall, Story, and Richardson. It is plausible that "Immunity of Religion" was written by Hunt, based on his letter to Adams. Indeed, Adams's use of the word *inspection* suggests that Hunt's letter may have been a manuscript of an essay sent to Adams for comment before publication. This is consistent with the theory that Adams was familiar with the review and its criticisms when he made revisions to the sermon for the second edition. A published volume of Hunt's speeches and miscellaneous papers, edited by his nephew, however, does not mention this essay.[10]

The respected jurist Joseph Hopkinson contributed reviews of legal works to the *American Quarterly Review,* as did Philadelphia attorney Peter S. Du Ponceau.[11] Interestingly, Adams reported that both men had been sent copies of his sermon. Moreover, both were learned attorneys, and Du Ponceau, in particular, had published widely on constitutional issues. It is possible that one of these men wrote the review.

In his sermon, Adams highlighted the manifestations, if not the de facto establishment, of general, nondenominational Christianity in the official charters and practices of the states and nation. The review writer, by contrast, emphasized disestablishment provisions in state constitutions that, it was argued, fostered freedom of religion and liberty of conscience. Adams ably maintained the nonpreferentialist position embraced by many religious traditionalists; the review writer effectively advanced the strict separationist perspective espoused by many Jacksonians, liberal religionists, and secularists. These documents reveal an increasingly polarized debate over the secularization of American society and an intensifying struggle to define the prudential and constitutional role of religion in public life.

NOTES

1. "Immunity of Religion," *American Quarterly Review* 17, no. 34 (June 1835): 319-40. The title suggests a theme developed by James Madison in an 1822 letter written to Edward Livingston: "I observe with particular pleasure the view you have taken of the immunity of Religion from civil jurisdiction, in every case where it does not trespass on private rights or the public peace. This has always been a favorite principle with me." Letter from James Madison to Edward Livingston, 10 July 1822, reprinted in Gaillard Hunt, ed., *The Writings of James Madison,* 9 vols. (New York: G.P. Putnam's Sons, 1900-1910), 9:100.

2. Frank Luther Mott, *A History of American Magazines, 1741-1850* (1930; Cambridge, Mass.: Belknap Press of Harvard Univ. Press, 1957), pp. 271-76.

3. *State v. Chandler,* 2 Harrington 553, 554 (Del. 1837). See the letter from Thomas Jefferson to Major John Cartwright, 5 June 1824, reprinted in Andrew A. Lipscomb and Albert Ellery Bergh, eds., *The Writings of Thomas Jefferson,* 20 vols., Library Ed. (Washington, D.C.: Thomas Jefferson Memorial Association, 1903-4), 16:48-51.

4. Mott noted that articles in the journal were unsigned. Interestingly, however, he revealed that in the 1920s "on the shelves of the Cadmus Book Shop, New York," there was a file that contained "the authors' names written in for many articles, in a contemporary hand, and may reasonably be supposed to have belonged to one of the editors or someone in their councils"(*History of American Magazines,* p. 276, n. 21). The Cadmus Book Shop, unfortunately, is no longer listed as a business in New York.

5. The reviewer drew attention to the fact that Adams was not an attorney, chastising him for "assum[ing] the part of a lawyer." "Immunity of Religion," p. 338 [148].

6. Ibid., p. 339 [148]. Thomas Cooper, *A Treatise on the Law of Libel and the Liberty of the Press* (New York: G.F. Hopkins, 1830).

7. Hunt graduated first in his class from South Carolina College in 1825. Edwin L. Green, *A History of the University of South Carolina* (Columbia, S.C.: State Co., 1916), p. 432.

8. Lucian Lamar Knight, comp., *Library of Southern Literature,* vol. 15, *Biographical Dictionary of Southern Authors* (Atlanta: Martin and Hoyt Co., 1907-10), p. 215; *The South in the Building of the Nation,* 12 vols. (Richmond, Va.: Southern Historical Publication Society, 1909), 11:528.

9. Adams's handwritten notes appended to his personal copy of the first edition of his sermon in the William L. Clements Library, University of Michigan, p. 9.

10. William Henry Hunt, ed., *Selected Arguments, Lectures and Miscellaneous Papers of Randell Hunt* (New Orleans: F.F. Hansell and Brother, 1896). This volume includes a lengthy biographical profile of Randell Hunt.

11. Mott, *History of American Magazines*, p. 276.

Immunity of Religion

A Sermon preached in St. Michael's Church, Charleston, February 13th, 1833, before the Convention of the Protestant Episcopal Church of the Diocese of South Carolina, by the Rev. J. ADAMS, D.D., President of the College of Charleston, South Carolina, and (ex officio) Horry Professor of Moral and Political Philosophy. Published at the request of the Bishop and Clergy of the Protestant Episcopal Church of South Carolina.

The author of this sermon is well known throughout South Carolina, as an accomplished scholar, a learned divine, and a gentleman of exemplary purity of life. We have occasionally heard him lecture on moral philosophy—and never without pleasure. His extensive literary attainments, his clear and simple style, his mild demeanour, and the respect which his character commands, qualify him peculiarly for the instruction of youth.

We have heard him also with pleasure in the pulpit. His discourses are generally argumentative, and abound with manly sentiments and moral reflections. But in the sermon now before us, Mr. Adams has aimed a blow at the Constitution of the United States. With a rash hand, he has endeavoured to overturn one of the main pillars of our liberty. He has invaded, and attempted to destroy freedom of conscience, and on its ruins to erect intolerance and odious discriminations for religion's sake.

We are aware that Mr. Adams would unhesitatingly deny that he had any such intention. But such is the inevitable tendency of the doctrines he advocates.

Before we proceed any further we would remark, that we are humble believers in the truth of the Christian Scriptures. The argument of Mr. Hume against the belief of miracles is not, in our opinion, entitled to much consideration. It is more probable, he contends, that human testimony is false, or that men are mistaken, than that the miracles should be true.

We readily admit that men are often mistaken, and that they sometimes lie "for the lie's sake," as Lord Bacon truly, though coarsely expresses it. We should therefore examine their testimony in favour of miracles with the most scrupulous care, and, if there be a reasonable room for doubt, reject it. But we must not shut our eyes against the light. We must not reject as wholly insufficient that evidence which would satisfy us in the most important transactions of life. In fact, human testimony is the only kind of evidence we can have in the case. Let that which appears miraculous occur every day, and it will soon cease to be considered a miracle; it will be regarded as the natural operation of fixed laws. No one will deny, we presume, that God *can* perform a miracle—that he *can,* if he think fit, suspend the ordinary operation of natural laws; for to deny this, is to limit his power. If a miracle occur then, and we ourselves do not witness it, we can only learn it from evidence.

Now, what evidence have we that the miracles mentioned in the New Testament were performed?

1. It is proved by the testimony of eye-witnesses; of persons who actually saw them performed, and who had no interest in deceiving us.

2. These witnesses suffered persecution, and even laid down their lives in support of what they said.

3. The miracles were not denied for centuries after by the opponents of Christianity, who, on the contrary, admitted that they were performed, but attributed them to the power of evil spirits.

We consider this evidence as strong as the nature of the case will admit. But if a shadow of doubt as to the truth of the Christian Scriptures were left by the external evidence, that is removed by the internal evidence of their Divine authority. The wonderful and exact fulfillment of the prophecies, cannot otherwise be accounted for. That in pretending to foretell events, an individual might occasionally hit upon a truth, we have no doubt. But that so many predictions, such precise prophecies, should be so exactly fulfilled, can only be accounted for on the supposition of a Divine inspiration. Mr. Channing delivered, some years ago in Boston, an admirable essay on the internal evidence of Christianity. It is written in a glowing style, and with much force of argument. In it he urges, that if there were no other proof of the truth of Christianity, this would be sufficient, viz. the fact that twelve ignorant, uneducated men, without any extraordinary advantages of mind, had prescribed a code of morals infinitely superior to any that the wisest and most learned men of antiquity framed: a code of morals not only adapted to the then situation of the world, but to all the various changes and modifications that have since taken place—and which, the more man improves in civilization, seems better and better adapted to the high purposes for which it was framed. This argument is entitled to greater consideration, from the reflection that time, which is thus continually developing the excellence of Christianity, exhibits defects in all *human* institutions.

We will not fatigue our readers by dwelling longer on arguments in favour of Christianity, arguments with which they are sufficiently familiar, and to which we have nothing new to add. Our object was rather to express our belief, than to "give a reason for the faith that is in us."

While, however, we are believers and followers of Christ, we must declare ourselves decidedly opposed to any connexion between church and state. Such a connexion will necessarily create a marked distinction between those who believe, and those who do *not* believe the religion upheld and protected by law. Hence a discrimination in civil rights will gradually arise. One set, or rather one sect of men, will be protected and rewarded, while another will be proscribed and persecuted. Freedom of conscience will be invaded. With freedom of opinion freedom of speech must fall—and liberty will soon expire.

This is not a picture drawn by an over-excited imagination; it is the truth, as portrayed by the pencil of history. Yet Mr. Adams has the boldness to hazard the following assertion,—

"If the Roman emperors had been satisfied to receive the new religion *without distinction of sects, as the broad ground of all the great institutions of the empire,* it is impossible to show or to believe, that such a measure would not have been both *wise* and *salutary.* The misfortune was, that there soon came to be a legal preference of one form of Christianity over all others." Page 5.

Now, Christianity may be considered but as one of the larger sects into which mankind is divided. Any argument that would prove the wisdom of making one particular form of religion the ground of all the great institutions of an empire, would prove the wisdom of making one form of Christianity the ground of those institutions. Let us take a case, and apply the argument.

The Roman Catholic religion is deemed by many a system of idolatry, of bigotry, and of superstition. We have heard several intelligent and well educated persons contend that it is opposed to civil liberty—that its fundamental doctrines interfere with the right of free judgment—impose an unnatural and tyrannical restraint on the mind, and inculcate a slavish submission to persons in authority. We have heard the same individuals contend that Unitarians are not, in the strict sense of the term, Christians—because, say they, the Unitarians deny the divine nature of Jesus, which is of the essence of Christianity; teach the most shocking and blasphemous doctrine on the nature of the Godhead; and are gradually introducing a culpable carelessness about religious concerns, infidelity, and even atheism.

A person entertaining these views, may be supposed to argue in the following manner:—

"The Unitarian sect, by introducing carelessness concerning the duties of religion, are gradually, though perhaps unconsciously, undermining the only sure foundation of public morals. Their influence on society must therefore be baleful. So too with the Roman Catholics. By dispensations and indulgences, by absolution and an absurd belief in purgatory, their religion gives a sanction to immorality and licentiousness, and destroys the sense of moral responsibility. Thus do extremes meet. The superstition of the Catholic is not less pernicious than the irreligion of the Unitarian. In vain do we look to monkish records for the mild spirit and beneficial effects of Christianity. For them we must look to THE REFORMATION. The REFORMATION has done much for individuals. It has inculcated charity, peace, and goodwill among men. It has destroyed superstition, introduced purity of morals, and taught us that the path of virtue is the road to God.—It has done much for nations. It has taught them to do good to one another. It has taught them that the prosperity and happiness of neighbouring nations, is a source of mutual comfort and enjoyment. It has diminished the horrors of war, by softening the lot of captives, abolishing the odious practices of the dark and gothic ages, and in a word, by teaching that the rights of humanity should never be disregarded. Why should not then Christianity, as established at the reformation, be incorporated in our laws? Why should not a religion so pure, so beneficial, be connected with, and protected by our laws and constitutions?"

How would Mr. Adams answer this, if it were urged by one expressing the opinions of a large majority of the people? He is precluded from arguing that civil government can not rightly interfere with religion. We have heard him already assert that it would have been both "*wise and salutary*" to connect one form of religion with all the great institutions of government. If "one form of religion," why not "one form of Christianity?"—especially when that is the only true form.

There is, and there can be, no middle ground between perfect liberty and tyranny on this subject. Give government the right to interfere, to pass laws for the protection of Christianity, and it will necessarily have to determine what *is* Christianity, and what laws are necessary for the *protection* of Christianity. In other words, it will have an unlimited power on the subject.

In page nineteenth, the author, addressing himself to this point, says:—

"No power less efficacious than Christianity, can permanently maintain the public tranquillity of the country, and the authority of law. We must be a Christian nation, if we wish to continue a free nation."

And, that he may not be misunderstood, he adds in a note:—

"With a view of illustrating this subject, by uniting high authority with great clearness of argument, the author subjoins a part of the opinion of the late Chief Justice Parsons, of Massachusetts, in the case of Barnes *vs.* First Parish in Falmouth, contained 6 Mass. Reports, p. 404, &c. In this case, the Court had occasion to vindicate Art. 3. Part I. of the Constitution of that State (p. 29.) So far as the Massachusetts' Constitution and the argument vindicating it make a discrimination between *Christian* denominations, they do not meet the concurrence of the author, but he considers the main positions of the Chief Justice incontrovertible, and his course of reasoning highly instructive and convincing."

The reasoning of the late Chief Justice Parsons of Massachusetts, is to the following effect: There are moral duties flowing from the disposition of the heart, and not subject to the control of human legislation. Secret offences cannot be prevented unless civil government derive assistance from some superior power, whose laws extend to the temper and disposition of the human heart. Legislators have, therefore, in all ages, had recourse to religion. It is not against freedom of conscience to establish a particular form of religion by law, and to compel persons to pay a tax for its support, although they may think the established religion false. It is simply a call on the citizen for money for the public use, and is in no sense a matter of conscience. The public has a right to levy taxes, and make appropriations; and no individual is at liberty to withhold the tax, because he dislikes the appropriation. Otherwise, there will soon be an end of all government. The object of a public religious establishment is, to teach and enforce a system of correct morals—and to secure obedience to important laws by a Divine sanction.

Now, "the main positions of the Chief Justice," which Mr. Adams pronounces "incontrovertible," and "the course of reasoning" which he is pleased to declare "highly instructive and convincing," urge the necessity for government to call in religion to its aid, and the right of government to establish and protect by law, and uphold by taxes, any religion it may deem proper. Why not Unitarianism then?—or Catholicism?—or Protestantism?—if the majority think fit. It is true, that Mr. Adams censures discriminations between *Christian* denominations; but he urges no reason for this censure—and we venture to assert that he can urge none—which will not apply with equal force to all religious discriminations. Admit his principle—which, veil it as he may, is discrimination between religious denominations—and a discrimination in favour of a particular sect will follow, as a matter of course. Admit the giant's foot, and his body will soon appear.

The truth is, the main positions of Chief Justice Parsons are utterly indefensible, and his argument is worse than futile. We would not detract a tithe of a hair from the just reputation of this distinguished jurist. He was indeed a man of transcendental abilities—a shining light and an ornament to the bench and to his country, fit to be ranked with the Kents and Marshalls. We venerate his memory—but we cannot venerate his errors. Upon the principles advocated by him, in the opinion cited with high commendation by the author of the sermon now before us, it would be impossible to prove *any* tax improper.—We pass by this, however, and confine ourselves to the point immediately before us.

Civil government is intended for the regulation of social man—for the promotion and security of human happiness here on earth. It is intended for this world—not the next. It should protect us in the enjoyment of our personal rights and property. It should not interfere with our opinions and faith. Its business is with our temporal or present interests, not with our future or eternal welfare. As long as a citizen discharges well his duty to society, he is a good citizen. Civil government should regulate the duty of man towards man. It should not interfere with the relations between man and his Creator. Offences against society should be punished by society.

Offences against God should be left to God. It argues great folly, as well as impiety, to suppose the Deity so weak as to require aid from society, or so negligent as to suffer offenders to escape with impunity. Deorum injuriæ, diis curiæ [wrongs done to the gods (are) concerns for the gods], was the wise and humble maxim of Pagans. We should not be less wise or humble— nor should we arrogantly usurp the province of the Almighty.

What is religion? The term is derived from *re* and *ligo*—to bind back— to tie again. It is the tie or bond that unites man to the Deity. It consists in the service of God. HE alone can judge who worships in sincerity and truth.

Opinion is involuntary. A man cannot believe as he wishes. I am writing with a candle before me. Can I believe that there is no such thing before me? I look at my hat; it is black. Can I, if I wish to do so, believe it white? I cannot. I am forced to believe the evidence of my senses. My very nature, my organization, my structure, compels me to do so.

I am a Christian. I have examined the evidence, internal and external, for and against Christianity. I am forced to believe it true. It is the conclusion of my mind after a candid examination. I cannot believe otherwise. Suppose I were in Turkey. Would the Turkish government have a right to punish me because I am not a Mahometan? Can an involuntary opinion be the subject of praise or blame? Can government rightly interfere with religious opinions? It cannot. Every man has, by the eternal law of nature, a right to worship God according to his own conscience. In the eloquent language of Mr. Brougham—now Lord Brougham—"The great truth has finally gone forth to all the ends of the earth, that man shall no more render an account to man for his belief, over which he has himself no control. Henceforward, nothing shall prevail upon us to praise or to blame any one for that which he can no more change than he can the hue of his skin, or the height of his stature. Civil government, we repeat, cannot rightly interfere with religious belief or opinion. It should look simply to the actions, to the conduct of individuals. History paints in strong colours the danger of a connexion between religion and government. Church and state have never been united without making the former subservient to the latter—without making religion, which should purify and ennoble the mind, a base instrument of tyranny and oppression."

In South Carolina, legal provision was made for the establishment of religious worship according to the church of England, for the erecting of churches, and the maintenance of clergymen. Mr. Adams notices this, and subjoins the following remarks:

"It is the testimony of history, however, that ever since the time of Constantine, *such an union of the ecclesiastical with the civil authority, has given rise to flagrant abuses and gross corruptions.* By a series of gradual, but well contrived usurpations, a Bishop of the

Church, claiming to be the successor of the Chief of the Apostles and the Vicar of Christ, had been seen for centuries to rule the nations of Christendom with the sceptre of despotism. The argument against the use of an institution arising from its abuse, is not valid, unless, when after sufficient experience, there is the best reason to conclude, that we cannot enjoy the use without the accompanying evils flowing from the abuse of it. Such perhaps is the case in regard to the union between any particular form of Christianity and civil government. IT IS AN HISTORICAL TRUTH, ESTABLISHED BY THE EXPERIENCE OF MANY CENTURIES, THAT WHENEVER CHRISTIANITY HAS IN THIS WAY BEEN INCORPORATED WITH THE CIVIL POWER, THE LUSTRE OF HER BRIGHTNESS HAS BEEN DIMMED BY THE ALLIANCE."—p. 6.

Now, Christianity has never been incorporated in any other way with the civil power. It became a religion exclusively established by law, for the first time, under Constantine, in the year of our Lord 325. Ever since that time, then, according to Mr. Adams, "the union of the ecclesiastical with the civil authority has given rise to flagrant abuses and gross corruptions!" No matter under what particular form Christianity has been united with civil government, invariably "the lustre of her brightness has been dimmed!!" Is not this evidence sufficiently strong to prove the impropriety of a connexion between church and state? Is the experience of fifteen centuries not enough? Must we again make an experiment, founded on a principle that has ever proved a fruitful source of evils? Shall we thus tamper with human happiness? We trust not. Christianity stands in need of no unequal protection. Give her a fair field, and the legitimate weapons of reason, and she must and will prevail. The fortress of error will be compelled to surrender, and the gentle sway of the Gospel will be universally acknowledged.

Having thus briefly pointed out the impropriety of any connexion between church and state, we will proceed to a more particular examination of Mr. Adams's sermon. He introduces his subject in the following manner:

"No nation on earth, perhaps, ever had opportunities so favourable to introduce changes in their institutions as the American people; and by the time of the Revolution, a conviction of the impolicy of a further union of Church and State according to the ancient mode, had so far prevailed, that all the States, in framing their new constitutions of government, either silently or by direct enactment, discontinued the ancient connexion.

"A question of great interest here comes up for discussion. In thus discontinuing the connexion between Church and Commonwealth—did these States intend to renounce all connexion with the Christian religion? Or did they intend to disclaim all preference of one sect of Christians?

★ ★ ★ ★ ★

"Did the people of the United States, when, in adopting the Federal Constitution, they declared, that 'Congress shall make no law respecting an establishment of religion or prohibiting the free exercise thereof,' expect to be understood as abolishing the national religion?"—pp. 7, 8.

It is an historical question, says Mr. Adams, and to arrive at a correct conclusion, recurrence must be had to the ordinary means for adjusting inquiries of this nature. Accordingly he refers,

1. To the charters of the colonies, and other similar documents as to the settlement of this continent.

2. To the rise and progress of our colonial growth; and

3. To the Constitutions of the several States, and to the Constitution of the United States; from which he deduces this principle:—

"THE PEOPLE OF THE UNITED STATES HAVE RETAINED THE CHRISTIAN RELIGION AS THE FOUNDATION OF THEIR CIVIL, LEGAL AND POLITICAL INSTITUTIONS; WHILE THEY HAVE REFUSED TO CONTINUE A LEGAL PREFERENCE TO ANY ONE OF ITS FORMS OVER ANY OTHER."—pp. 12, 13.

It is evident, on the first blush of the question, that the "colonial charters," and "the rise and progress of our colonial growth," can have nothing to do with the question, whether, under our present constitutions, there is any connexion between religion and civil government. That is a question to be decided by the constitutions themselves. But let us examine the three sources whence Mr. Adams draws his conclusion.

And 1. as to "the charters of the colonies, and the settlement of this continent." He contends, that the originators and early promoters of the discovery and settlement of this continent, had the propagation of Christianity before their eyes, as one of the principal objects of their undertaking—and refers, as an evidence of this, to the charters of Massachusetts, Virginia, Pennsylvania, and Rhode Island—(pp. 8, 9.) Now, granting this to be true, although we doubt that it is so, what reference has it to the question, whether we have an established "NATIONAL RELIGION?" We answer, none. The United States had no national existence previous to the 4th of July, 1776, when they first assumed a station among the nations of the earth. Indeed, even then, and under the Articles of Confederation, they can scarcely be considered as having done more than prepared for the establishment of civil national institutions. The Constitution of 1789 is the very basis, the foundation-stone of those institutions—and with that Constitution our inquiries should commence. But the inquiry is concluded by the Constitution itself—*i.e.* by the first article of the amendments to the Constitution, which says, "*Congress shall make no law respecting an establishment of religion, or prohibiting the free exercise thereof.*" In a legal and constitutional sense, then, we have no "*established national religion.*" The language is inapplicable to the United States; it is unconstitutional language—language at war with the great principles of freedom on which our institutions are built. Mr. John Adams was right, when he wrote to the Dey of Algiers, that "the Constitution is, in no sense, founded on the Christian religion."

Our author, having cited the colonial charters, and paid a well merited compliment to our ancestors, remarks:—"We very much mistake, if we suppose ourselves so much advanced before them, that we cannot be benefited by becoming acquainted with their sentiments, their characters, and their labours." The mistake against which Mr. Adams here warns us, is a creature of his own imagination—a man of straw, set up by himself, that he may obtain a fancied victory. No one supposes it useless to learn the sentiments, characters, and labours of our ancestors. They serve, in some instances, as beacons, to warn—in others, as examples, to imitate. We acquire wisdom from the experience of our predecessors, and should live to little purpose, if we were to shut our eyes against the light of history.

We come now to the second source whence Mr. Adams draws his conclusion. "If we advert," says he, "for a moment, to the rise and progress of our colonial growth," we will find, that "wherever a settlement was commenced, a church was founded," and that "according to the views which had prevailed in Europe, since the days of Constantine, a legal preference of some one denomination over all others, prevailed in almost all the colonies," (pp. 10, 11.) Granted, we say: but this evidently has nothing at all to do with the question under the existing Constitution. It may be instructive to read the laws passed by our ancestors on the subject of religion. But every good man, and lover of his country, blushes at the superstition, bigotry, and intolerance, with which they were too often tainted. Need we refer to history? Let us look for a moment to the pilgrim fathers, to the colony at Plymouth. Speaking of them, a judicious writer observes:

"Much as we respect that noble spirit which enabled them to part with their native soil—by some held dearer than friends, relatives, or children, and by every generous bosom preferred even to life itself—we must condemn the proceedings which ensued. In the first moment when they began to taste of Christian liberty themselves, they forgot that others had a right to the same enjoyment. Some of the colonists, who had not emigrated through motives of religion, retaining a high veneration for the ritual of the English church, refused to join the colonial state establishment, and assembled separately to worship. But their objections were not suffered to pass unnoticed, nor unpunished. Endicott called before him the two principal offenders, and though they were men of respectability, and amongst the number of original patentees, he expelled them from the colony, and sent them home in the first ships returning to England. Had this inquisitorial usurpation been no further exercised, some apology, or at least palliation, might be framed. More interesting and painful consequences, however, not long afterwards, resulted. The very men who had countenanced this violation of Christian duties, lived to see their own descendants excluded from church communion; to behold their grandchildren, the smiling infants at the breast, denied the sacred rite of baptism." ★ ★ ★ "The first general court was held at Charlestown, on board the ship Arabella. A law was passed, declaring that none should be admitted as freemen, or be entitled to any share in the government, or even to serve as jurymen, except those who had been received as members of the church; *by which measure, every person whose mind was not of a particular structure, or accidentally impressed with peculiar ideas, was at once cast out of society, and stripped of his civic rights.*"

"This fanatical spirit continued to increase. The restless disposition of Williams had caused his banishment from Salem; and Coddington, a wealthy merchant of Boston, having, with seventy-six others, been banished from Massachusetts, for holding eighty erroneous opinions, and favouring the religion of Ann Hutchinson, purchased an island—and named it Rhode island—which includes the previous settlement by Williams. They received a charter from the British Parliament. By this it was ordered, that none were ever to be molested for any difference of opinion in religious matters. Yet the very first Assembly convened under this authority, excluded Roman Catholics from voting at elections, and from every office in the government. In 1656, a number of Quakers having arrived from England and Barbadoes, and given offence to the clergy of the established church, by the novelty of their religion, at that time, certainly, a little extravagant, were imprisoned, and by the first opportunity sent away. A law was then made, which prohibited masters of vessels from bringing any Quakers into Massachusetts, and themselves from coming there, under a penalty, in case of a return from banishment, as high as death. In consequence of this several were hanged. Toleration was preached against, as a sin in rulers that would bring down the judgment of Heaven upon the land. Mr. Dudley died with a copy of verses in his pocket, of which the two following lines make a part:

> Let men of God, in court and churches watch,
> O'er such as do a toleration hatch.

The Anabaptists were the next object of persecution. Many were disfranchised, and some banished."

But why multiply examples? It affords us no pleasure to dwell on the follies of our ancestors. They cannot affect the question at issue between us and the author of the sermon now before us. To know the connexion of Christianity with the civil government of the United States, we must look to the Constitution of the United States, and that declares, as we have already seen, "Congress shall make no law respecting an establishment of religion, or prohibiting the free exercise thereof." Jews, Turks, Infidels, Christians, ALL stand on the same footing. Mr. Jefferson, in a letter acknowledging the receipt of a discourse on the consecration of a synagogue, says: "Your sect, by its sufferings, has furnished a remarkable proof of the universal spirit of religious intolerance, inherent in *every* sect; disclaimed by all while feeble, and practised by all when in power. Our laws have applied the only antidote to this vice—protecting our religious, as they do our civil rights, by placing all on an equal footing. But more remains to be done; for, though we are free by the law, we are not so in practice; public opinion erects itself into an inquisition, and exercises its office with as much fanaticism as fans the flame of an *auto da fé.*"

We are prepared now to examine the third source whence Mr. Adams draws his conclusion—we mean the Constitutions of the several States, and the Constitution of the United States.

"In perusing the twenty-four Constitutions of the United States," says he, p. 11, "we find all of them recognising Christianity as the well known AND WELL ESTABLISHED RELIGION of the communities, whose legal, civil, and political foundations, these Constitutions are." And again, in pp. 15 and 16, he remarks, by way of a seeming inference: "Thus, while all others enjoy full protection in the profession of their opinions and practice, Christianity is THE ESTABLISHED RELIGION of the nation, its institutions and usages are sustained by legal sanctions, and many of them are incorporated with the fundamental law of the country."

So far is this from being true, that, we will venture to assert, in nearly all the twenty-four Constitutions it is assumed that there is NO *established* religion, and that there should be no preference of any one religious denomination over another—whether Jews, Christians, Pagans, or Turks.

Some of the State Constitutions were framed *flagrante bello,* during the storm of the Revolution—while the public mind was engrossed with political subjects. It needs be a matter of little surprise, that, under such circumstances, and when there was in most of the colonies a legal preference of one form of Christianity over all others, there should be found some provisions in favour of Christianity. Thus, in the Constitution of *Maryland,* adopted 14th April, 1776, Article 35 prescribes, that every person, before entering on any office of honour, profit or trust, shall make a declaration of belief in the Christian scriptures—thereby excluding from office all Jews. In the Constitution of *New Jersey,* adopted July 2d, 1776, the nineteenth section declares "all persons, professing a belief in the faith of any *Protestant* sect, eligible to offices of profit or trust." And in the Constitution of *North Carolina,* adopted December 18th, 1776, the thirty-second section provides, that no person who shall deny the being of God, or the truth of the *Protestant* religion, or the Divine authority either of the Old or New Testament, or who shall hold, &c., shall be capable of holding any office or place of profit or trust in the civil department within that state. So that these two states went a step farther than Maryland, and excluded Roman Catholics as well as Jews.

The Constitutions of *New Hampshire,* (Part 1, Art. 6,) and of *Massa-*

chusetts, (Part 1, Art. 3,) invest the respective legislatures of those states with "power to require, and direct them to require, the several towns, parishes, precincts, and other bodies politic, or religious societies, to make provision for the support and maintenance of public *Protestant* teachers of piety, religion, and morality." These provisions are utterly indefensible. Nothing can justify the power thus given to the legislatures to invade the rights of conscience, and to compel an individual to pay for the propagation of a doctrine which he believes to be false, and fraught with mischief!

The Constitution of *Virginia* refers to Christianity, but gives it no preference over other religious denominations; on the contrary, the sixteenth article of the "Bill of Rights," made by Virginia June 12, 1776, and prefixed to her Constitution of 1830, expressly provides against such preference. So, in the third article of the "Declaration of Rights" of the inhabitants of *Vermont,* July 4, 1793, after declaring the right of all men to worship God according to their own consciences, it is laid down, that "no authority can or ought to be vested in, or assumed by any power whatever, that shall in any case interfere with, or in any manner control the rights of conscience, in the free exercise of religious worship."

The Constitution of *Maine,* adopted October 29th, 1819, does not contain the word Christian. It is not even said to have been adopted "in the year of Lord," &c., but simply, "in Convention, October 29th, 1819." It declares the natural and unalienable right to worship God according to conscience, and rejects all religious tests and discriminations. (See Article 1, Section 3.)

So, too, in the Constitution of *New York,* the word Christian is not to be found. It is dated, "Done in Convention at, &c., in the year 1821." Art. 7, Sec. 3, provides, that "the free exercise and enjoyment of religious profession and worship, without discrimination or preference, shall for ever be allowed in this state to all mankind."

In like manner, *Kentucky,* in the 3d and 4th Sections, Art. 10, of her Constitution, recognises the rights of conscience, and declares, "that no preference shall ever be given by law to any religious societies or modes of worship: That the civil privileges or capacities of any citizen shall in no wise be diminished or enlarged on account of his religion." The style of its date is similar to that of Maine or New York. It is this: "Done in Convention at Frankfort, the 17th day of August, 1799."

The Constitution of *Illinois,* adopted 26th August, 1818, recognises the right of all men to worship God according to the dictates of their consciences, and provides against any preference to religious establishments and against religious tests. (Art. 8, Sec. 3 and 4).

The Constitution of *Alabama,* adopted in 1819, is equally explicit. Article 1, Section 7, is in the following words: "There shall be no establishment of religion by law; no preference shall ever be given by law to any religious sect, society, or denomination, or mode of worship; and no religious test shall ever be required as a qualification to any office or public trust under this state."

The 4th and 5th Sections of the 13th Article of the Constitution of *Missouri*, adopted in 1820, runs thus: "All men have a natural and indefeasible right to worship God according to the dictates of their own consciences: no man can be compelled to erect and support, or to attend any place of worship, or to maintain any minister of the gospel or teacher of religion: no human authority can control or interfere with the rights of conscience: no person can ever be hurt, molested, or restrained in his religious professions or sentiments if he do not disturb others in their religious worship." "No person, on account of his religious opinions, can be rendered ineligible to any office of profit or trust under this state. No preference can ever be given by law to any sect or mode of worship: and no religious corporation can ever be erected in this state."

Indiana, in the 1st Article, 3d Section, of her Constitution, adopted in 1816, makes similar provisions in language equally strong.

Louisiana, in her Constitution, makes no reference to the subject of Christianity. No religious tests are prescribed; but offices and honours are open to all citizens.

The Constitution of *Georgia,* Article 4, Section 10, after declaring the rights of conscience, &c. provides: "No one religious society shall ever be established in this state in preference to any other; nor shall any person be denied the enjoyment of any civil right, merely on account of his religious principles."

The Constitution of *Ohio,* Article 8, Section 3, has a similar provision. True, it declares that "religion, morality, and knowledge shall for ever be encouraged by legislative provision," but it adds, "not inconsistent with the rights of conscience." Besides, it provides that "no preference shall ever be given by law to any religious society or mode of worship."

The Constitution of *Pennsylvania,* (Article 9th, Section 3d,) and the Constitution of *Tennessee,* (Article 11th, Sections 3d and 4th,) assert the rights of conscience, and declare that "no preference shall ever be given by law to any religious establishments or modes of worship." It is true, the latter, in 8th Article, Section 2d, and the former in 9th Article, Section 4, exclude from office "those who deny the existence of God, or a future state of rewards and punishments." But this is no provision in favour of Christianity. The followers of Mahomet, the Jews, and most Pagans, believe these.

Mr. Adams has misrepresented the Constitution of *Delaware,* by garbling the 1st Article, Section 1. The Constitution declares, that "through Divine goodness, all men have by nature the right of worshipping and serving God according to the dictates of their consciences." It then proceeds:

"ARTICLE 1, § 1. ALTHOUGH it is the duty of all men frequently to assemble together for the public worship of the author of the universe; and piety and morality, on which the prosperity of communities depends, are thereby promoted; YET *no man shall, or ought to be compelled to attend any religious worship, to contribute to the erection or support of any place of worship, or to the maintenance of any ministry, against his own free will and consent; and no power shall or ought to be vested in, or assumed by any magistrate, that shall in any case interfere with, or in any manner control the rights of conscience, in the free exercise of religious worship. Nor shall a preference be given by law to any religious societies, denominations, or modes of worship.*

§ 2. No religious test shall be required as a qualification to any office or public trust under this state."

Mr. Adams omits the word "although" in the first section, and ends with the word "promoted," leaving out all that we have italicised. Even in the mangled form presented by him, the section simply expresses the duty of all men publicly to assemble and worship God—a duty which Jews and others feel as well as Christians. But in its proper form, it denies the right of any human power to interfere with religious opinions.

Mr. Adams cites Article 7, Section 1, Constitution of *Connecticut,* which makes some regulations concerning societies of Christians, and the manner in which individuals may separate therefrom; but he does not notice the very first Article, which in the 3d Section declares, that "the exercise and enjoyment of religious profession and worship *without discrimination,* shall for ever be free to all persons in the state."

We have now briefly examined the constitutions of all the states except South Carolina, and have fully sustained our assertion, that in nearly all the twenty-four constitutions freedom of conscience has been recognised as one of the unalienable rights of man, and that no preference is allowed to any religious denomination—whether it consist of Jews, Christians, Pagans, or Turks. The principle obtained from the foregoing examination is then this—viz. THE PEOPLE OF THE SEVERAL STATES—ALTHOUGH A VAST MAJORITY OF THEM WERE CHRISTIANS—RESOLVED, IN FRAMING THEIR CONSTITUTIONS, TO DESTROY ALL CONNEXIONS BETWEEN CHURCH AND STATE. Of course, we except those who have, in spite of reason and the experience of more than fifteen centuries, established a preference for certain sects—a preference which Mr. Adams himself affects to deprecate.

In order to complete our examination of the constitutions, we must refer to the Constitution of South Carolina and the Constitution of the United States. Before we do so more particularly, we will notice two expressions which are to be found not only in those constitutions, but in several already examined. We do this, not because the expressions themselves call for any comment—but because an ingenious though sophistical argument has been built upon them.

The expressions are: 1. "If any bill shall not be returned by the president (or governor) within ten days, (the number differs in different states,) SUNDAYS EXCEPTED" &c. 2. "Done in Convention, &c., in the YEAR OF OUR LORD" &c.

Upon the first expression, Mr. Adams has borrowed the argument of Mr. Frelinghuysen in the United States' Senate. Upon the second, so far as we are informed, he is entitled to the credit of originality. Both expressions, he contends, are recognitions of Christianity.

We have already remarked, that many of the state constitutions were framed in the midst of war and confusion—when the public mind was engrossed with political subjects. Ninety-nine hundredths of the people were, and still are thoroughly convinced of the truth of the Christian scriptures. The exception of Sundays, above cited, notwithstanding the many political reasons which may be urged in its favour, is to be attributed to this general conviction. Public opinion will have its effect; and we are only surprised that more expressions of this occasional kind are not to be found in the constitutions. But to infer from this that the people of the several states have retained the Christian religion as the foundation of their civil, legal, and political institutions, is worse than absurd. It is building up weakness. It is like an attempt to construct an inverted pyramid—to rear an immense superstructure with a point for a base. But if we are shocked at so sweeping an inference from such premises, what must we think, when we reflect that the inference is directly contradicted by the various provisions already cited from the constitutions themselves?

These remarks will apply with equal, perhaps greater force, to the dates of some constitutions—"*Done, &c., &c., in the year of our Lord.*" Besides, it has become a sort of fashion in dating papers to say, "in the year of our Lord." C'est une façon de parler—a mere mode of speech. This perhaps may be traced to the fact, that we are Christians. It does not show that Christianity is the foundation of our civil, legal, and political institutions. On the contrary, assuming with our author that the date of the Constitution of the United States—"*in the year of our Lord*"—refers back to the words, "We the people of the United States," it would only amount to this, that the people of the United States, although professing themselves Christians, were so thoroughly convinced of the impropriety of any and every connexion between church and state, that they laid it down as a fundamental law, "Congress shall make no law respecting an establishment of religion, or prohibiting the free exercise thereof."

We will now examine more particularly the Constitution and laws of South Carolina, so far as this subject is concerned. Mr. Adams refers to the

Carolina charters of 1662–1663, and of 1665. But these have nothing to do—as we have already seen—with the relation of Christianity to civil government under the present Constitution. We therefore dismiss them. In like manner we would dismiss the Constitution of South Carolina, 1778; but Mr. Adams contends, that the Constitution of 1790, which is at present the fundamental law of the state, is no more than an alteration or amendment of the Constitution of 1778. Let him speak for himself:

"This Constitution itself *decides,* that it is no more than an alteration or amendment of the preceding Constitution of the State. (*See Constitution of South Carolina of 1790, Art.* 8. *Sect.* 2.) The Constitution of 1778, then, is still in force, except so far as it has 'been altered or amended' by the Constitution of 1790; and the 38th Section of the former is still in force, except so far as it has 'been altered or amended' by Article 8th of the latter.["] Note E, p. 37.

What is the 38th section, alluded to by our author?

It declares the Christian Protestant religion the established religion of the state. It then provides that Protestant societies may be incorporated, provided fifteen members subscribe the following articles—and not otherwise:—

1. That there is one God, and a future state of rewards and punishments.

2. That God is publicly to be worshipped.

3. That the Christian religion is true.

4. That the Old and New Testaments are of Divine inspiration, and the rule of faith and practice.

5. That every witness, when called on, shall speak truth, &c.

We have studied with some attention the Constitutions of South Carolina, and cannot but express our surprise at Mr. Adams' assertion, that the Constitution of 1790 itself, decides that the Constitution of 1778 is still of force, except so far as it has been altered or amended. There is not a word in the present Constitution to support the assertion. The Constitution of 1790, wholly superseded that of 1778. But Mr. Adams refers for support to the 2d Section, 8th Article Constitution of South Carolina. This relates solely to the rights preserved to corporate bodies and societies. No constitutional lawyer of any reputation can be found bold enough—we had almost used a harsher term—to say, "that the Constitution of 1790 leaves Christianity, *i.e.* Christianity without distinction of sects—precisely as it found it established by the Constitution of 1778." The Constitution abolishes all distinction of religious denominations. The follower of Moses is seated in our legislative hall by the follower of Jesus. The object of each is alike his country's honour, and his country's good.

We cannot argue the seal off the bond: we cannot argue the words out of the Constitution. The language is too clear to be misunderstood. Let us read the 8th article, to the 2d section of which Mr. Adams refers:—

"ARTICLE VIII.

SECTION 1. The free exercise and enjoyment of religious profession and worship, WITHOUT DISCRIMINATION OR PREFERENCE shall for ever hereafter, be allowed within this State to all mankind, &c.

SECTION 2. The rights, privileges, immunities, and estates of both civil and religious societies, and of corporate bodies, shall remain as if the Constitution of this State had not been altered or amended."

The meaning of this is palpable. The civil and religious societies, which have under the old Constitution acquired property and rights, shall not be deprived of their estates and privileges. But henceforth the free exercise of religious worship and profession, *without discrimination or preference,* shall for ever be allowed within this state to all mankind. Yet Mr. Adams contends that Christianity—without distinction of sects—is the established religion of the state! "It is too manifest," says he, "to require argument, that the Constitution of 1790 leaves Christianity—that is, Christianity without distinction of sects—precisely as it found it established by the Constitution of 1778." So that, according to him, "the free exercise of religious profession and worship," means only "the profession of Christianity!" And the establishment, the legal and constitutional establishment of Christianity, makes no discrimination or preference between the Jew and the Christian. The framers of the Constitution built no temple for intolerance. The cornerstone of their structure was liberty—liberty in its broadest and most general sense—liberty of speech, liberty of the press, liberty of conscience—the right to worship God in any way man thinks fit.

But Mr. Adams says:—

"It has hitherto been supposed, that our judges, our legislators, and our statesmen, ought to be influenced by the spirit, and bound by the sanctions of Christianity, both in their public and private conduct; but no censure can be rightfully attached to them for refusing to comply, if nothing of this kind is required by the commissions under which they act, and from which their authority is derived."—Page 16.

How is this? Jews hold offices of honour and trust under the general government: many hold commissions in the militia of the several states; many in the army and navy of the United States: Jews have been sent abroad as consuls: Jews are to be found in the legislative halls of South Carolina, New York, &c. Are *they* bound by the sanctions of *Christianity,* in their public and private conduct? Do the commissions under which they act, require any thing of this kind? Will they not consider this constitutional doctrine of

Mr. Adams somewhat strange? We have dwelt too long on this point. Proceed we to another.

Mr. Adams says:—

"The statute of December 12th, 1712, in adopting the Common Law of England as the Law of South Carolina, (*Grimké's Laws of South Carolina*, p. 99,) made Christianity a part of our fundamental law, it being a well established principle that Christianity is a part of the Common Law of England."*

We would remark now, in the first place, that in adopting the common law of England, South Carolina did not adopt it unreservedly. She only adopted such portions of it as were consistent with her Constitution and laws. She did not, and she could not deprive herself of the power of altering that common law, when applied to herself. If Christianity, then, were a part of the common law, she certainly had a right to abolish it if she thought proper. This right she exercised in framing her Constitution in 1790.

This is a complete reply to the argument, that the statute of 1712 incorporated Christianity with the laws of South Carolina, even if we admit his dictum—that it is a well settled "principle, that Christianity is a part of the common law of England."

But we deny that Christianity ever was a part of the common law of England. We do not know how we can better express our opinion on this subject, than by copying the following extract of a letter from Mr. Jefferson to Major Cartwright, dated Monticello, June 5, 1824.

"I was glad to find in your book a formal contradiction at length of the judiciary usurpation of legislative powers; for such the judges have usurped in their repeated declarations that Christianity is a part of the common law. The proof of the contrary which you have adduced is incontrovertible, to wit, that *the common law existed while the Anglo-Saxons were yet Pagans; at a time when they had never yet heard the name of Christ pronounced, or knew that such a character had existed.* But it may amuse you to show, when and by what means they stole this law upon us.

"In a case 'quare impedit,' in the Year Book, 34. H. 6. fo. 38 (1458), a question was made, how far the ecclesiastical law was to be respected in a common law court?

---

* "Sec. 11, Sergeant & Rawle, pp. 400, 401, where the Supreme Court of Pennsylvania says, that 'from the time of Bracton, Christianity has been received as part of the Common Law of England.' To this effect, the opinions of Lord Chief Justice Hale, (the great and good Lord Hale) Lord Chief Justice Raymond, and Lord Mansfield, are quoted. The Court refer to the King *vs.* Taylor, 1 Vent. 293, 3 Keb. 607—The King *vs.* Woolston, 2 Stra. 834. Fitz. 64. Raym. 162. Fitz. 66.—Evans *vs.* Chamberlain of London. Furneaux's Letters to Sir W. Blackstone. Appx. to Black. Com. and 2 Burns' Eccles. Law, p. 95—also, 8 Johnson, 292, where the Supreme Court of New York quote the same authorities, and add Emlyn's Preface to the State Trials, p. 8. Whitlock's Speech, 2 State Trials, 273. Tremaine's Pleas of the Crown, 226. S.C. The King *vs.* Williams, tried before Lord Kenyon in 1797."

And PRISOT, C. J., gives his opinion in these words: 'A tielx Leis que ils de Saint Eglise ont en *ancien scripture,* covient a nous a doner credence; car ceo common Ley, surquel touts mans leis sont fondes. Et auxy Sir, nous sumus obliges de conustre nostre ley. Et, Sir, si poit apperer a nous que l'evesque ad fait comme un ordinary fera en tiel cas, a dong nous devons ces adjuger bon, ou autrement nemy' [It is proper for us to give credence to such laws as they of the Holy Church have in ancient scripture (or writing); for this is common law, on which all manner of laws are founded. And also Sir, we are obliged to recognize their law (of the Holy Church). And, Sir, if it may appear to us that the bishop has acted like an Ordinary would act in such a case, then, we must adjudge these good, or otherwise not], &c. See S.C., Fitzh. Abr. qu: im. 89. Bro: Abr. qu: imp. 12. FINCH, in his first book, c. 3. is the first afterwards who quotes this case, and misstates it thus:—'To such laws of the church as have warrant in *holy scripture,* our law giveth credence,' and cites PRISOT, mistranslating '*ancien scripture*' into '*holy scripture;*' whereas PRISOT palpably says, 'to such laws as those of holy church have in *ancien writing,* it is proper for us to give credence;' to wit, to their ancient written laws. This was in 1613, a century and a half after the dictum of PRISOT. WINGATE, in 1658, erects this false translation into a maxim of the common law, copying the words of FINCH, but citing PRISOT. (Wingatis max. 3.) And SHEPPARD, tit. religion in 1675, copies the same mistranslation, quoting the Y.B., Finch and Wingate. HALE expresses it in these words; 'Christianity is parcel of the laws of England.' 1. *Ventr.* 293: 3. *Keb.* 607; but quotes no authority.

"By these echoings and re-echoings, from one to another, it had become so established in 1728, that in the case of the *King vs. Woolston,* 2 Str. 834, the court would not suffer it to be debated, whether to write against Christianity was punishable in the temporal courts at common law! WOOD, therefore, 409, ventures still to vary the phrase, and says, 'that all blasphemy and profaneness are offences by the common law,' and cites 2. *Str.*

"Then BLACKSTONE, in 1763, IV. 59, repeats the words of Hale, that Christianity is part of the common law of England, citing *Ventris and Strange;* and finally, LORD MANSFIELD, with a little qualification, in *Evans' case,* in 1767, says, 'that the essential principles of revealed religion are parts of the common law,' thus engulphing bible, testament, and all, into the common law, without citing any authority.

"And thus far we find this chain of authorities hanging, link by link, one upon another, and all ultimately upon one and the same hook, and that a mistranslation of the words 'ancien scripture,' used by PRISOT. FINCH quotes PRISOT; WINGATE does the same: SHEPPARD quotes PRISOT, FINCH, and WINGATE: HALE cites nobody; the court in *Woolston's case* cites HALE; WOOD cites *Woolston's case;* BLACKSTONE quotes *Woolston's case* and HALE; and LORD MANSFIELD, like HALE, ventures it on his own authority.

"Here I might defy the best read lawyer to produce another scrip of authority for this judicial forgery; and I might go on further to show how some of the Anglo-Saxon clergy interpolated into the text of Alfred's laws, the 20th, 21st, 22d, and 23d chapters of Exodus, and the 15th of the Acts of the Apostles, from the 23d to the 29th verse. But this would lead my pen and your patience too far. What a conspiracy this between church and state!!!"

We might safely rest here; but the question before us is too important to suffer us to pass by other authorities.

Richard Carlisle published "Paine's Age of Reason." In 1818, he was prosecuted for blasphemy and convicted, and sentenced on the 19th November, 1819, to three years' imprisonment, and to fines of £1500. He was, under various indictments and convictions, confined six years.

On the 30th June, 1825, Mr. Brougham presented a petition to the House of Commons in his behalf. In the petition it is urged,

"That Lord Hale was the first who asserted Christianity to be part or parcel of the law of the land: that but a few years before this unfair addition to the common law, Lord Chief Justice Coke, always considered as good an authority as Sir Matthew Hale, distinctly laid it down as law in mentioning the case of Caudrey; so in causes ecclesiastical and spiritual, as *blasphemy,* apostacy from Christianity, heresies, schisms, &c., *the conusance whereof belongeth not to the common law of England;* the same are to be determined and decided by ecclesiastical judges, according to the king's ecclesiastical laws of this realm; and he gives as a reason, for as before it appeareth the deciding of matters, so many and of so great importance is not within the conusance of the common law.★

"That before the abolition of the star chamber, and the decay of the ecclesiastical courts, no cases of blasphemy towards the Christian religion were known to the common law courts.

"That no statute can be found which has conferred authority on the common law courts, to take conusance of a charge of blasphemy toward the Christian religion, as assumed by Sir Matthew Hale.

"That it therefore clearly appears, that *that* and the subsequent conusance of such cases by the common law courts, have been an unjust usurpation of power, and an unlawful creation of law, contrary to the common and statute laws of this realm.

"That later in the middle of the 18th century, Lord Mansfield decided, that the common law did *not* take conusance of matters of opinion: whence it appears, by this and the authority of Lord Coke, the immediate predecessor of Sir Matthew Hale, that the judges are not unanimous on the subject; and that Sir Matthew Hale evidently warped the common law to punish an individual who had not committed an infringement of that or any other law; and that such has been the conduct of the judges in the case of your petitioner and others."

Mr. Brougham supported the petition in a very able and eloquent argument. None of the law officers of the crown attempted a reply. The fine was remitted by a warrant of the king, dated 12th November, 1825.

We will now refer to the argument of Carlisle, in 12 Repub. 652. It was to the following effect.

★ 5 Coke's Rep. IV. a. 33d year of Elizabeth.

The common law has been loosely described as that to which the memory of man runneth not to the contrary. But the time of legal memory has been more accurately defined, to be any time within the first year of Richard I.

Now the Christianity that existed before that time was that of the Roman Catholic church—and that Christianity the church of England pronounces "idolatrous and damnable."

Parliament, in 1713, pronounced it blasphemy to impugn the doctrine of the Trinity; and in 1813 declared it lawful to impugn that doctrine.

What then is the Christianity which is part and parcel of the common law of England?

We would ask Mr. Adams what was the Christianity which South Carolina adopted, in adopting the common law of England, when the Protestant religion was the established religion of the state? Was the *Protestant* religion ever a part of the common law? We have seen that it was not. But if ever, it was clearly repealed when South Carolina in her Constitution declared, that the free exercise of religious profession and worship, without discrimination or preference, should for ever be allowed within her limits to all mankind. Mr. Adams refers to the speech of Whitelock, 2 State Trials, 275. The reference is unfortunate; in that very page we find the lord commissioner, Whitelock, mentioning a case where the bishop committed a man for *heresy*, "for denying that tithes were due to the parson." Does Mr. Adams acknowledge this to be law?

The reference to Emlyn's preface to the State Trials is equally unfortunate. The preface contains some judicious remarks—among them, the following concerning indictments for blasphemous libels: "It is customary to insert the words 'falsò et malitiosé scripsit [one wrote falsely and maliciously], &c.' and indeed they are the very gist of the indictment, and absolutely necessary to constitute the offence; for as no words can be blasphemy, (viz. a reproachful reflection on God or religion,) which are true—(for truth can be no reflection on the God of truth)—so no opinion, however erroneous, can merit that denomination, unless uttered with a malicious design of reviling God or religion. Yet how often have persons been found guilty on these indictments, without any proof of the falsehood of the positions, or of the malice of him who wrote them. Nay, sometimes there is a great deal of reason to think they were published from no other principle but a sincere love and regard for truth."

We come now to the decision in the case of the People *vs.* Ruggles, cited by Mr. Adams from 8th Johnson's Reports, 292. In that case, the Supreme Court of New York relied on the authorities already examined, and shown to be illegal. Their positions are utterly untenable. The decision was made in 1811; we have not the then Constitution of New York by us, but it

is clear as the sun at mid-day, that the case is overruled by the 7th Art. 3d
Sec. Constitution New York, adopted in 1821. The words of the section
are: "The free exercise and enjoyment of religious profession and worship,
without discrimination or preference, shall for ever be allowed in this state
to all mankind." We will not dwell longer on this point; but in taking our
leave of it, we must advise Mr. Adams, who seems fond of quoting decisions, whenever he again assumes the part of a lawyer, to bear in mind what
the books say, viz. "The LAW and the *opinion of the judge* are not always con-
vertible terms, or one and the same thing; since it sometimes may happen
that the judge may *mistake* the law."

It appears then that the assertion, that Christianity is a well established
principle of the common law, is erroneous. It is a judicial forgery, a usurpation of legislative powers by the court, a bench-made, judge-enacted law,
unsupported by proper legal authority. They who wish to see this subject
fully treated, will do well to peruse "Cooper's Law of Libel"—particularly
that portion of it which treats of ecclesiastical libels. It is replete with learning and argument; its style is clear, vigorous, and striking, although occasionally rough and abrupt; it is sometimes witty, and sometimes eloquent; it
exhibits great power of condensation, notwithstanding it is frequently dis-
figured by repetitions; it is always fearless in the expression of opinions,
and its legal argument is unanswerable.

Mr. Adams, having noticed the common law, proceeds to quote an act
passed by South Carolina in 1712, prohibiting persons from travelling on
Sunday, or employing their slaves at work on that day. But this law is obso-
lete. Persons are continually travelling on Sunday. The mail is carried and
opened on Sunday. Passengers crowd the stages on Sunday. In fact, this act
of 1712 is repealed by the Constitution of 1790. With regard to not employing slaves at work on Sunday, we would observe, that public opinion—which
is stronger than the law—causes this to be observed. Independently of our
own individual religious profession, which induces us to observe the Sabbath, we are satisfied that in a political point of view, the observance of the
day is attended with beneficial effects. These have been frequently pointed
out. It is a day of rest for those who have laboured hard throughout the rest
of the previous week. As such, it invigorates both body and mind. The certain prospect of a holiday is exceedingly exhilarating. It diffuses cheerful-
ness over the heart. It gives the poor an opportunity to prepare for its
enjoyment. It insures them a period of rest, which would otherwise depend
on the caprice of the task-master. Sunday is indeed a day of jubilee and rest,
of enjoyment and ease. Ordinary occupations are suspended: and if a cheerful heart be pleasant in the sight of God, to that day HE must look with
peculiar delight! It is unnecessary to dwell on the advantages of Sunday as a
period of rest for cattle—for horses, mules, oxen, &c.

These and other considerations, make it politic to have a fixed day of rest: and no reason can be given for preferring any other day to Sunday.

Mr. Adams seems to have a high relish for old laws on the subject of religion; and, we have no doubt, will pay equal reverence to those which regulate the conduct, and those which regulate the belief of individuals. There is an act intended to provide for the security of the province of South Carolina, and more especially of church-going people. It is to be found in pages 185 and 186, *Grimké's Public Laws*. It was enacted in 1743, made perpetual by revival act of 1783, and has never since been repealed. We commend it to Mr. Adams' notice. It enacts that "all male persons, under sixty years of age, who shall go on Sunday or Christmas-day, to any church or place of worship, without a gun or a good pair of horse-pistols in good order and fit for service, with at least six chargers of gunpowder and ball; or who shall not carry the same into the church or other places of Divine worship, shall forfeit and pay the sum of 20s. current money." We trust that hereafter Mr. Adams will not neglect the duty prescribed by this act, and that every Sunday he will be seen with a gun on his shoulder, in conformity with the law.

We have thus, at the risk of being tedious, in most instances laid before our readers the very words of the several provisions in most of our constitutions, on the subject of religion. It is the only fair way of examining the question now before us—a question of vital importance—a question between liberty and tyranny, between the rights of conscience on the one hand, and intolerance, bigotry, and superstition on the other. The argument on the common law will apply to most of the states—so that while we have apparently been confining ourselves to the law of South Carolina, we have in truth been discussing the general law of the country.

We have seen that the connexion of Christianity with civil government has been, for fifteen centuries, invariably productive of the most flagrant abuses and the grossest corruptions. We have shown that there is, and there can be no middle ground between perfect liberty of conscience and despotism—since to give government power to protect Christianity for instance, is to give it power to declare what *is* Christianity, and what is necessary for its protection—in other words to give it unlimited power. We have shown also that opinion, faith, belief, are involuntary; that no human power can rightly interfere with them; that the object of civil government should be the regulation and promotion of human happiness here on earth; and that it should confine itself to the *conduct* of individuals, and regulate the duty of man towards man; but should not interfere with the relation between man and God. We have shown that most of the states, in framing their constitutions, have been influenced by these considerations; that in our country, Christianity has no connexion with the law of the land, or our political institutions; but that although a vast majority of the people of the United States are Christians, they have refused to give the general government power to make any laws on the subject, and have guaranteed to every man liberty of conscience, without discrimination or preference of any sect.

Christianity requires no aid from force or persecution. She asks not to be guarded by fines and forfeitures. She stands secure in the armour of truth and reason. She seeks not to establish her principles by political aid and legal enactments. She seeks mildly and peaceably to establish them in the hearts of the people.

EPILOGUE

Reflections on the
Church-State Debate

Adams's sermon and the responses to it provide a vivid reminder that religion was a dynamic factor in the founding of the American republic. Sadly, scholarly accounts of history have often discounted or even ignored the role of religion in the life of the nation. Popular perceptions of the nation's mission and purpose, though, have been framed by religious themes. The pursuit of religious liberty motivated many European colonists to settle in the New World. Furthermore, as Adams observed, "[t]he originators and early promoters of the discovery and settlement of this continent, had the propagation of Christianity before their eyes, as one of the principal objects of their undertaking."[1] Religion was arguably the most influential force in shaping the political identity and culture of the new nation.

A struggle to define the prudential and constitutional role of religion in public life has persisted since the inception of the republic. The early 1830s, in particular, was a season of uncertainty and transition for American church-state relations. The forces that prompted a reconsideration of church-state arrangements included democratization and secularization. In 1833 Massachusetts became the last state to terminate a formal establishment; nonetheless, federal and state governments continued to support a multitude of religious institutions, missions, and practices. For example, legislative chaplains and religious education were often subsidized by the public treasury, religious observances were recognized in the official calendar, and, in several state constitutions, religious test oaths coexisted with religious liberty and nonestablishment provisions. The rapid transition from state church to disestablishment raised novel and ponderous questions. Can a society remain virtuous, stable, and prosperous without the props of religion and morality? Did the American people intend to discontinue all *public* expressions and acknowledgments of traditional religion when they boldly opted for a disestablished society? What role, if any, should religion play in the formulation of public policy? Did separation of church and state mean something less than a wholly secular polity? Questions like these prompted

Adams to join a national conversation on religion and politics, and they continue to agitate the public mind nearly two centuries later.

The documents compiled in this book reveal that by the 1830s two distinct and popular views on the appropriate relationship between religion and politics were firmly entrenched in American political thought. On the one hand, there was the view, endorsed by Adams and Story, that religion provided an indispensable support for social order and civic virtue. Civil society, therefore, had an interest in nurturing and encouraging public assistance for religion and religious institutions. Not all who embraced this view, it should be emphasized, advocated a formal, exclusive ecclesiastical establishment, much less a theocracy, although some religious traditionalists agitated for an official state church.

On the other hand, there was the view, espoused by Madison and the author of "Immunity of Religion," that true and genuine religion flourished when it relied on the voluntary support of believers and eschewed all corrupting endorsements of the civil authority. Neither religion nor the state, it was argued, depended on an alliance with the other in order to survive and prosper. Most who held this view fervently and sincerely denied that they were hostile to religion or thought it unimportant. Rather, it was maintained that religion was too important to subject it in any way to governmental control. There were, no doubt, a few extremists who advocated a secular order because they were hostile to traditional, orthodox Christianity and thought it incompatible with a rational, enlightened polity.

The underlying themes and concerns of church-state debate are virtually unchanged since Adams delivered his sermon. The place of religion in a pluralistic society and the secularization of public life are sources of controversy today, just as they were in Adams's day. Indeed, some disputes that aroused passion in the early republic continue to provoke bitter argument. The style and intensity of church-state debate in the 1830s also characterize debate today. Contending sides tend to caricature or even misrepresent the other's position. Despite suggestions to the contrary, Adams did not advocate theocracy (at least not in the strictest sense of the word), any more than Madison championed infidelism or doctrinaire secularism. Adams was not intolerant of religious minorities, and Madison was not indifferent to religion and the concerns of the religious community.[2] Significantly, Adams and Madison eschewed the extreme positions of exclusive establishment and strict separation respectively. Adams's "middle course" and Madison's "line of separation" were attempts to craft moderate responses to delicate political and constitutional questions. Those aligned with Adams and Madison, however, were often less moderate in their approaches and rhetoric. Participants in the debate have frequently talked past each other and often have unnecessarily inflamed passions and nurtured distrust of their opponents' motives. In the pages that follow, the two contrasting views presented in this book will be briefly summarized, with every effort made to avoid misrepresentation or caricature.

Jasper Adams succinctly and passionately articulated the concerns of religious traditionalists. He lamented the diminishing respect for and influence of religion in American public life and decried efforts to minimize the contributions of Christianity to the civil constitutions and laws of the republic. Adams blamed Thomas Jefferson for promoting a secular polity in which "Christianity has no connexion with the law of the land, or with our civil and political institutions."[3] He thought this notion, which he feared was "gradually gaining belief among us," would inevitably "tend to degrade [Christianity] and to destroy its influence among the community."[4] Moreover, it would ultimately prove detrimental to our national standing. "Christianity," he wrote, "has been the chief instrument by which the nations of Christendom have risen superior to all other nations;—but if its influence is once destroyed or impaired, society instead of advancing, must infallibly retrograde."[5] Adams believed, as did many religious traditionalists of the day, that only the Christian religion provided an ethical code capable of sustaining a stable social order and a virtuous people.

Adams's argument rested on important premises. First, he believed in a superintending deity, a dispenser of rewards and punishments, involved in the affairs of men and nations. And nations, he said, have the same duty as individuals to behave in conformity with Divine precepts.[6] Second, "religion" and "politics" were, in Adams's view, not separate categories but interrelated components of a seamless whole. All political systems, he believed, inevitably reflect a moral and attendant religious ethic. Moreover, from a perspective informed by a Manichean dualism, Adams believed that the United States stood at a historic crossroads, and the political order had to choose the "faith" of either orthodox Christianity or infidelity.

History was important to Adams. It provided an intellectual framework for interpreting not only the past and the unfolding present but also the nation's future. He believed that religion had played a vital and pervasive role in the nation's founding. Indeed, American history was a resplendent record of Divine providence. The continent, he claimed, was discovered and settled by pious individuals who were called to build "a city set upon a hill."[7] The grand American experiment could not be understood apart from its religious foundations:

The Christian religion was intended by them ["our pious forefathers"] to be the corner stone of the social and political structures which they were founding. . . .

The Colonies, then, from which these United States have sprung, were originally planted and nourished by our pious forefathers, in the exercise of a strong
and vigorous Christian faith. They were designed to be Christian communities.[8]

A brief survey of the constitutions and uniform practices of the various states similarly revealed that "Christianity [was] the well known and
well established religion of the communities."[9] Although the American
people declined to give any one church or denomination a preferred legal
status, they "RETAINED THE CHRISTIAN RELIGION AS THE FOUNDATION
OF THEIR CIVIL, LEGAL AND POLITICAL INSTITUTIONS." In a spirit of tol-
erance, Adams hastened to add, the states "all grant the free exercise and
enjoyment of religious profession and worship, with some slight discriminations, to all mankind."[10]

The federal Constitution, Adams continued, similarly preserved civil
government's vital relationship with religion. "The first amendment . . .
leaves the entire subject [of religion] in the same situation in which it found
it; and such was precisely the most suitable course."[11] State ecclesiastical
establishments were left untouched by the Constitution, and the framers
wisely denied the federal government all jurisdiction over religion because
it was deemed too delicate and too important a subject to be entrusted to its
guardianship. Congress, then, must permit the Christian religion to remain
in the same state in which it was at the time the Constitution was adopted.
Legislators "have no commission to destroy or injure the religion of the
country. Their laws ought to be consistent with its principles and usages.
They may not rightfully enact any measure or sanction any practice calculated to diminish its moral influence, or to impair the respect in which it is
held among the people."[12]

The American people, Adams concluded, wisely declined to establish
a *national* church; thus they avoided giving legal preference to one form of
Christianity over all others. They also prudently refrained from the opposite extreme of creating a strictly secular political order in which civil government severs all connection with religion. Instead, they "wisely chose the
middle course."[13] This arrangement renounced an exclusive ecclesiastical
establishment but retained a public and influential role for religion as the
foundation of civil institutions and the public ethic. Christianity thus remained, in an informal, nondenominational sense, the national religion. The
First Amendment nonestablishment provision, in short, merely proscribed
Congress from conferring upon one church or denomination special favors
and advantages that it denied others. The institutional separation of church
and state was not designed to silence the community of faith, and it did not
require the Christian ethic to be divorced from public concerns.

The central theme of Adams's argument was that religion was essential to preserve and promote civic virtue. He agreed with George Washington that religion provided an indispensable support for social order and stability, and that a free and virtuous civil polity could not endure without the restraining authority of religion.[14] This was particularly true in a nation as diverse, high-spirited, and free of government regulation as the United States. "Especially it is to Christianity, that we are indebted for the steady self-control, and power of habitually subjecting our passions to the sway of reason and conscience, which have preserved us to this day, a free and a united people."[15] A belief in a superintending deity and a future state of rewards and punishments, he maintained, instilled in the minds of men a sense of moral responsibility and civic duty. "[I]f our religion is once undermined, it will be succeeded by a decline of public and private morals, and by the destruction of those high and noble qualities of character, for which as a community we have been so much distinguished[.]"[16] According to Adams, the unmistakable lesson of history is that if religion is denied "the sustaining aid of the civil Constitutions and law of the country," then religion's influence in the community will be destroyed.[17] And if Christian influence is "destroyed or impaired, society instead of advancing, must infallibly retrograde."[18] In a sweeping declaration, Adams forcefully and passionately summarized his thesis:

No nation on earth, is more dependent than our own, for its welfare, on the preservation and general belief and influence of Christianity among us. Perhaps there has never been a nation composed of men whose spirit is more high, whose aspirations after distinction are more keen, and whose passions are more strong than those which reign in the breasts of the American people. These are encouraged and strengthened by our systems of education, by the unlimited field of enterprise which is open to all; and more especially by the great inheritance of civil and religious freedom, which has descended to us from our ancestors. It is too manifest, therefore, to require illustration, that in a great nation thus high spirited, enterprising and free, public order must be maintained by some principle of very peculiar energy and strength;—by some principle which will touch the springs of human sentiment and action. Now there are two ways, and two ways only by which men can be governed in society; the one by physical force; the other by religious and moral principles pervading the community, guiding the conscience, enlightening the reason, softening the prejudices, and calming the passions of the multitude. Physical force is the chief instrument by which mankind have heretofore been governed; but this always has been, and I trust will always continue to be inapplicable in our case. My trust, however, in this respect, springs entirely from a confidence, that the Christian religion will continue as heretofore to exert upon us, its tranquilizing, purifying, elevating and controlling efficacy. No power less efficacious than Christianity, can permanently maintain the public tranquillity of the country, and the authority of law. We must be a Christian nation, if we wish to continue a free nation. We must make our election:—to be swayed by the gentle reign of moral and Christian principle, or ultimately, if not soon, by the iron rod of arbitrary sway.[19]

Adams believed that a nation and its people could not thrive without religious and moral principles pervading the community, informing the public ethic, and promoting civic virtue.[20] True religion, he argued, was the most effectual instrument for making a virtuous people, and thereby securing a stable society. If social order and national prosperity depended on true religion, then civil magistrates had an obligation to defend, encourage, and support religion. Moreover, civil society could not tolerate acts inimical to religion. Constitutional protection for religious exercise fostered an environment in which religion could flourish, free from governmental restraint, and religious spokesmen could speak boldly without inhibition or fear of retribution against immorality and corruption in the public arena. This moral voice raised in high places was essential to preserve the political order. Religion was thus vital to national survival, and religious liberty ensured that religion was available to provide this indispensable support.

James Madison espoused a new faith in a secular polity in which ecclesiastical authority is separated from civil government and support for religion is left entirely "to the voluntary provisions of those who profess it."[21] Madison's commitment to church-state separation did not signal indifference, much less hostility, toward religion. Rather, he believed that a secular, separationist policy was in the best interests of true religion, civil government, and a free society and that it was the surest guarantor of liberty of conscience.[22] "[T]here are few . . . enlightened judges," Madison opined, "who will maintain" that the Old World system of "establishment of a particular religion without any, or with very little toleration of others, . . . has been favourable either to Religion or to government."[23]

"[T]he prevailing opinion in Europe," and the one suggested in Adams's sermon, had "been, that Religion could not be preserved without the support of Government, nor Government be supported without an established Religion, that there must be at least an alliance of some sort between them."[24] Madison believed, to the contrary, that true religion prospered in the marketplace of ideas unrestrained by the monopolistic control of the civil authority.[25] He thought it a contradiction to argue that discontinuing state support for Christianity would precipitate its demise, since "this Religion both existed and flourished, not only without the support of human laws, but in spite of every opposition from them." If Christianity depends on the support of civil government, the pious confidence of the faithful in its "innate excellence and the patronage of its Author" will be undermined.[26] The best and purest religion, Madison thus concluded, relied on the spontaneous, voluntary support of the devoted and eschewed all entanglements with civil government—including those fostered by financial support or compulsion.[27]

Madison was also unpersuaded by the argument that leaving religion "entirely to itself" would demoralize society, erode respect for civil authority, and unleash individual and collective licentiousness destructive of social stability.[28] He argued that the bold disestablishment experiment in his native Virginia and neighboring southern states supported his conclusion. Discontinuation of legal support for the established church and reliance on "spontaneous support of the people" had resulted in "greater purity & industry of the pastors & in the greater devotion of their flocks."[29] The continuing vitality of religion in Virginia fifty years after "legal support of Religion was withdrawn," Madison wrote, "sufficiently prove, that it does not need the support of Government. And it will scarcely be contended that government has suffered by the exemption of Religion from its cognizance, or its pecuniary aid."[30]

A figure of speech is perhaps the most significant and interesting feature of Madison's letter to Adams. He abandoned Jefferson's image of a "wall of separation" in favor of a more subtle metaphor that acknowledged the complex and ambiguous intersection of religion and civil government: "I must admit, moreover, that it may not be easy, in every possible case, to trace the *line of separation,* between the rights of Religion & the Civil authority, with such distinctness, as to avoid collisions & doubts on unessential points."[31] Madison's metaphor more precisely describes the actual church-state relationship in the United States than Jefferson's "wall." Jefferson's metaphor "connotes antagonism and suspicion" between "two distinct and settled institutions in the society once and for all time separated by a clearly defined and impregnable barrier."[32] Madison's "line" is fluid, adaptable to changing relationships, and unlike Jefferson's "wall," it can even be overstepped in the interest of fostering the full and uninhibited expression of religious belief.

Madison viewed the concepts of religious liberty and church-state separation as dependent principles. Religious freedom could not endure, he thought, as long as civil government enforced belief in religious dogma or was entangled with an ecclesiastical hierarchy; and civil government could only disengage itself from sectarian quarrels in a milieu of social and intellectual freedom. Therefore, Madison believed that an institutional separation of church and state was the preferred means for fostering religious freedom. Separation of church and state, however, was not an end in itself; it was merely a useful means to the end of expansive religious freedom. His motivation, it is clear, was to promote the best and purest religion and to protect liberty of conscience from invasion by the state.[33]

Jasper Adams's sermon and the responses to it have a strikingly modern quality. The language and themes of church-state debate today are much the same as they were in the 1830s. Only the occasional archaic word or phrase suggests that the documents reprinted here are the product of an earlier generation. Furthermore, many controversies that inspire bitter disputes today would be familiar to Adams, Madison, Marshall, and Story. Adams, for example, was alarmed by the prospect that instruction in Christian values and principles would no longer form "the basis of the education of our youth."[34] Subsidizing religion from the public purse was disquieting to Madison. These issues are as current as the front page of the morning newspaper. The more things change, the more things stay the same.

Adams perceptively identified the central historical and constitutional question: When the American people discontinued the Old World system of exclusive ecclesiastical establishments, did they "intend to renounce all connexion with the Christian religion? Or did they only intend to disclaim all preference of one sect of Christians over another, as far as civil government was concerned; while they still retained the Christian religion as the foundation of all their social, civil and political institutions?"[35] From this question flow many other issues that troubled church-state relations in Adams's era and continue to provoke controversy today. Can a society promote civic virtue and moral character in its citizens without the guiding hand of religion? Does the U.S. Constitution permit religion to inform the public mind and influence the formulation of public policy? Does the First Amendment nonestablishment provision mandate a religiously neutral state or a wholly secular polity, in which all vestiges of traditional religious influences are divorced from public life and policy? To what extent, if any, may civil government facilitate, aid, and encourage religious practices and expression (including the display of religious symbols) in the public square? Can civil government recognize and accommodate religious institutions and rituals in the official life of the nation?

Both Madison and Adams anticipated an intensifying struggle to redefine the public role of religion in an increasingly secular culture; however, they articulated very different prescriptions for resolving prospective church-state conflicts. Madison foresaw the emergence of a pluralistic, religiously diverse society and believed that disestablishment was the surest means for avoiding sectarian conflict and promoting religious liberty. He argued that leaving religion to the voluntary support of those who profess it was best for religion and best for civil government. Adams anticipated the emergence of a dominant secular culture and the inevitable conflict with traditional religious values. He thought the secularization of public life not only deviated from American tradition but also, he feared, threatened to loosen the bonds of social order and to undermine the very foundations of a self-governing people. Adams argued that insofar as national prosperity was linked to a vibrant religious ethic, civil government had a duty to preserve and promote general, nondenominational religious values in the community.

Adams's sermon was born of the consternation and alienation of conservative, evangelical Protestants marginalized by an encroaching secularism that they believed threatened to divorce religious values from the public ethic and to limit religious expression to the private realm. Adams embraced a faith profoundly public in character that made normative claims and involved moral judgments he thought vital to the body politic. The urgency with which his message was delivered emphasized the startling erosion of religious influence in mid-nineteenth-century America. A Christian ethic was no longer shared by all in public life; rather, Christians were reduced to one more interest group competing with others in the political arena for the allegiance of the American people. These concerns continue to spark church-state conflict, and they have revived political activism among religious traditionalists today.

The consequences of secularization and a restricted role for religion in the public square are debated today as vigorously as ever. A chorus of voices, from diverse perspectives, has warned of an intensifying "culture war" that pits religious traditionalists against secularists—those who believe religious values must inform the public ethic versus those who would restrict religious influence to the private sphere of life.[36] There is deepening concern and renewed debate about the moral fabric of American society and the contribution of religion to the content of the public ethic. Adams surely would have identified with these concerns.

The issues raised and debated by Adams, Madison, and others whose views are presented in this book were alive in the public mind long before Adams put pen to paper, and they remain a source of discussion and controversy today. Despite all the impulses or tendencies of an advanced industrial society toward secularization, by virtually all conventional yardsticks of religious commitment Americans continue to be among the most "religious" people on earth.[37] Thus, there seems little prospect that tensions between traditional religion and secular politics will fade away. These tensions are exacerbated by civil government's expansion into and regulation of traditional domains of organized religion, and by a growing diversity of and competition among religious sects. Questions concerning the propriety and constitutionality of religious themes in the public life of the nation will, no doubt, continue to provoke energetic debate. These are issues that, like the poor, will be with us always.[38]

Notes

1. Jasper Adams, *The Relation of Christianity to Civil Government in the United States. A Sermon, Preached in St. Michael's Church, Charleston, February 13th, 1833, before the Convention of the Protestant Episcopal Church of the Diocese of South-Carolina*, 2d ed. (Charleston, S.C.: A.E. Miller, 1833), p. 8 [43].

2. The author of "Immunity of Religion" emphasized his adherence to orthodox Christianity in an apparent effort to insulate himself from a charge of infidelity or political atheism. Madison may have had the same objective when in his letter to Adams he described the "Christian Religion" as the "best & purest religion." Letter from James Madison to Jasper Adams, Sept. 1833, in Adams's handwritten notes appended to his personal copy of the first edition of his sermon in the William L. Clements Library, University of Michigan, p. 12 [117], hereinafter cited as Author's Notes.

3. Adams, *Relation*, p. 7 [42].

4. Ibid., pp. 7, 17 [42, 49].

5. Ibid., p. 18 [50].

6. Adams wrote: "If, then, we permit this chief cause [i.e., Christianity] of all our choicest blessings to be destroyed or counteracted in its effects; what can we expect from the dealings of a righteous Providence, but the destiny of a people who have rejected the counsel of God against themselves? [Luke 7:30] If we refuse to be instructed by the Divine assurance, we shall be made to feel by the intensity of our sufferings, 'that righteousness exalteth a nation, and that sin is a reproach to any people' [Proverbs 14:34]." Adams, *Relation*, p. 19 [51].

7. Matthew 5:14.

8. Adams, *Relation*, pp. 9, 10 [44, 44-45].

9. Ibid., p. 11 [45].

10. Ibid., p. 12 [46]; emphasis in the original.

11. Ibid., p. 13 [46].

12. Ibid., p. 13 [47].

13. Ibid., p. 15 [48].

14. Adams cited with approval George Washington's statement in his "Farewell Address" on the relationship of religion to national prosperity: "Of all the dispositions and habits, which lead to political prosperity, religion and morality are indispensable supports. . . . And let us with caution indulge the supposition, that morality can be maintained without religion. Whatever may be conceded to the influence of refined education on minds of peculiar structure, reason and experience both forbid us to expect, that national morality can prevail in exclusion of religious principle" (*Relation*, p. 60, n. I [99]). For the complete speech, see "Farewell Address," 19 Sept. 1796, in John C. Fitzpatrick, ed., *The Writings of George Washington*, vol. 35 (Washington, D.C.: GPO, 1940), pp. 214-38. For a discussion of this idea in the political thought of the founding era, see Fred J. Hood, *Reformed America: The Middle and Southern States, 1783-1837* (University: Univ. of Alabama Press, 1980), pp. 7-26.

15. Adams, *Relation*, p. 25 [55].

16. Ibid., p. 23 [54].

17. Ibid., p. 17 [50].

18. Ibid., p. 18 [50]. Justice Joseph Story concurred: "My own private judgement has long been, (& every day's experience more & more confirms me in it,) that government can not long exist without an alliance with religion *to some extent;* & that Christianity is indispensable to the true interests & solid foundations of all

free governments. . . . I know not, indeed, how any deep sense of moral obligation or accountableness can be expected to prevail in the community without a firm persuasion of the great Christian Truths promulgated in your South Carolina constitution of 1778." Letter from Joseph Story to Jasper Adams, 14 May 1833, Author's Notes, p. 4 [115]; emphasis in the original.

19. Adams, *Relation*, pp. 19-20 [51-52].

20. Adams elaborated on this theme in a speech entitled *The Moral Causes of the Welfare of Nations: An Oration, Delivered 1st November, 1834, in the Chapel, before the Society of Graduates of the College of Charleston* (Charleston, S.C.: J.S. Burges, 1834).

21. Letter from James Madison to Jasper Adams, Sept. 1833, Author's Notes, p. 12 [117].

22. The author of "Immunity of Religion" argued that the union of church and state inevitably condones discrimination and erodes religious and civil rights. "Such a connexion [between church and state] will necessarily create a marked distinction between those who believe, and those who do *not* believe the religion upheld and protected by law. Hence a discrimination in civil rights will gradually arise. One set, or rather one sect of men, will be protected and rewarded, while another will be proscribed and persecuted. Freedom of conscience will be invaded. With freedom of opinion freedom of speech must fall—and liberty will soon expire." "Immunity of Religion," *American Quarterly Review* 17, no. 34 (June 1835): 320-21 [128-29]; emphasis in original.

23. Letter from James Madison to Jasper Adams, Sept. 1833, Author's Notes, p. 12 [118].

24. Ibid., pp. 12-13 [118].

25. The author of "Immunity of Religion" similarly argued: "Christianity stands in need of no unequal protection. Give her a fair field, and the legitimate weapons of reason, and she must and will prevail. The fortress of error will be compelled to surrender, and the gentle sway of the Gospel will be universally acknowledged" (p. 325 [133]). The reviewer returned to this theme in the concluding paragraph: "Christianity requires no aid from force or persecution. She asks not to be guarded by fines and forfeitures. She stands secure in the armour of truth and reason. She seeks not to establish her principles by political aid and legal enactments. She seeks mildly and peaceably to establish them in the hearts of the people" (p. 340 [150]).

26. James Madison, "Memorial and Remonstrance against Religious Assessments," reprinted in Robert A. Rutland et al., eds., *The Papers of James Madison,* vol. 8 (Chicago: Univ. of Chicago Press, 1973), p. 301.

27. See the letter from James Madison to Edward Livingston, 10 July 1822, reprinted in Gaillard Hunt, ed., *The Writings of James Madison,* 9 vols. (New York: G.P. Putnam's Sons, 1900-1910), 9:102-3: "[R]eligion & Govt. will both exist in greater purity, the less they are mixed together. . . . Religion flourishes in greater purity, without than with the aid of Govt."

28. Letter from James Madison to Jasper Adams, Sept. 1833, Author's Notes, p. 14 [120].

29. Ibid., p. 13 [118-20].

30. Ibid., p. 14 [120].

31. Ibid.; emphasis added.

32. Terry Eastland, "In Defense of Religious America," *Commentary* 71, no. 6 (June 1981): 39; Sidney E. Mead, "Neither Church nor State: Reflections on James Madison's 'Line of Separation,'" *Journal of Church and State* 10 (1968): 350.

33. For an examination of Madison's church-state views, see Robert S. Alley, ed., *James Madison on Religious Liberty* (Buffalo, N.Y.: Prometheus, 1985); Daniel L.

Dreisbach, *Real Threat and Mere Shadow: Religious Liberty and the First Amendment* (Westchester, Ill.: Crossway, 1987), pp. 135-58; Adrienne Koch, *Madison's "Advice to My Country"* (Princeton, N.J.: Princeton Univ. Press, 1966), pp. 3-49; William Lee Miller, *The First Liberty: Religion and the American Republic* (New York: Alfred A. Knopf, 1986), pp. 77-150; Lance Banning, "James Madison, the Statute for Religious Freedom, and the Crisis of Republican Convictions," in *The Virginia Statute for Religious Freedom: Its Evolution and Consequences in American History,* ed. Merrill D. Peterson and Robert C. Vaughan (New York: Cambridge Univ. Press, 1988), pp. 109-38; Eva T.H. Brann, "Madison's 'Memorial and Remonstrance': A Model of American Eloquence," in *Rhetoric and American Statesmanship,* ed. Glen E. Thurow and Jeffrey D. Wallin (Durham, N.C.: Carolina Academic Press, 1984), pp. 9-46; Irving Brant, "Madison: On the Separation of Church and State," *William and Mary Quarterly,* 3d ser., 8 (1951): 3-24; Donald L. Drakeman, "Religion and the Republic: James Madison and the First Amendment," *Journal of Church and State* 25 (1983): 427-45; Charles J. Emmerich, "The Enigma of James Madison on Church and State," in *Religion, Public Life, and the American Polity,* ed. Luis E. Lugo (Knoxville: Univ. of Tennessee Press, 1994), pp. 51-73; Gaillard Hunt, "James Madison and Religious Liberty," in *Annual Report of the American Historical Association for the Year 1901* 1 (1902): 163-71; Thomas Lindsay, "James Madison on Religion and Politics: Rhetoric and Reality," *American Political Science Review* 85 (1991): 1321-37; Joseph M. Lynch, "Madison's Religion Proposals Judicially Confounded: A Study in the Constitutional Law of Conscience," *Seton Hall Law Review* 20 (1990): 418-77; Neal Riemer, "Madison: A Founder's Vision of Religious Liberty and Public Life," in *Religion, Public Life, and the American Polity,* ed. Lugo, pp. 37-50; Marvin K. Singleton, "Colonial Virginia as First Amendment Matrix: Henry, Madison, and Assessment Establishment," *Journal of Church and State* 8 (1966): 344-64; and Paul J. Weber, "James Madison and Religious Equality: The Perfect Separation," *Review of Politics* 44 (1982): 163-86.

34. Adams, *Relation,* p. 17 [49].

35. Adams, *Relation,* pp. 6-7 [42].

36. See, for example, James Davison Hunter, *Culture Wars: The Struggle to Define America* (New York: Basic, 1991); Stephen Bates, *Battleground: One Mother's Crusade, the Religious Right, and the Struggle for Control of Our Classrooms* (New York: Poseidon, 1993); Stephen L. Carter, *The Culture of Disbelief: How American Law and Politics Trivialize Religious Devotion* (New York: Basic, 1993); Richard John Neuhaus, *The Naked Public Square: Religion and Democracy in America* (Grand Rapids, Mich.: William B. Eerdmans, 1984); John W. Whitehead, *Religious Apartheid: The Separation of Religion from American Public Life* (Chicago: Moody Press, 1994); and John W. Whitehead, *The Second American Revolution* (Elgin, Ill.: David C. Cook, 1982).

37. See Kenneth D. Wald, *Religion and Politics in the United States,* 2d ed. (Washington, D.C.: Congressional Quarterly Press, 1992), pp. 7-15.

38. Matthew 26:11; Mark 14:7; John 12:8.

APPENDIX ONE

The Life and Works of Jasper Adams

Jasper Adams was born in East Medway, Massachusetts, on 27 August 1793. He was a descendant of Henry Adams (ca. 1583–1646) of Braintree, who immigrated to the Massachusetts Bay Colony in 1638 and was the patriarch of the renowned Adams family.[1] The son of a New England farmer, Jasper Adams received college preparatory instruction under the tutelage of the Reverend Luther Wright.[2] In 1815 he graduated from Brown University, where he was second in his class.[3] Adams taught at Phillips Academy in Andover, Massachusetts, for the next three years, during two of which he also pursued divinical studies at Andover Theological Seminary.[4] In 1818 he returned to Brown as a tutor, and the following year he was elected professor of mathematics and natural philosophy. Adams's curriculum vitae in the Brown University catalog indicates that he received the degrees of A.M. in 1819 from Yale College and D.D. in 1827 from Columbia College, New York.[5]

As a student at Brown, Adams apparently "adopted the religious views which governed him through life."[6] Although reared in the Presbyterian Church, he gravitated toward the Episcopal communion. His religious convictions were nurtured at Andover, and in 1820 he was ordained a priest in the Protestant Episcopal Church.

Adams remained at Brown until 1824, when he was appointed president of the College of Charleston. He arrived in South Carolina to find the institution financially embarrassed, lacking suitable facilities, and declining in academic reputation.[7] Frustrated by the reluctance of the trustees to endorse his plans for institutional revitalization, he resigned in 1826 and moved to Geneva, New York, where he was elected the first president of Geneva (Hobart) College.[8]

After an eighteen-month tenure at Geneva, Adams in 1828 was induced by the trustees at the College of Charleston to return.[9] Adams had developed strong attachments to South Carolina, especially through his marriage to a Charlestonian woman.[10] Moreover, he found the rigors of northern winters detrimental to his frail constitution. Adams was reluctant, however, to return to Charleston except on his own terms. "A country of

frost and snow," he remarked, "does not suit me as well as the mild sky of
S.C., but I would prefer living here in the snow twice as deep as it is to
seeing things drag along as they did when I was in Charleston before."[11]
With a renewed appreciation for his talents, the college trustees acceded to
his sweeping demands, and he continued for nine years—often turbulent
ones—as college president.[12] During his second administration the college
was reorganized, the academic program restructured and strengthened, en-
rollment nearly doubled, and capital improvements initiated.[13]

By 1836, however, the college once again faced difficulties, not unlike
those of a decade earlier. Adams resigned his post and devoted his energy
to completing a treatise on moral philosophy.[14] In 1838 he was appointed
chaplain and professor of ethics, geography, and history at the U.S. Military
Academy at West Point, New York. After two years he returned to South
Carolina's warmer climate, where he took charge of a private seminary in
Pendleton, South Carolina. He died a year later, on 25 October 1841, after a
brief illness.[15] Adams was buried on the grounds of St. Paul's Episcopal
Church in Pendleton.[16]

Adams was recognized in his own day as "a good scholar, an unusu-
ally able administrator, and a man of great practical wisdom, energy, and
determination."[17] The Reverend Charles Cotesworth Pinckney noted on
Adams's death that "[a]s a *writer* and a *man of letters,* Dr. A[dams] also held a
prominent place in our land. . . . His learning was extensive and profound—
his thirst for knowledge very great—his information remarkably correct,
and his research deep and indefatigable."[18] Among his surviving works are
the treatise on moral philosophy and a handful of published lectures and
sermons, including the convention address on the relation of Christianity
to civil government. Jasper Adams's greatest legacy undoubtedly is the transformation of the College of Charleston from little more than a grammar
school into a reputable institution of higher education. One college historian opined, "From his accession the real greatness and true fame of the
college seems to date."[19]

THE WORKS OF JASPER ADAMS

"An Address, Delivered on Whitsun Tuesday, 1830, being the Anniversary
of the Charleston Protestant Episcopal Sunday School Society. By the
Rev. Jasper Adams, D.D., Principal of Charleston College." *Gospel
Messenger, and Southern Episcopal Register* 7, no. 81 (Sept. 1830): 257-64.
*A Baccalaureate Address, Delivered in St. Paul's Church, 3d November, 1835, at the
Annual Commencement of the College of Charleston.* Charleston, S.C.: Jas.
S. Burges, 1835. 16pp.

Characteristics of the Present Century: A Baccalaureate Address to the Graduates of the College of Charleston, So. Ca., Delivered in St. Paul's Church, at the Annual Commencement, 31st October, 1834. Charleston, S.C.: Burges and Honour, 1836. 11pp.

Elements of Moral Philosophy. Cambridge, Mass.: Folsom, Wells and Thurston, 1837. xxviii, 492pp.

An Eulogium, Pronounced 23d January, 1835, in the Chapel of the College of Charleston, before the Trustees, Faculty and Students; on the Life and Character of the Late Elias Horry, Esq. Charleston, S.C.: A.E. Miller, 1835. 26pp.

"A Historical Sketch of the College of Charleston." *American Quarterly Register* 12 (Nov. 1839): 164-77.

An Inaugural Discourse, Delivered in Trinity Church, Geneva, New-York, August 1, 1827. Geneva, N.Y.: James Bogert, 1827. 56pp.

Laws of Success and Failure in Life; An Address, Delivered 30th October, 1833, in the Chapel of the College of Charleston, before the Euphradian Society. Charleston, S.C.: A.E. Miller, 1833. 52pp.

The Moral Causes of the Welfare of Nations: An Oration, Delivered 1st November, 1834, in the Chapel, before the Society of Graduates of the College of Charleston. Charleston, S.C.: J.S. Burges, 1834. 40pp.

The Relation of Christianity to Civil Government in the United States. A Sermon, Preached in St. Michael's Church, Charleston, February 13th, 1833, before the Convention of the Protestant Episcopal Church of the Diocese of South-Carolina. Charleston, S.C.: A.E. Miller, 1833. 56pp.

The Relation of Christianity to Civil Government in the United States. A Sermon, Preached in St. Michael's Church, Charleston, February 13th, 1833, before the Convention of the Protestant Episcopal Church of the Diocese of South-Carolina. 2d ed. Charleston, S.C.: A.E. Miller, 1833. 64pp.

A Sermon, Preached in St. Michael's Church, Charleston, on the Morning of Advent Sunday, 29th November, 1835. Charleston, S.C.: James S. Burges, 1836. 32pp.

A Sermon, Preached in St. Paul's Church, on the morning of Advent Sunday, 30th November, 1834, being the day of the late Total Eclipse of the Sun. Charleston, S.C.: J.S. Burges, 1835. 36pp.

"Sermon No. X. Delivered at the Lecture Founded by the Late Chief Justice Pinckney, in St. Philip's Church, Nov. 9, 1825, by the Rev. Jasper Adams, A.M., Principal of Charleston College." *Gospel Messenger, and Southern Episcopal Register* 3, no. 25 (Jan. 1826): 1-8.

"Sermon No. XV. A Sermon, Delivered in St. Philip's Church, Charleston, on Wednesday, May 10, 1826, at the Lecture founded by the Hon. Chief Justice Pinckney. By the Rev. Jasper Adams, A.M., Principal of Charleston College." *Gospel Messenger, and Southern Episcopal Register* 3, no. 32 (Aug. 1826): 225-34.

NOTES

1. John Adams and John Quincy Adams, distant cousins of Jasper Adams, are among the famous sons of this family. On the Adams family, see Andrew N. Adams, ed., *A Genealogical History of Henry Adams, of Braintree, Mass., and His Descendants; also John Adams, of Cambridge, Mass., 1632-1897* (Rutland, Vt.: Tuttle, 1898).

2. [Charles Cotesworth Pinckney], *The Sermon, Delivered at Pendleton, by the Rector of Christ Church, Greenville, on the Occasion of the Death of the Rev. Jasper Adams, D.D.* (Charleston, S.C.: A.E. Miller, 1842), p. 4 [172] (this sermon is reprinted in this volume as Appendix 4 and in *Charleston Gospel Messenger, and Protestant Episcopal Register* 18, no. 215 [Feb. 1842]: 321-25); E.O. Jameson, ed., *The History of Medway, Massachusetts, 1713-1885* (Providence, R.I.: J.A. and R.A. Reid, 1886), p. 335. For a brief sketch of the life of the Reverend Luther Wright, see Jameson, pp. 111-12, 442.

3. [Pinckney], *Sermon*, p. 4 [172]. According to the 1815 Brown University program of commencement exercises, Adams delivered a salutatory address.

4. Allen Johnson, ed., *Dictionary of American Biography*, vol. 1 (New York: Scribner's, 1928), p. 72, hereinafter cited as *DAB;* Jameson, *History of Medway*, p. 335.

5. *Historical Catalogue of Brown University, Providence, Rhode Island, 1764-1894* (Providence, R.I.: P.S. Remington, 1895), p. 65. See also Jameson, *History of Medway*, p. 336. The registers of graduates of both Yale University and Columbia University indicate that the degrees from these institutions were awarded *ad eundem gradum*. It was not uncommon for reputable colleges of this era, as an intercollegiate courtesy, to grant degrees *ad eundem gradum* to graduates in good standing from other colleges who applied and paid a fee for the "honorary" degree.

6. [Pinckney], *Sermon*, p. 4 [172].

7. J.H. Easterby, *A History of the College of Charleston, Founded 1770* (Charleston, S.C., 1935), pp. 74-77; Colyer Meriwether, *History of Higher Education in South Carolina* (Washington, D.C.: GPO, 1889; Spartanburg, S.C.: Reprint Co., 1972), pp. 58-59; *DAB* 1:72; and "A Historical Sketch of the College of Charleston, South Carolina," *American Quarterly Register* 12 (Nov. 1839): 169-72. The brief history of the college in the *American Quarterly Register,* according to Easterby, was "written, it seems certain, by Mr. Adams himself" (*History*, p. 74).

8. *The National Cyclopædia of American Biography*, vol. 12 (New York: James T. White and Co., 1904), p. 520.

9. For an unflattering assessment of Adams and his brief tenure as the first president of Geneva College, see Warren Hunting Smith, *Hobart and William Smith: The History of Two Colleges* (Geneva, N.Y.: Vail-Ballou, 1972), pp. 55-58.

10. Adams married Mercy D. Wheeler (1799-1821) of East Medway on 16 May 1820. She died eighteen months later, in November 1821, during their residence in Providence. Adams remarried in 1826. His second wife was Placidia Mayrant of Charleston. She died in September 1873 and was buried next to her husband in Pendleton, South Carolina.

11. Adams, as quoted in Easterby, *History,* p. 78.

12. The terms Adams set as conditions for his return are outlined in "Historical Sketch," pp. 172-73; Easterby, *History,* pp. 77-78.

13. Meriwether, *History of Higher Education,* pp. 59-60; *DAB* 1:72; *National Cyclopædia* 12:521. See also Easterby, *History,* pp. 78-89; "Historical Sketch," pp. 173-77.

14. Jasper Adams, *Elements of Moral Philosophy* (Cambridge, Mass.: Folsom, Wells and Thurston, 1837). For a brief discussion of Adams's contribution to nineteenth-

century literature on moral philosophy, see D.H. Meyer, *The Instructed Conscience: The Shaping of the American National Ethic* (Philadelphia: Univ. of Pennsylvania Press, 1972), pp. 71, 147-48.

15. Adams's family remained in Pendleton following his death in 1841. In July 1849 Jasper's daughter, Ann Richardson Adams (1828-50)—also known as Anzie—married Dr. John Caldwell Calhoun Jr. (1823-55), the son of the famous South Carolina statesman. The marriage was cut tragically short when Anzie died in childbirth in September 1850. See Ernest McPherson Lander Jr., *The Calhoun Family and Thomas Green Clemson: The Decline of a Southern Patriarchy* (Columbia, S.C.: Univ. of South Carolina Press, 1983); and Edwin H. Vedder, *Records of St. Pauls Episcopal Church of Pendleton, South Carolina* (Greenville, S.C.: A Press, 1982), pp. 37, 48, 124.

16. Adams's gravestone bears the following inscription:

JASPER ADAMS,
D.D, LL.D., F.R.S.
"NIL PATRIA HOC HABUISSE
VIRO PRAECLARIUS IN SE
NEC SANCTUM MAGIS, ET MIRUM,
CARUMQUE VIDETUR."
LUCRETIUS.

These lines from the poet Lucretius are translated: "The fatherland is seen to have had nothing in it more eminent than this man, nor anything more holy, admirable or beloved." Lucretius, *De Rerum Natura* 1.729-30.

17. *DAB* 1:72.

18. [Pinckney], *Sermon*, p. 6 [175]; emphasis in the original.

19. *History of Charleston College* (1896), quoted in *DAB* 1:72.

APPENDIX TWO

Obituary of the
Reverend Jasper Adams, D.D., from the
Pendleton Messenger, 12 November 1841

Died in the neighborhood of Pendleton [South Carolina], on the 25th of October, the Rev. JASPER ADAMS, D.D., after a few days illness, in the 48th year of his age. In the sudden and unexpected dissolution of this distinguished man; the Church of which he was an able Minister; his afflicted family and the community, upon whose affections he had and was still rapidly gaining have sustained an irreparable loss. Few have been called to fill more distinguished stations than Dr. Adams. He was first tutor and then Professor of Mathematics in Brown University; then President of the Charleston College; also of Geneva College in the State of N.Y.; afterward Chaplain and Professor of Moral Philosophy in the U.S. Academy, at West Point. His return to the State of his adoption and affection, was with the hope of raising the standard of literary attainment and of contributing as he was pre-eminently qualified, his aid in producing this desirable result. But in the inscrutable wisdom of Almighty God, this expectation was suddenly frustrated, and a bereaved family; an afflicted and weeping community, mourn over this grievous dispensation of God's righteous providence. Though denied the privilege of communicating to his distressed family his feelings in his last illness, we feel every assurance that his peace was made with God; his faith in Christ was genuine and unwavering, and his life Godly, righteous and sober. "Blessed are the dead who die in the Lord, yea even so saith the Spirit, for they rest from their labors and their works do follow them." May we bow in deep humility under this righteous dispensation, and by God's Grace be enabled to say with afflicted Job, "The Lord gave and the Lord hath taken away, blessed be the name of the Lord."

The grave of the Reverend Jasper Adams, St. Paul's Episcopal Church, Pendleton, South Carolina. Photograph courtesy of the Religion and Public Policy Research Fund.

APPENDIX THREE

The Sermon, Delivered at Pendleton, by the Rector of Christ Church, Greenville, on the Occasion of the Death of the Rev. Jasper Adams, D.D.

The following eulogy was published in 1842 by the printer A.E. Miller in Charleston, South Carolina. The rector of Christ Church, Greenville, was the Reverend Charles Cotesworth Pinckney (1812–98). The scion of a prominent Charleston family, Pinckney graduated first in his class from the College of Charleston in 1831, then under Jasper Adams's administration. In 1834 the college conferred a master's degree on him. He studied at Virginia Theological Seminary, Alexandria, and was ordained to the ministry of the Protestant Episcopal Church. During a long and distinguished ministry, he served as rector of St. James', Santee; Christ Church, Greenville; and Grace Church, Charleston. From 1866 to 1898 he was a trustee of the College of Charleston, which awarded him the honorary degrees of D.D. in 1877 and LL.D. in 1895. See J.H. Easterby, *A History of the College of Charleston, Founded 1770* (Charleston, S.C., 1935), pp. 263, 264, 332. Pinckney is best remembered as the author of *The Life of General Thomas Pinckney* (Boston: Houghton, Mifflin, 1895), a biography of his famous grandfather. See generally John Howard Brown, ed., *Lamb's Biographical Dictionary of the United States,* vol. 6 (Boston: Federal Book Co., 1903), p. 272; and Mabel L. Webber, comp., "The Thomas Pinckney Family of South Carolina," *South Carolina Historical and Genealogical Magazine* 39 (1938): 15–35.

II. *Kings,* xx. 1,
"AND THE PROPHET ISAIAH, THE SON OF AMOS, CAME TO HIM AND SAID UNTO HIM, THUS SAITH THE LORD, SET THINE HOUSE IN ORDER: FOR THOU SHALT DIE."

Thus spake the Lord to Hezekiah by the mouth of his servant Isaiah, and thus He speaks to us by His word and providence, daily reminding us of our mortality, and warning us by many a providential dispensation to "set our house in order"—to prepare to die. Yet it is a lesson to which we are slow to learn—a warning which we are most reluctant to take. We know that we must die: but how little do we realize the fact. There is but one thing certain to all the sons of men, but one future event which we can surely foretell. It is the certainty of our own death, and yet there are few improbabilities in life which we do not contemplate more than this only certainty on this side the grave! Though we see the ravages of death all

The Reverend Charles Cotesworth Pinckney.
Courtesy of the South Carolina Historical Society.

around: though we see generation giving place to generation, as wave suc-
ceeds wave; though we see, as we have lately seen, one taken from our midst
to swell the conscript band which death is daily gathering, yet how little do
we feel that we are floating with the wave—soon to break on the shores of
eternity—our names are already upon the conscript lists, and that at any
day, and at any hour, we may be summoned to join the pale army on its
march to the regions of the dead. We know these things: but how little do
we realize them!

In the whole compass of human duties, I know not one more difficult
than to realize the truth of our own mortality, and live in daily preparation
for that event. I know not a higher attainment in philosophy, or in religion,
than an habitual recollection of our "latter end," and an habitual "setting of
our house in order" for the reception of our Lord. I know nothing which
requires a more watchful, devotional spirit, than thus to make our life a
preparation for death, by daily doing, or daily leaving undone, what we
should wish performed or omitted when we stand before the judgment seat.

But difficult as is this duty, wisdom demands that it be done, and God
warns us to be "wise;" to "consider our latter end"—and as a means of in-
citing you to this duty, and of assisting you in its discharge, I would call
your attention to the recent instance of mortality in this congregation. So
sudden and unexpected a loss should not be passed by without notice, for it
is due to the living that this hasty summons should be improved—that this
warning voice, this *"memento mori"* should be laid to heart, that it may
strengthen us to "set our house in order"—to "prepare to meet our God"—
and it is due to the dead that some respect be paid to the memory of one,
who bore the sacred character of a Christian Minister—who has held many
important and honorable posts, and occupied no mean station in the ranks
of literature and learning. We should first give you a brief sketch of the life
of our deceased brother; then point out some truly commendable traits of
his character, and conclude with some practical reflections suggested by the
melancholy event.

The Rev. Jasper Adams, D.D., was born in East Midway [*sic*], Mass.,
in 1793. He was the son of a New-England farmer, and lived for the first
sixteen years of his life upon his father's farm, where he obtained a plain
English education. At seventeen years of age he determined to go to College, and begun his preparatory studies—and so diligent was his application, that he made sufficient progress in the Classics and Mathematics to
enter College the following year. He entered Brown University, (Providence,
R.I.) at eighteen, and completed his collegiate course there, taking the second appointment in his class.

It was during his residence in College that he adopted the religious
views which governed him through life—for, though educated a Presbyterian, he admitted the force of the Episcopal arguments, and when he felt
the duty of publicly joining the visible Church of Christianity, he united
himself to the Episcopal communion. It was there also that he decided on
his future course. He had designed studying medicine—but the religious
feelings which led him to the Church, led him to her ministry, and he resolved to qualify himself for its solemn duties. From College he removed
to Andover to pursue the study of divinity, and accepted the place of assis-
tant teacher in an Academy there for three years. Receiving an invitation

from Brown University, he removed there as tutor, and the following year was appointed Professor of Mathematics in that institution. About this time he was ordained Deacon in the Church of Christ by the Rt. Rev. Alexander Griswold, Bishop of the Eastern Diocese, and soon after received Priest's orders at the hands of the same venerable man.

He retained his situation in Brown University, until his removal to Charleston in 1824, to take charge of the College in that city. Not finding the state of the institution what he expected, he did not continue long in Charleston, but accepted an invitation to the Presidency of Geneva College in New-York. After spending eighteen months there, he was induced by the Trustees of the Charleston College to return to the Presidency of that institution, which had just been placed on a new footing. In consequence of this arrangement, he removed again to Carolina in 1827, and continued for nine years President of the College, which he succeeded in raising to a flourishing condition. Subsequent difficulties however led to his resignation of that post, and in the interval of leisure thus afforded, he completed and published a work which he had been for some time preparing, on Moral Philosophy. It appeared in 1837.

In the following year he was appointed Chaplain and Professor of Moral Philosophy in the United States Academy at West Point. He discharged the duties of this station for two years, and then returned to this State, and settled in this district just a twelvemonth since. He purposed devoting himself to the education of youth, and was contemplating the establishment of a large Episcopal school, after the plan of the Rev. Dr. Hawkes' in New-York. But death hath cut short his course, and frustrated all his earthly plans, and hurried him to the eternal world to give an account of his stewardship. Though the summons was sudden, we trust that it did not find him unprepared—for he had made his peace with God, we have reason to believe, and had a friend and "advocate at God's right hand," to plead his cause, and throw over his trembling soul that robe of spotless righteousness, in which alone the sinner can presume to stand the scrutiny of our final judge. For if he was "in Christ," then was he secure—"for there is no condemnation to them that are in Christ Jesus." Jesus has "borne their sins," and their penalty too. Jesus "has redeemed them," and "sanctified them, and justified" them. Jesus hath prepared for them a "mansion in his father's house," into which he will bring them, and they "shall enter in," and "sup with him, and he with them"—for he hath promised respecting all the sheep of his fold, that "no man shall pluck them out of his hand." This hope we trust and believe that our deceased brother possessed, and therefore we trust that death found him not unprepared—for though the warning was brief, and the time of his sickness short, yet we believe that he was a man who always thought much of death, and lived in habitual view of his "latter end," and it is a consolation to his friends to know that he expressed himself both ready and willing to die. Oh, the blessedness of such a frame of mind! Oh, the joy of such a hope in Jesus! "Blessed saith the Spirit, are the dead who die in the Lord"—and "blessed" says the Saviour "is that servant whom his Lord, when he cometh, shall find watching"—"Yea blessed is that servant." Thus speaks the Scripture, and great must be the blessing, "for I wot he whom thou blessest, is blest, and he whom thou cursest is curst."

Such is an outline of the life and death of our departed friend.

We next designed speaking of the deceased in the different relations which he sustained, as a minister, a teacher, and a friend of literature and learning. As a *preacher of righteousness,* Dr. Adams appears to have been acceptable to those under his ministry. Nevertheless in the providence of God he seems to have been but little called to the exercise of this office. Even since his ordination he has preached whenever and wherever his services were needed, rather in the way of the occasional supply, than as settled Pastor. The only Church of which he had pastoral charge, was St. Andrew's, near Charleston, of which he was Rector for two years, uniting his ministerial duties with the discharge of his other labors in the Charleston College. Several of the sermons which he delivered in Charleston were published by request of his auditors, and will well repay perusal. They all exhibit deep thought, and as might be expected from a man of so much research, embody a large store of useful information. In style they are plain, didactic and logical. But the opportunities which you had the last winter of listening to his discourses, while he occupied your pulpit, render it unnecessary for me to say more of his ministerial character.

As a teacher, I can say more of the deceased, for this was the occupation in which his life was spent. For nearly thirty years he has been an instructor of youth, and has had upwards of two thousand young men under his professional care. In this capacity I can speak with sincerity and with pleasure of Dr. Adams' fidelity and skill—for I speak from an experience of several years acquaintance as my instructor; when I say that he was the most *laborious, conscientious, painstaking,* and *successful* teacher I have ever met—and seldom did he fail in inducing those committed to his charge to make some progress in learning. Being himself most punctual and indefatigable, he was remarkably successful in inspiring even the languid and careless with a desire of improving their opportunities, and such was his patient perseverance towards the most reluctant scholar, that few could resist his efforts if they continued under his care.

His fidelity to his trust in this respect was worthy of all praise, for I know not an earthly employment which demands a larger share of perseverance and laborious self-denial, than the instruction of young men—and he who perseveres in a conscientious discharge of unthankful duty amidst discouragement and ill-success, exhibits the very highest degree of moral courage, and of honorable devotion to a confided trust.

That Dr. Adams possessed these requisites of a faithful teacher, I think would be cheerfully conceded by all who enjoyed the benefits of his instruction.

As a *writer* and a *man of letters,* Dr. A. also held a prominent place in our land. His labors in the acquisition and dispensation of knowledge are worthy of commemoration, for no man lives in vain who contributes any thing to the stock of human knowledge, or exerts an influence favorable to the progress of literature and useful learning. Such a man has done something for his generation. He has contributed to aid in the elevation, and improvement of humanity, and done his share in the advancement of his race towards that intellectual and moral perfection, which the philosopher hopes, and the Christian knows, we should yet attain upon earth. Dr. A's. literary character was calculated to produce this effect. His learning was extensive and profound—his thirst for knowledge very great—his information remarkably correct, and his research deep and indefatigable. Though he has written a great deal in the shape of lectures upon morals, history, constitutional and international law, he has not published much of his writings, with the exception of the sermons to which I have referred, upon the day of the total eclipse in 1834, upon the approach of a comet in 1835, and his Convention sermon on the connexions between Christianity and our civil government, (which is a valuable production,) and several addresses before literary bodies, his only published work is his treatise on Moral Philosophy—a work which does him credit in my estimation, for it bases the science of morals more decidedly than Paley has done, upon the only foundation on which they can ever rest—the *revelation of God's will by Jesus Christ.* It is a work of great labor and research, and entitles its author to a station among the learned of our land—and we shall regard its use as an evidence of an approximation towards a Christian standard of morality in our seats of learning.

If I were now asked what was the most prominent trait of Dr. A's. character, I should reply, *patient indefatigable industry.* He was a most faithful economist of time. In all my intercourse with him I never remember to have found him unemployed. He was always gathering or strewing; always acquiring or imparting knowledge, or stowing it away for future use. By this energy he gained whatever he possessed, for he was more indebted to his own efforts than to nature, for his literary acquisitions. Beginning his education at an advanced period, by faithful industry he became a distinguished scholar. As a student, a teacher, and a writer, he was most industrious and persevering—and in each relation of life, he exhibited a character for faithful perseverance in what he thought the path of duty, which may be held up to our imitation.

For this is unquestionably the most important ingredient in human character. It can accomplish more than all genius, and eloquence, and wealth. It is irresistible. It can remove mountains, conquer difficulties, attain all human blessings, and gain the kingdom of heaven—for in spiritual, as in temporal things, it is "the hand of the diligent that maketh rich"—and he who pursues any object with untiring energy and industry, will generally succeed as regards earthly things—always succeed as regards heavenly—for there are few attainments in science, or in religion, which cannot be gained by patient persevering industry in its pursuit.

But what avails these traits, or these acquirements? "There is one event which happeneth alike to all"—"the rich and the poor," the learned and the ignorant, "the wise man and the fool," all alike must die—neither riches, nor learning, nor health, can avoid the decree. "It is appointed unto all men once to die, and after this, the judgment"—"for we must all appear before the judgment seat of Christ, that every one may receive the things done in his body, whether they be good or bad"—death and judgment are the two themes on which this event shall preach to you. "Be ye also ready" is the language of that new made grave. Men and brethren, are ye ready? ready for death, ready for judgment, ready for heaven? Is your house set in order? Is your soul prepared for the Lord? Is sin cast out? Is every offence removed? Is every duty to God and man discharged? and your heart decked with holiness, and purity, and love? Is Christ your Saviour and your friend? Is heaven the home for which you sigh? and for which you are daily ripening? Are you habitually preparing, and habitually prepared, for death, for judgment, and eternity? Through these solemn scenes you soon must pass, to enter on eternal joy, or eternal woe. Seize, then, the present hour—lay hold upon "the rock, Christ Jesus"—"work out your own salvation with fear and trembling"—seek a robe of Jesus' sheltering righteousness—wrap it close around your naked soul—"Be ready." Hark! "Behold the bridegroom cometh"— ["]they that are ready, enter in, and the door is shut." Take heed, my brethren, lest ye be too late. "Now is the accepted time—now is the day of salvation[.]" "Be ye also ready"—keep your "lamps burning"—watch and pray for the day of the Lord, and it shall come with joy, not with sorrow— for the day of your death shall be to you the birth-day to life and salvation.

APPENDIX FOUR

The Publication and Distribution of Adams's Sermon

Bound into Jasper Adams's personal copy of the first printed edition of the sermon are his handwritten notes detailing the preparation, revision, publication, and distribution of the convention address.[1] These notes reveal that Adams consulted eminent jurists on technical legal points addressed in the sermon, and that he found their comments useful "in revising the sermon for the second edition," which was published in 1833, the same year as the first edition.[2] Adams also recounted the manner in which the tract had been distributed and, more important, to whom it had been sent. He meticulously reproduced endorsements soliciting comments on the printed sermon sent to prominent individuals. These notes provide a documentary history of the printed convention sermon and the national discussion it generated.

South Carolina Judge John Smythe Richardson recommended that the sermon be "widely disseminated . . . [as] the best antidote to the threatening spread of infidelity."[3] Toward that end, Judge Richardson, Charleston attorney Thomas Smith Grimké, and perhaps others contributed funds to publish and distribute the printed sermon. According to Adams's notes, the Society for the Advancement of Christianity in South Carolina sent copies to more than a hundred individuals.[4] The author sent copies to nearly a hundred additional institutions and individuals, including family members, personal friends, and faculty, trustees, and benefactors of the College of Charleston.[5]

The lists of recipients, according to Adrienne Koch, included "almost every important figure of the day."[6] Among those who received the sermon were the president and vice-president of the United States and former presidents and vice-presidents, members of the cabinet, influential members of Congress, and other public officials; justices of the U.S. Supreme Court, other federal and state jurists, and leading attorneys and constitutional commentators; prominent South Carolina politicians and establishment figures; scholars, writers, and intellectuals of national reputation; members of the clergy; College of Charleston trustees, faculty colleagues, alumni, and benefactors; and Adams's friends and family members. Many of the individuals

A page from Jasper Adams's handwritten notes listing the recipients of his printed sermon. Courtesy of the William L. Clements Library.

who received the sermon were prominent and influential leaders of the pro-liferating voluntary religious societies championed by evangelical Protes-tants, such as the American Bible Society, the American Tract Society, and various domestic and foreign missionary societies.

On the cover of copies sent to Mr. Madison and Chief Justice Marshall, Adams reported that he placed the following endorsement: "If it suits the much respected patriot & statesman to whom this is sent, to write the au-thor a few lines expressive of his opinion of the validity of the argument herein contained, it will be received as a distinguished favour."[7] Similar re-quests were extended to Justice Story and others.[8]

Adams copied out in full the comments he received from Madison, Marshall, Story, and Richardson and preserved this handwritten record an-nexed to his own copy of the sermon.[9] Of these letters, only a rough draft of Madison's letter has been previously published.[10] This draft, which dif-fers in some respects from Adams's version, was reprinted in Gaillard Hunt's edition of the collected papers of James Madison; however, it was misdated as written in "1832," and the recipient was identified only as "Rev. ———— Adams."[11] Hunt was apparently unaware of the context in which the letter was written.

Adams's meticulous handwritten notes on the preparation, publica-tion, and distribution of his sermon reveal a man with an eye on posterity. He clearly recognized the significance of the letters from Madison, Marshall, and Story and sought to preserve their statements on a controversial consti-tutional issue. He was also, no doubt, eager to document his own contribu-tion to the literature on church and state and his role in initiating this fruitful exchange of ideas. This collection of documents and Adams's notes provide a unique record of the evolving relationship between religion and politics in the early republic.

ADAMS'S LISTS OF THE RECIPIENTS OF HIS SERMON

Among Adams's handwritten notes bound into his personal copy of the first edition of the sermon are the following two lists of individuals and institutions that were sent a copy of the sermon.[12] The names below appear in the order that Adams placed them. Names that Adams abbreviated or may have misspelled are provided in the column on the right. Brackets have been used where Adams's handwriting is illegible and there is uncertainty about the proper transcription of a name. Question marks accompany a few names where it is thought Adams may have misstated a name or initial. Most of the individuals included in these lists are briefly identified in the col-umn on the right.[13] An effort was made to identify, first, the position held by the recipient in 1833 and, second, other notable posts and achievements for which the person is remembered. Inscriptions in Adams's hand on copies of the sermon preserved in various archives around the country indicate that Adams sent the sermon to individuals not included in these lists.

Adams reported that the "Society for the Advancement of Christianity in So. Carolina has sent copies to the following persons":[14]

Column One.

Andrew Jackson.	U.S. president (1829–37).
Martin Van Buren.	U.S. vice-president (1833–37), former member of the U.S. Senate from New York and U.S. secretary of state, and later U.S. president (1837–41).
Edward Livingston.	U.S. secretary of state, and former member of the U.S. House and Senate from Louisiana.
Levi Woodbury.	U.S. secretary of the navy, former member of the U.S. Senate from New Hampshire, and later U.S. secretary of the treasury and Associate Justice of the U.S. Supreme Court.
Louis McLane.	U.S. secretary of the treasury, former member of the U.S. House and Senate from Delaware, and later U.S. secretary of state.
Lewis Cass.	U.S. secretary of war, and later member of the U.S. Senate from Michigan and U.S. secretary of state.
Roger B. Taney.	U.S. attorney general, and later U.S. secretary of the treasury and Chief Justice of the U.S. Supreme Court.
Bishop William White.	Protestant Episcopal bishop of Pennsylvania.
" A.V. Griswold.	Alexander Viets Griswold, Protestant Episcopal bishop of the Eastern Diocese.
" T.C. Brownell.	Thomas Church Brownell, Protestant Episcopal bishop of Connecticut and president of Washington (Trinity) College.
" H.U. Onderdonk.	Henry U. Onderdonk, Protestant Episcopal bishop of Pennsylvania.
" Wm Meade.	William Meade, Protestant Episcopal bishop of Virginia.
" Wm M. Stone.	William M. Stone, Protestant Episcopal bishop of Maryland.
" B.T. Onderdonk.	Benjamin T. Onderdonk, Protestant Episcopal bishop of New York.

" Levi S. Ives.   Protestant Episcopal bishop of North Carolina.

" John H. Hopkins. John Henry Hopkins Jr., Protestant Episcopal bishop of Vermont.

" Benj. B. Smith.   Benjamin Bosworth Smith, Protestant Episcopal bishop of Kentucky.

" C.P. M'Ilvaine.   Charles P. McIlvaine, Protestant Episcopal bishop of Ohio and president of Kenyon College.

" G.W. Doane.   George Washington Doane, Protestant Episcopal bishop of New Jersey.

Daniel Webster.   Member of the U.S. Senate from Massachusetts, former member of the U.S. House, and later U.S. secretary of state.

C.C. Pinckney.   Charles Cotesworth Pinckney, lieutenant governor of South Carolina (1832–34) and College of Charleston trustee.

Judge David Johnson. South Carolina judge, and later governor of South Carolina (1846–48).

" Wm Harper.   William Harper, South Carolina judge and legislator, member of the U.S. Senate, and former Speaker of the South Carolina House (1828).

" J.B. O'Neale.   John Belton O'Neall, South Carolina judge, and former South Carolina legislator and Speaker of the South Carolina House (1824–28).

" Job Johnson.   Job Johnston, South Carolina judge.

Column 2

Judge Robt Gantt. Richard Gantt[?], South Carolina judge.

" B.[G.]   Baylis John Earle[?], South Carolina judge and legislator.

" Wm D. Martin.   William D. Martin, South Carolina judge, and former South Carolina legislator and member of the U.S. House.

" Josiah J. Evans.   South Carolina judge, former South Carolina legislator, and later member of the U.S. Senate.

R. Barnwell Smith.   Robert Barnwell Smith (Rhett), South Carolina attorney general, former South Carolina legislator, and later member of the U.S. House and Senate.

Waddy Thompson.   South Carolina legislator and judge, and later member of the U.S. House.

Thomas T. Player.   Thompson T. Player[?], South Carolina legislator.

F.H. Elmore.	Franklin H. Elmore, solicitor for the southern circuit (South Carolina), and later member of the U.S. House and Senate from South Carolina.
Henry Deas.	South Carolina legislator and College of Charleston trustee.
Rich. Cunningham.	Richard Cunningham, South Carolina legislator.
Henry L. Pinckney.	Henry Laurens Pinckney, South Carolina legislator, Speaker of the South Carolina House (1830–33), member of the U.S. House, and College of Charleston trustee.
Rich^d [J.] Manning.	Richard Irvine Manning[?], South Carolina legislator, former governor of South Carolina (1824–26), and later member of the U.S. House.
Angus Patterson.	South Carolina legislator.
James Chesnut.	South Carolina legislator.
Robt B. Campbell.	Robert Blair Campbell, South Carolina legislator, and later member of the U.S. House.
A.P. Butler.	Andrew Pickens Butler, South Carolina legislator, and later South Carolina judge and member of the U.S. Senate.
Wm R. Hill.	William Randolph Hill, South Carolina legislator.
Jacob Axson.	South Carolina legislator, judge, and College of Charleston trustee.
L.E. Dawson.	Laurence Edwin Dawson, South Carolina legislator.
Peter W. Fraser.	Peter William Fraser, South Carolina legislator.
J.W. Phillips.	
J.S. Richardson.	John Smythe Richardson, South Carolina judge, and former South Carolina legislator, Speaker of the South Carolina House (1810), and South Carolina attorney general.
Samuel Bacot.	South Carolina legislator.
Patrick Noble.	South Carolina legislator, Speaker of the South Carolina House (1818–23, 1833–35), lieutenant governor (1830–32), and later governor of South Carolina (1838–40).
D.L. Wardlaw.	David Lewis Wardlaw, South Carolina legislator and judge, and later Speaker of the South Carolina House (1836–41).
W.A. Bull.	William A. Bull, South Carolina legislator, and former lieutenant governor of South Carolina (1824–26).

Column 3

J.H. Harrison. — John Hampton Harrison, South Carolina legislator.

Fred. A. Porcher. — Frederick Augustus Porcher, South Carolina legislator.

Thos. Pinckney. — Thomas Pinckney, South Carolina legislator and College of Charleston trustee.

Thos. W. Boone. — Thomas W. Boone.

John C. Calhoun. — Member of the U.S. Senate from South Carolina, former U.S. vice-president (1825–32), and later U.S. secretary of state.

Wm C. Preston. — William Campbell Preston, South Carolina legislator, and later member of the U.S. Senate and president of South Carolina College.

[Jas. K. Erving]. [K.B.] Montgomery. — James K. Ervin[?], South Carolina legislator.

A.F. Pay. — Austin Ford Peay[?], South Carolina legislator.

Stephen D. Miller. — Member of the U.S. Senate from South Carolina, and former South Carolina legislator, member of the U.S. House, and governor of South Carolina (1828–30).

J.O. Dunovant. — John Dunovant[?], South Carolina legislator.

William Rice. — South Carolina legislator and College of Charleston trustee.

F.W. Higgins. — Francis Bernard Higgins[?], South Carolina legislator.

Turner Richardson. — South Carolina legislator.

John Dodd. — South Carolina legislator.

Robt. Barnwell. — Robert Woodward Barnwell, member of the U.S. House from South Carolina, former South Carolina legislator, and later president of South Carolina College and member of the U.S. Senate and the Confederate Senate.

Thos. R. Mitchell. — Thomas R. Mitchell, member of the U.S. House from South Carolina.

J.[W. Felder]. — John Myers Felder[?], member of the U.S. House from South Carolina, and former South Carolina legislator.

George McDuffie. — Member of the U.S. House from South Carolina, and later governor of South Carolina (1834–36) and member of the U.S. Senate.

Warren R. Davis.	Warren Ransom Davis, member of the U.S. House from South Carolina.
Wm C. Nuckolls.	William T. Nuckolls[?], member of the U.S. House from South Carolina.
James Blair.	Member of the U.S. House from South Carolina.
J.K. Griffin.	John King Griffin, member of the U.S. House from South Carolina, and former South Carolina legislator.
S. Hammond.	Samuel Hammond[?], South Carolina secretary of state, and former member of the U.S. House from Georgia.
R.J. Turnbull.	Robert James Turnbull, South Carolina leader of the nullification and states' rights movements, and College of Charleston trustee.
James Hamilton.	James Hamilton Jr., College of Charleston trustee, and former South Carolina legislator, member of the U.S. House, and governor of South Carolina (1830–32).
Ed^d R. Laurens.	Edward Rutledge Laurens, South Carolina legislator.
Wm Johnson.	William Johnson, Associate Justice of the U.S. Supreme Court.
[Daniel] E. Huger.	Daniel Elliot Huger, former South Carolina legislator, judge, College of Charleston trustee, and later member of the U.S. Senate from South Carolina.

Column 4

Gabriel Duval.	Associate Justice of the U.S. Supreme Court.
Smith Thompson.	Associate Justice of the U.S. Supreme Court.
John McLean.	Associate Justice of the U.S. Supreme Court.
Henry Potter.	U.S. district judge.
Jeremiah Cuyler.	U.S. district judge.
Thomas Randall.	U.S. district judge.
James Webb.	U.S. district judge.
J.Q. Adams.	John Quincy Adams, member of the U.S. House from Massachusetts, and former U.S. president (1825–29) and U.S. secretary of state.
Josiah Quincy.	President of Harvard University, and former Massachusetts legislator and member of the U.S. House from Massachusetts.

Richd M. Johnson.	Richard M. Johnson, member of the U.S. House from Kentucky, former member of the U.S. Senate, and later U.S. vice-president (1837–41).
Peleg Sprague.	Member of the U.S. Senate from Maine, and former member of the U.S. House from Maine.
Wilson Lumpkin.	Governor of Georgia (1831–35), former member of the U.S. House from Georgia, and later member of the U.S. Senate.
Levi Lincoln.	Governor of Massachusetts (1825–34), and later member of the U.S. House from Massachusetts.
Prentiss Mellen.	Chief Justice of the Maine Supreme Court, and former member of the U.S. Senate from Massachusetts.
Samuel Dinsmoor.	Governor of New Hampshire (1831–34), and former member of the U.S. House from New Hampshire.
Wm M. Richardson.	William M. Richardson, Chief Justice of the New Hampshire Supreme Court, and former member of the U.S. House from Massachusetts.
Lemuel Shaw.	Chief Justice of the Massachusetts Supreme Court.
Artemas Ward.	Chief Justice of the Massachusetts Court of Common Pleas, and former member of the U.S. House from Massachusetts.
Peter O. Thacher.	Peter Oxenbridge Thacher, Boston municipal court judge.
Reuben H. Walworth.	New York chancellor, and former member of the U.S. House from New York.
John Savage.	Chief Justice of the New York Supreme Court, and former member of the U.S. House from New York and federal prosecutor.
William Cranch.	Chief Judge of the U.S. Circuit Court for the District of Columbia.
William Rawle.	Attorney, former federal prosecutor in Pennsylvania, and constitutional commentator.
Wm Meredith.	William Meredith, Pennsylvania legislator, and later a federal prosecutor, state attorney general, and U.S. secretary of the treasury.
John Sergeant.	Member of the U.S. House from Pennsylvania.
P.S. Du Ponceau.	Peter Stephen Du Ponceau, Philadelphia attorney and constitutional commentator.
Nicholas Biddle.	President of U.S. Bank.

Joseph Hopkinson.	U.S. district judge, and former member of the U.S. House from Pennsylvania.
James Kent.	New York chancellor, former Chief Justice of the Supreme Court of Errors and Appeals of New York, and noted legal scholar.
Ste^n van Rensalaer.	Stephen van Rensselaer, New York militia leader, legislator, educator, and former member of the U.S. House from New York.
William Wirt.	Former U.S. attorney general and federal prosecutor.
Thos. McAuley.	Thomas McAuley, Presbyterian clergyman.
[Jno.] B. Francis.	John Brown Francis[?], Governor of Rhode Island (1833–38), and later member of the U.S. Senate.
[Jno. P.] Richardson.	John Peter Richardson[?], South Carolina legislator, and later member of the U.S. House and governor of South Carolina (1840–42).
H.W. De Saussure.	Henry William DeSaussure, South Carolina judge and College of Charleston trustee.
Henry Clay.	Member of the U.S. Senate from Kentucky, and former Speaker of the U.S. House and U.S. secretary of state.
William Drayton.	Member of the U.S. House from South Carolina and College of Charleston trustee (president).
Joseph Story.	Associate Justice of the U.S. Supreme Court and noted legal scholar.
John Marshall.	Chief Justice of the U.S. Supreme Court.
Horace Binney.	Member of the U.S. House from Pennsylvania and constitutional attorney.
Elihu H. Bay.	Elihu Hall Bay, South Carolina judge and attorney general.
James H. Smith.	James H. Smith (Rhett), South Carolina legislator and College of Charleston trustee.
James L. Petigru.	Leader of South Carolina Union Party, College of Charleston trustee, and former South Carolina legislator and South Carolina attorney general.

Column 5

Adams further reported that he sent copies of the sermon to the following persons and institutions. Many individuals on this list were family members, personal friends, faculty colleagues, or supporters of the College of Charleston.[15]

William E. Bailey.	College of Charleston faculty member.
Stephen Lee.	College of Charleston faculty member.
Charles B. Cochran.	College of Charleston faculty member.
Henry M. Bruns.	College of Charleston faculty member.
Oliver M. Smith.	College of Charleston faculty member.
[Samuel] A. Burns.	College of Charleston faculty member.
Thomas S. Grimkè.	Thomas Smith Grimké, Charleston attorney, College of Charleston trustee, and former South Carolina legislator.
Robert Y. Hayne.	Governor of South Carolina (1832–34), and former member of the U.S. Senate, Speaker of the South Carolina House (1818), and College of Charleston trustee.
Dr John Dickson.	College of Charleston faculty member.
Dr James [Manning].	
Mrs Ann Mayrant.	
[Samuel] Mayrant.	Brother of Adams's second wife.
Col. James Gadsden.	Diplomat.
John G. Polhill.	Associate Justice of the Georgia Supreme Court (and Adams's former classmate at Brown University).
University of Georgia.	
University of Alibama.	University of Alabama.
Charleston Lib. Society.	Charleston Library Society.
University of N. Carolina.	University of North Carolina.
Joseph E. Worcester.	Joseph Emerson Worcester, lexicographer and publisher.
Miss Anna Adams.	Adams's sister.
[Rev^d McGoodwin].	
Lewis Wheeler.	Father of Adams's first wife.
Miss M.S. Quincy.	
James C. Courtenay.	College of Charleston faculty member.
Sewall Harding.	Congregationalist clergyman in Waltham and Medway, Massachusetts (Adams and Harding married sisters, and they were contemporaries at Brown University).
Samuel [Toney].	
B.B. Edwards.	Bela Bates Edwards, editor of *American Quarterly Register,* and later professor of sacred literature at Andover Theological Seminary.
Joseph Clarke.	
Joshua W. Toomer.	South Carolina legislator and College of Charleston trustee.

Charles Fraser.	Charleston attorney and College of Charleston trustee (secretary and treasurer).
Frances Moore.	
James S. Guiguiard.	Cousin of Adams's second wife.
Mrs Wm Lowndes.	
[ ].	
[Rev. Mc Bragg].	
William Lloyd.	
Mrs Louisa McAllister.	
Henry Middleton.	Former South Carolina legislator, governor of South Carolina (1810–12), member of the U.S. House, diplomat, and College of Charleston trustee.

Column 6

Horatio Mason.	Husband of Adams's sister.
Thomas R. Dew.	Professor of history, metaphysics, and political economy, and later president of the College of William and Mary.
Alvan Bond.	Congregationalist clergyman and professor of sacred literature at Theological Seminary, Bangor, Maine (and Adams's former classmate at Brown University).
Dr Thomas [Sowalls].	
William Ruggles.	Professor of mathematics at Columbian College in the District of Columbia.
James Watson Williams.	New York attorney and journalist, and later mayor of Utica, New York (and Adams's former student at Geneva College).
Furman Theo. Seminary.	Furman Theological Seminary.
Luther Wright.	Congregationalist clergyman in Medway, Massachusetts (and Adams's secondary school tutor).
Moses Stuart.	Professor of sacred literature at Andover Theological Seminary.
Library of And^r Seminary.	Library of Andover Seminary.
Library of Yale College.	
Alexandria Seminary.	
Harvard University.	
N. York P.E. Theo. Seminary.	New York Protestant Episcopal Theological Seminary.
Joseph W. [F? —].	

N.B. Crocker.   Nathan Bourne Crocker, Rector of St. John's
                         Church in Providence, Rhode Island, and trustee
                         of Brown University.
Romeo Elton.   Professor of Latin and Greek at Brown Univer-
                         sity and Baptist clergyman (and Adams's contem-
                         porary at Brown University).
Wᵐ G. Goddard.   William Giles Goddard, professor of moral phi-
                         losophy and metaphysics at Brown University.
Francis Wayland.   President of Brown University, Baptist clergyman,
                         and influential moral philosopher.
Miss Lucy [Ann Lippitt].
Presᵗ Nathan Lord.   President Nathan Lord, president of Dartmouth
                         College and Congregationalist clergyman.
Dartmouth College.
Amherst College.
Bowdoin College.
Williams College.
Washington College [Ct.].
Wesleyan University.
Columbia College, N.Y.
John Pott[er].
Princeton College.
Union College.
Geneva College.
Kenyon College.
Mʳˢ Eliza Francis.
Josiah W. Gibbs.   Librarian and professor of sacred literature at Yale
                         College.
University of Vermont.
Middlebury College.
University of Pennsylvania.
Luther Bailey.   Congregationalist clergyman in Medway, Massa-
                         chusetts.
Philadelphia Library.
Mass. Hist. Society.   Massachusetts Historical Society.
Nicholas Brown.   Brown University trustee and the university's
                         most famous benefactor.
Bowen Adams.   Adams's brother.
Elizabeth Big[e]low.   Adams's sister.
Miss Lightwood.
Columbia Theo. Sem-
     inary.   Columbia Theological Seminary.

NOTES

1. Jasper Adams's personal copy of the first printed edition of his sermon and the attached handwritten notes are located in the William L. Clements Library, University of Michigan. (References to the handwritten material bound into Adams's copy of the sermon are hereinafter cited as Author's Notes.)

Richard W. Ryan, curator of books at the Clements Library, noted: "Both the outside wrapper (bound in) and the title page are included with this [Adams's printed sermon]. You will note that the handwriting at the top of the wrapper resembles that of the manuscript pages. The notation '1st ed. the author's own copy' at the bottom of this page is in another hand." Letter from Richard W. Ryan to Daniel L. Dreisbach, 17 Sept. 1991.

2. Author's Notes, p. 10. This statement was made in reference to "10 pages of foolscap [written by Thomas Smith Grimké to Adams], containing comments on the text & notes of this sermon. Some of these comments are somewhat severe," Adams reported, "but they were written with the most friendly intentions" (Author's Notes, p. 10). Adams had earlier noted that Grimké, a respected attorney in South Carolina, had criticized him for his mistaken interpretation of the relation of the South Carolina "constitution of 1790 to that of 1778" (Author's Notes, p. 8). Therefore, Adams requested Judge J.S. Richardson and Justice Story to offer their opinions on this legal point. Adams copied out in full the responses from Richardson and Story.

Adams also reported that "Randall [sic] Hunt, Esq. sent for my inspection, a letter containing 29 pages of letter paper, closely written, controverting the chief positions of the sermon." According to Adams, Hunt's arguments accorded with the views of Thomas Jefferson and Thomas Cooper (Author's Notes, p. 9).

The few substantive differences between the first and second editions of the sermon are mainly in Adams's copious notes.

3. Letter from J.S. Richardson to Jasper Adams, 21 March 1833, Author's Notes, pp. 1-2 [121].

4. The history and mission of the society is described in Albert Sidney Thomas, "The Protestant Episcopal Society for the Advancement of Christianity in South Carolina," *Historical Magazine of the Protestant Episcopal Church* 21 (Dec. 1952): 447-60.

5. Adams's lists of the recipients of the sermon appear at the end of this Appendix.

6. Adrienne Koch, *Madison's "Advice to My Country"* (Princeton, N.J.: Princeton Univ. Press, 1966), p. 43.

7. Author's Notes, p. 15.

8. Adams indicated that he specifically requested Justice Story to address several technical legal points concerning constitutional interpretation. Author's Notes, p. 8.

Adams also sent a copy of the printed sermon to Horace Binney, an eminent Philadelphia attorney and a leading authority on constitutional law. In return for the sermon, Binney was requested to send to Adams a copy of his eulogy for Chief Justice Tilghman of the Pennsylvania Supreme Court. "After some time," Adams reported, "a copy of the Eulogium was received with this endorsement. 'Revᵈ J. Adams, D.D. from the author, a very inadequate return for the "Convention Sermon," full of striking & profound reflections upon a subject of increasing interest to every Christian Patriot in the United States'" (Author's Notes, p. 1).

9. Adams also reproduced a letter from James Watson Williams requesting a copy of the sermon and portions of letters from Thomas Smith Grimké and Mrs. Eliza Francis, wife of Dr. John W. Francis of New York.

10. Marshall's letter is cataloged in Irwin S. Rhodes, *The Papers of John Marshall: A Descriptive Calendar,* vol. 2 (Norman: Univ. of Oklahoma Press, 1969), p. 417.

11. Gaillard Hunt, ed., *The Writings of James Madison,* 9 vols. (New York: G.P. Putnam's Sons, 1900-1910), 9:484-88. Hunt identified the source of this manuscript as the Chicago Historical Society. The society's Archives and Manuscript Department, however, has no record that this letter was ever in its collection. The Library of Congress does have a rough draft of this letter in its Madison Papers that corresponds with Hunt's version and may have been purchased from the Chicago Historical Society. See James Madison Papers, Manuscript Division, Library of Congress.

12. Author's Notes, pp. 10-11.

13. Biographical information on many individuals included in these lists was gleaned from leading dictionaries and encyclopedias of American biography, including the *Dictionary of American Biography, Appletons' Cyclopædia of American Biography, The National Cyclopædia of American Biography,* and *Who Was Who in America: Historical Volume, 1607-1896.* Useful sources for biographical information on South Carolina legislators of this era are Emily Bellinger Reynolds and Joan Reynolds Faunt, eds., *Biographical Directory of the Senate of South Carolina, 1776-1964* (Columbia: South Carolina Archives Department, 1964); N. Louise Bailey, Mary L. Morgan, and Carolyn R. Taylor, *Biographical Directory of the South Carolina Senate, 1776-1985,* 3 vols. (Columbia: Univ. of South Carolina Press, 1986); and Alexander Moore, ed., *Biographical Directory of the South Carolina House of Representatives,* vol. 4, *1816-1828* (Columbia: South Carolina Department of Archives and History, 1992). John Belton O'Neall's *Biographical Sketches of the Bench and Bar of South Carolina,* 2 vols. (Charleston, S.C.: S.G. Courtenay and Co., 1859), is an excellent source for information on South Carolina judges.

14. Author's Notes, p. 10.

15. For comprehensive lists of College of Charleston trustees, administrators, faculty, and students, see J.H. Easterby, *A History of the College of Charleston, Founded 1770* (Charleston, S.C., 1935).

SELECTED BIBLIOGRAPHY

There is an extensive body of scholarly works on religion and politics in America. A variety of perspectives, emphases, and disciplines have enriched this literature. The following is a bibliography of selected works on the history of religion and religious liberty in America from colonial times to the mid–nineteenth century and on the social and intellectual forces that shaped political culture and church-state relations in the early republic. Emphasis has been placed on the ample scholarship that examines the framing of the First Amendment provisions governing the relations between religion and civil government in the United States. For a comprehensive bibliography of works on church and state in the colonial and early national periods, see John F. Wilson's edited volume *Church and State in America: A Bibliographical Guide* (1986).

Abzug, Robert H. *Cosmos Crumbling: American Reform and the Religious Imagination.* New York: Oxford Univ. Press, 1994.

Adams, Arlin M., and Charles J. Emmerich. *A Nation Dedicated to Religious Liberty: The Constitutional Heritage of the Religion Clauses.* Philadelphia: Univ. of Pennsylvania Press, 1990.

———. "William Penn and the American Heritage of Religious Liberty." *Journal of Law and Religion* 8 (1990): 57-70.

Adams, Jasper. *The Relation of Christianity to Civil Government in the United States. A Sermon, Preached in St. Michael's Church, Charleston, February 13th, 1833, before the Convention of the Protestant Episcopal Church of the Diocese of South-Carolina.* 2d ed. Charleston, S.C.: A.E. Miller, 1833.

Ahlstrom, Sydney E. *A Religious History of the American People.* New Haven, Conn.: Yale Univ. Press, 1972.

Albanese, Catherine L. *Sons of the Fathers: The Civil Religion of the American Revolution.* Philadelphia: Temple Univ. Press, 1976.

Aldrich, P. Emory. "The Christian Religion and the Common Law." *American Antiquarian Society Proceedings* 6 (April 1889–April 1890): 18-37.

Alley, Robert S., ed. *James Madison on Religious Liberty.* Buffalo, N.Y.: Prometheus, 1985.

Amos, Gary T. *Defending the Declaration: How the Bible and Christianity Influenced the Writing of the Declaration of Independence.* Brentwood, Tenn.: Wolgemuth and Hyatt, 1989.

Anderson, M.B. "Relations of Christianity to the Common Law." *Albany Law Journal* 20 (4 Oct. 1879): 265-68, (11 Oct. 1879): 285-88.

Antieau, Chester James, Phillip Mark Carroll, and Thomas Carroll Burke. *Religion under the State Constitutions.* Brooklyn, N.Y.: Central Book Co., 1965.

Antieau, Chester James, Arthur T. Downey, and Edward C. Roberts. *Freedom from*

Federal Establishment: Formation and Early History of the First Amendment Religion Clauses. Milwaukee: Bruce, 1964.

Bailyn, Bernard, ed. *The Ideological Origins of the American Revolution.* Cambridge, Mass.: Belknap Press of Harvard Univ. Press, 1967.

———, ed. *Pamphlets of the American Revolution, 1750-1776.* Vol. 1, *1750-1765.* Cambridge, Mass.: Belknap Press of Harvard Univ. Press, 1965.

Bainton, Roland H. *The Travail of Religious Liberty.* New York: Harper and Brothers, 1951.

Baird, Robert. *Religion in America; or, An Account of the Origin, Progress, Relation to the State, and Present Condition of the Evangelical Churches in the United States. With Notices of the Unevangelical Denominations.* New York: Harper and Brothers, 1844.

Baker, John S., Jr. "The Establishment Clause as Intended: No Preference among Sects and Pluralism in a Large Commercial Republic." In *The Bill of Rights: Original Meaning and Current Understanding,* edited by Eugene W. Hickok Jr. Charlottesville: Univ. Press of Virginia, 1991.

———. "James Madison and Religious Freedom." *Benchmark* 3, nos. 1-2 (1987): 71-78.

Baldwin, Alice M. *The New England Clergy and the American Revolution.* Durham, N.C.: Duke Univ. Press, 1928.

Banning, Lance. "James Madison, the Statute for Religious Freedom, and the Crisis of Republican Convictions." In *The Virginia Statute for Religious Freedom: Its Evolution and Consequences in American History,* edited by Merrill D. Peterson and Robert C. Vaughan. New York: Cambridge Univ. Press, 1988.

Bellah, Robert N. "Civil Religion in America." *Daedalus: Journal of the American Academy of Arts and Sciences* 96 (Winter 1967): 1-21.

———. "The Revolution and Civil Religion." In *Religion and the American Revolution,* edited by Jerald C. Brauer. Philadelphia: Fortress, 1976.

Bercovitch, Sacvan. *The American Jeremiad.* Madison: Univ. of Wisconsin Press, 1978.

Berman, Harold J. "Religion and Law: The First Amendment in Historical Perspective." *Emory Law Journal* 35 (1986): 777-93.

Berns, Walter. *The First Amendment and the Future of American Democracy.* New York: Basic, 1976.

Beth, Loren P. *The American Theory of Church and State.* Gainesville: Univ. of Florida Press, 1958.

Billington, Ray Allen. *The Protestant Crusade, 1800-1860: A Study of the Origins of American Nativism.* New York: Macmillan, 1938; New York: Rinehart, 1952.

Blakely, William Addison, ed. *American State Papers on Freedom in Religion.* 3d ed. Washington, D.C.: Religious Liberty Association, 1943.

Blau, Joseph L. "'The Christian Party in Politics.'" *Review of Religion* 11 (1946-47): 18-35.

———. "The Wall of Separation." *Union Seminary Quarterly Review* 38 (1984): 263-88.

Bodo, John R. *The Protestant Clergy and Public Issues, 1812-1848.* Princeton, N.J.: Princeton Univ. Press, 1954; Philadelphia: Porcupine, 1980.

Boles, John. *The Great Revival, 1787-1805: The Origins of the Southern Evangelical Mind.* Lexington: Univ. Press of Kentucky, 1972.

Boller, Paul F., Jr. "George Washington and Religious Liberty." *William and Mary Quarterly,* 3d ser., 17 (1960): 486-506.

Bonomi, Patricia U. *Under the Cope of Heaven: Religion, Society, and Politics in Colonial America.* New York: Oxford Univ. Press, 1986.

Borden, Morton. "Federalists, Antifederalists, and Religious Freedom." *Journal of Church and State* 21 (1979): 469-82.

———. *Jews, Turks, and Infidels*. Chapel Hill: Univ. of North Carolina Press, 1984.

Botein, Stephen. "Religious Dimensions of the Early American State." In *Beyond Confederation: Origins of the Constitution and American National Identity*, edited by Richard Beeman, Stephen Botein, and Edward C. Carter II. Chapel Hill: Univ. of North Carolina Press, 1987.

Bradford, M.E. *Founding Fathers: Brief Lives of the Framers of the United States Constitution*. 2d ed., rev. Lawrence: Univ. Press of Kansas, 1994.

———. "Religion and the Framers: The Biographical Evidence." *Benchmark* 4, no. 4 (1990): 349-58.

Bradley, Gerard V. "Beguiled: Free Exercise Exemptions and the Siren Song of Liberalism." *Hofstra Law Review* 20 (1991): 245-319.

———. *Church-State Relationships in America*. Westport, Conn.: Greenwood, 1987.

———. "Imagining the Past and Remembering the Future: The Supreme Court's History of the Establishment Clause." *Connecticut Law Review* 18 (1986): 827-43.

———. "The No Religious Test Clause and the Constitution of Religious Liberty: A Machine That Has Gone of Itself." *Case Western Reserve Law Review* 37 (1987): 674-747.

Brady, Joseph H. *Confusion Twice Confounded: The First Amendment and the Supreme Court*. South Orange, N.J.: Seton Hall Univ. Press, 1954.

Brann, Eva T.H. "Madison's 'Memorial and Remonstrance': A Model of American Eloquence." In *Rhetoric and American Statesmanship*, edited by Glen E. Thurow and Jeffrey D. Wallin. Durham, N.C.: Carolina Academic Press, 1984.

Brant, Irving. *The Bill of Rights: Its Origin and Meaning*. Indianapolis: Bobbs-Merrill, 1965.

———. "Madison: On the Separation of Church and State." *William and Mary Quarterly*, 3d ser., 8 (1951): 3-24.

Brauer, Jerald C., ed. *Religion and the American Revolution*. Philadelphia: Fortress, 1976.

Breen, T.H. *The Character of the Good Ruler: A Study of Puritan Political Ideas in New England, 1630-1730*. New Haven, Conn.: Yale Univ. Press, 1970.

Brewer, David J. *The United States a Christian Nation*. Philadelphia: John C. Winston, 1905.

Bridenbaugh, Carl. *Mitre and Sceptre: Transatlantic Faiths, Ideas, Personalities, and Politics, 1689-1775*. New York: Oxford Univ. Press, 1962.

Bronner, Frederick L. "The Observance of the Sabbath in the United States, 1800-1865." Ph.D. diss., Harvard Univ., 1937.

Buckley, Thomas E. *Church and State in Revolutionary Virginia, 1776-1787*. Charlottesville: Univ. Press of Virginia, 1977.

Butler, Jon. *Awash in a Sea of Faith: Christianizing the American People*. Cambridge, Mass.: Harvard Univ. Press, 1990.

Butts, R. Freeman. *The American Tradition in Religion and Education*. Boston: Beacon, 1950.

Calhoon, Robert M. *Evangelicals and Conservatives in the Early South, 1740-1861*. Columbia: Univ. of South Carolina Press, 1988.

Carmody, Denise Lardner, and John Tully Carmody. *The Republic of Many Mansions: Foundations of American Religious Thought*. New York: Paragon House, 1990.

Carroll, Peter N., ed. *Religion and the Coming of the American Revolution*. Waltham, Mass.: Ginn-Blaisdell, 1970.

Carwardine, Richard J. *Evangelicals and Politics in Antebellum America*. New Haven, Conn.: Yale Univ. Press, 1993.

Cherry, Conrad, ed. *God's New Israel: Religious Interpretations of American Destiny.* Englewood Cliffs, N.J.: Prentice-Hall, 1971.

Clebsch, William A. *From Sacred to Profane America: The Role of Religion in American History.* New York: Harper and Row, 1968.

Cobb, Sanford. *The Rise of Religious Liberty in America: A History.* New York: Macmillan, 1902.

Conkin, Paul K. *The Uneasy Center: Reformed Christianity in Antebellum America.* Chapel Hill: Univ. of North Carolina Press, 1994.

"Constitutional Fiction: An Analysis of the Supreme Court's Interpretation of the Religion Clauses." *Louisiana Law Review* 47 (1986): 169-98.

Cord, Robert L. "Church-State Separation: Restoring the 'No Preference' Doctrine of the First Amendment." *Harvard Journal of Law and Public Policy* 9 (1986): 129-72.

———. "Original Intent Jurisprudence and Madison's 'Detached Memoranda.'" *Benchmark* 3, nos. 1-2 (1987): 79-85.

———. *Separation of Church and State: Historical Fact and Current Fiction.* New York: Lambeth, 1982.

Cornelison, Isaac A. *The Relation of Religion to Civil Government in the United States of America: A State without a Church, but not without a Religion.* New York: G.P. Putnam's Sons, 1895.

Corwin, Edward S. "The 'Higher Law' Background of American Constitutional Law." *Harvard Law Review* 42 (1928-29): 149-85, 365-409.

———. "The Supreme Court as National School Board." *Law and Contemporary Problems* 14 (1949): 3-22.

Costanzo, Joseph F. "Religious Heritage of American Democracy." *Thought* 30 (Winter 1955-56): 485-506.

———. *This Nation under God: Church, State and Schools in America.* New York: Herder and Herder, 1964.

Cousins, Norman, ed. *"In God We Trust": The Religious Beliefs and Ideas of the American Founding Fathers.* New York: Harper and Brothers, 1958.

Curry, Thomas J. *The First Freedoms: Church and State in America to the Passage of the First Amendment.* New York: Oxford Univ. Press, 1986.

De Jong, Norman. "Separation of Church and State: Historical Reality or Judicial Myth?" *Fides et Historia* 18, no. 1 (Jan. 1986): 25-37.

De Jong, Norman, with Jack Van Der Slik. *Separation of Church and State: The Myth Revisited.* Jordan Station, Ontario, Canada: Paideia, 1985.

Drakeman, Donald L. *Church-State Constitutional Issues: Making Sense of the Establishment Clause.* Westport, Conn.: Greenwood, 1991.

———. "Religion and the Republic: James Madison and the First Amendment." *Journal of Church and State* 25 (1983): 427-45.

Dreisbach, Daniel L. "A New Perspective on Jefferson's Views on Church-State Relations: The Virginia Statute for Establishing Religious Freedom in Its Legislative Context." *American Journal of Legal History* 35 (1991): 172-204.

———. *Real Threat and Mere Shadow: Religious Liberty and the First Amendment.* Westchester, Ill.: Crossway, 1987.

———. "Thomas Jefferson and Bills Number 82-86 of the Revision of the Laws of Virginia, 1776-1786: New Light on the Jeffersonian Model of Church-State Relations." *North Carolina Law Review* 69 (1990): 159-211.

Dunn, Charles W., ed. *American Political Theology: Historical Perspective and Theoretical Analysis.* New York: Praeger, 1984.

———, ed. *Religion in American Politics.* Washington, D.C.: Congressional Quarterly Press, 1989.

Eastland, Terry. "In Defense of Religious America." *Commentary* 71, no. 6 (June 1981): 39-45.

————, ed. *Religious Liberty in the Supreme Court: The Cases That Define the Debate over Church and State.* Washington, D.C.: Ethics and Public Policy Center, 1993.

Eckenrode, Hamilton James. *Separation of Church and State in Virginia: A Study in the Development of the Revolution.* Richmond, Va.: Davis Bottom, 1910.

Edwards, Martha L. "Religious Forces in the United States, 1815-1830." *Mississippi Valley Historical Review* 5 (1918-19): 434-49.

Eidsmoe, John. *Christianity and the Constitution: The Faith of Our Founding Fathers.* Grand Rapids, Mich.: Baker Book House, 1987.

Elazar, Daniel J. "The Political Theory of Covenant: Biblical Origins and Modern Developments." *Publius: The Journal of Federalism* 10, no. 4 (Fall 1980): 3-30.

————, ed. *Covenant in the Nineteenth Century: The Decline of an American Political Tradition.* Lanham, Md.: Rowman and Littlefield, 1994.

Elliott, Emory. "The Dove and the Serpent: The Clergy in the American Revolution." *American Quarterly* 31 (1979): 187-203.

Emmerich, Charles J. "The Enigma of James Madison on Church and State." In *Religion, Public Life, and the American Polity,* edited by Luis E. Lugo. Knoxville: Univ. of Tennessee Press, 1994.

Esbeck, Carl H. "Five Views of Church-State Relations in Contemporary American Thought." *Brigham Young University Law Review* (1986): 371-404.

Estep, William R. *Revolution within the Revolution: The First Amendment in Historical Context, 1612-1789.* Grand Rapids, Mich.: William B. Eerdmans, 1990.

Evans, M. Stanton. *The Theme Is Freedom: Religion, Politics, and the American Tradition.* Washington, D.C.: Regnery, 1994.

"First Amendment Religion Clauses: Historical Metamorphosis." *Northwestern University Law Review* 61 (1966): 760-76.

Fleet, Elizabeth, ed. "Madison's 'Detached Memoranda.'" *William and Mary Quarterly,* 3d ser., 3 (1946): 534-68.

Foster, Charles I. *An Errand of Mercy: The Evangelical United Front, 1790-1837.* Chapel Hill: Univ. of North Carolina Press, 1960.

Gaustad, Edwin Scott. "The Backus-Leland Tradition." *Foundations: A Baptist Journal of History and Theology* 2 (1959): 131-52.

————. "A Disestablished Society: Origins of the First Amendment." *Journal of Church and State* 11 (1969): 409-25.

————. *Faith of Our Fathers: Religion and the New Nation.* San Francisco: Harper and Row, 1987.

————. *Liberty of Conscience: Roger Williams in America.* Grand Rapids, Mich.: William B. Eerdmans, 1991.

————. *A Religious History of America.* Rev. ed. San Francisco: Harper and Row, 1990.

Gifford, Frank Dean. "The Influence of the Clergy on American Politics from 1763 to 1776." *Historical Magazine of the Protestant Episcopal Church* 10 (June 1941): 104-23.

Glenn, Gary D. "Forgotten Purposes of the First Amendment Religion Clauses." *Review of Politics* 49 (1987): 340-67.

Goen, C.C. *Broken Churches, Broken Nation: Denominational Schisms and the Coming of the American Civil War.* Macon, Ga.: Mercer Univ. Press, 1985.

Goldwin, Robert A., and Art Kaufman, eds. *How Does the Constitution Protect Religious Freedom?* Washington, D.C.: American Enterprise Institute, 1987.

Good, Douglas L. "The Christian Nation in the Mind of Timothy Dwight." *Fides et Historia* 7, no. 1 (1974): 1-18.

Greene, Evarts B. *Religion and the State: The Making and Testing of an American Tradition.* New York: New York Univ. Press, 1941.

Greene, Jack P., and William G. McLoughlin. *Preachers and Politicians: Two Essays on the Origins of the American Revolution.* Worcester, Mass.: American Antiquarian Society, 1977.

Grenz, Stanley J. "Church and State: The Legacy of Isaac Backus." *Center Journal* 2, no. 2 (Spring 1983): 73-94.

————. "Isaac Backus and Religious Liberty." *Foundations: A Baptist Journal of History, Theology, and Ministry* 22 (1979): 352-60.

Gribbin, William. "The Covenant Transformed: The Jeremiad Tradition and the War of 1812." *Church History* 40 (1971): 297-305.

Griffin, Clifford S. *Their Brothers' Keepers: Moral Stewardship in the United States, 1800-1865.* New Brunswick, N.J.: Rutgers Univ. Press, 1960.

Guliuzza, Frank, III. "The Practical Perils of an Original Intent-Based Judicial Philosophy: Originalism and the Church-State Test Case." *Drake Law Review* 42 (1993): 343-83.

Hall, Thomas Cuming. *The Religious Background of American Culture.* Boston: Little, Brown, 1930.

Hall, Timothy L. "Roger Williams and the Foundations of Religious Liberty." *Boston University Law Review* 71 (1991): 455-524.

Hamburger, Philip A. "A Constitutional Right of Religious Exemption: An Historical Perspective." *George Washington Law Review* 60 (1992): 915-48.

Handy, Robert T. "The American Tradition of Religious Freedom: An Historical Analysis." *Journal of Public Law* 13 (1964): 247-66.

————. *A Christian America: Protestant Hopes and Historical Realities.* 2d ed. New York: Oxford Univ. Press, 1984.

————. *A History of the Churches in the United States and Canada.* New York: Oxford Univ. Press, 1977.

————. "The Magna Charta of Religious Freedom in America." *Union Seminary Quarterly Review* 38 (1984): 301-17.

————. "The Protestant Quest for a Christian America, 1830-1930." *Church History* 22 (1953): 8-20.

————. *Undermined Establishment: Church-State Relations in America, 1880-1920.* Princeton, N.J.: Princeton Univ. Press, 1991.

Hanley, Mark Y. *Beyond a Christian Commonwealth: The Protestant Quarrel with the American Republic, 1830-1860.* Chapel Hill: Univ. of North Carolina Press, 1994.

Hart, Benjamin. *Faith and Freedom: The Christian Roots of American Liberty.* Dallas, Tex.: Lewis and Stanley, 1988.

————. "The Wall That Protestantism Built: The Religious Reasons for the Separation of Church and State." *Policy Review,* no. 46 (Fall 1988): 44-52.

Hartnett, Robert C. "The Religion of the Founding Fathers." In *Wellsprings of the American Spirit,* edited by F. Ernest Johnson. New York: Cooper Square, 1964.

Hatch, Nathan O. "The Christian Movement and the Demand for a Theology of the People." *Journal of American History* 67 (Dec. 1980): 545-67.

————. *The Democratization of American Christianity.* New Haven, Conn.: Yale Univ. Press, 1989.

————. *The Sacred Cause of Liberty: Republican Thought and the Millennium in Revolutionary New England.* New Haven, Conn.: Yale Univ. Press, 1977.

Headley, J.T. *The Chaplains and Clergy of the Revolution.* New York: Scribner's, 1864.

Healey, Robert M. *Jefferson on Religion in Public Education.* New Haven, Conn.: Yale Univ. Press, 1962.

Heimert, Alan. *Religion and the American Mind: From the Great Awakening to the Revolution.* Cambridge, Mass.: Harvard Univ. Press, 1966.

Hirsch, Elisabeth Feist. "John Cotton and Roger Williams: Their Controversy Concerning Religious Liberty." *Church History* 10 (1941): 38-51.

Holmes, Oliver W. "Sunday Travel and Sunday Mails: A Question Which Troubled Our Forefathers." *New York History* 20 (Oct. 1939): 413-24.

Hood, Fred J. *Reformed America: The Middle and Southern States, 1783-1837.* University: Univ. of Alabama Press, 1980.

———. "Revolution and Religious Liberty: The Conservation of the Theocratic Concept in Virginia." *Church History* 40 (1971): 170-81.

Howe, Daniel Walker. "The Evangelical Movement and Political Culture in the North during the Second Party System." *Journal of American History* 77 (1991): 1216-39.

Howe, Mark DeWolfe. *The Garden and the Wilderness: Religion and Government in American Constitutional History.* Chicago: Univ. of Chicago Press, 1965.

Hudson, Winthrop S. "The Issue of Church and State: A Historical Perspective." *Religion in Life* 46 (1977): 278-88.

———. *Religion in America: An Historical Account of the Development of American Religious Life.* 3d ed. New York: Scribner's, 1981.

Humphrey, Edward Frank. *Nationalism and Religion in America, 1774-1789.* Boston: Chipman Law, 1924.

Hunt, Gaillard. "James Madison and Religious Liberty." *Annual Report of the American Historical Association for the Year 1901* 1 (1902): 163-71.

Hyneman, Charles S., and Donald S. Lutz, eds. *American Political Writing during the Founding Era: 1760-1805.* 2 vols. Indianapolis: Liberty, 1983.

Ives, J. Moss. *The Ark and the Dove: The Beginning of Civil and Religious Liberties in America.* New York: Cooper Square, 1969.

———. "The Catholic Contribution to Religious Liberty in Colonial America." *Catholic Historical Review* 21 (1935): 283-98.

"Jefferson and the Church-State Wall: A Historical Examination of the Man and the Metaphor." *Brigham Young University Law Review* (1978): 645-74.

John, Richard R. "Taking Sabbatarianism Seriously: The Postal System, the Sabbath, and the Transformation of American Political Culture." *Journal of the Early Republic* 10 (1990): 517-67.

Johnson, F. Ernest, ed. *Wellsprings of the American Spirit.* New York: Cooper Square, 1964.

Jones, Archie Preston. "Christianity in the Constitution: The Intended Meaning of the Religion Clauses of the First Amendment." Ph.D. diss., Univ. of Dallas, 1991.

———. "The Christian Roots of the War for Independence." *Journal of Christian Reconstruction* 3, no. 1 (Summer 1976): 6-51.

Joyce, Lester Douglas. *Church and Clergy in the American Revolution: A Study in Group Behavior.* New York: Exposition, 1966.

Kerr, Harry P. "The Election Sermon: Primer for Revolutionaries." *Speech Monographs* 29 (1962): 13-22.

———. "Politics and Religion in Colonial Fast and Thanksgiving Sermons, 1763-1783." *Quarterly Journal of Speech* 46 (Dec. 1960): 372-82.

Kessler, Sanford. "John Locke's Legacy of Religious Freedom." *Polity* 17 (1985): 484-503.

———. "Locke's Influence on Jefferson's 'Bill for Establishing Religious Freedom.'" *Journal of Church and State* 25 (1983): 231-52.

———. "Tocqueville on Civil Religion and Liberal Democracy." *Journal of Politics* 39 (1977): 119-46.

———. *Tocqueville's Civil Religion: American Christianity and the Prospects for Freedom.* Albany: State Univ. of New York Press, 1994.

———. "Tocqueville's Puritans: Christianity and the American Founding." *Journal of Politics* 54 (1992): 776-92.

Ketcham, Ralph L. "James Madison and Religion—A New Hypothesis." *Journal of the Presbyterian Historical Society* 38 (June 1960): 65-90.

Kingsbury, Harmon. *The Sabbath: A Brief History of Laws, Petitions, Remonstrances and Reports, with Facts and Arguments, Relating to the Christian Sabbath.* New York, 1840.

Kirk, Russell. *The Roots of American Order.* LaSalle, Ill.: Open Court, 1974.

Kloppenberg, James T. "The Virtues of Liberalism: Christianity, Republicanism, and Ethics in Early American Political Discourse." *Journal of American History* 74 (June 1987): 9-33.

Koch, Adrienne. *Madison's "Advice to My Country."* Princeton, N.J.: Princeton Univ. Press, 1966.

Kohler, Max J. "The Fathers of the Republic and Constitutional Establishment of Religious Liberty." In *God in Freedom: Studies in the Relations between Church and State,* edited by Luigi Luzzatti. New York: Macmillan, 1930.

Kramer, Leonard J. "Muskits in the Pulpit: 1776-1783." *Journal of the Presbyterian Historical Society* 31 (Dec. 1953): 229-44, 32 (March 1954): 37-51.

———. "Presbyterians Approach the American Revolution." *Journal of the Presbyterian Historical Society* 31 (June 1953): 71-86, (Sept. 1953): 167-80.

Kruse, Clifton B. "The Historical Meaning and Judicial Construction of the Establishment of Religion Clause of the First Amendment." *Washburn Law Journal* 2, no. 1 (1962): 65-141.

Kurland, Philip B. "The Origins of the Religion Clauses of the Constitution." *William and Mary Law Review* 27 (1986): 839-61.

LaFontaine, Charles V. "God and Nation in Selected U.S. Presidential Inaugural Addresses, 1789-1945." *Journal of Church and State* 18 (1976): 39-60, 503-21.

Laycock, Douglas. "'Noncoercive' Support for Religion: Another False Claim about the Establishment Clause." *Valparaiso University Law Review* 26 (1991): 37-69.

———. "'Nonpreferential' Aid to Religion: A False Claim about Original Intent." *William and Mary Law Review* 27 (1986): 875-923.

Leedes, Gary C. "Rediscovering the Link between the Establishment Clause and the Fourteenth Amendment: The Citizenship Declaration." *Indiana Law Review* 26 (1993): 469-518.

Leon, D.H. "'The Dogma of the Sovereignty of the People': Alexis De Tocqueville's Religion in America." *Journal of Church and State* 14 (1972): 279-95.

Levy, Leonard W. *Constitutional Opinions: Aspects of the Bill of Rights.* New York: Oxford Univ. Press, 1986.

———. *The Establishment Clause: Religion and the First Amendment.* 2d ed. Chapel Hill: Univ. of North Carolina Press, 1994.

———. *Original Intent and the Framers' Constitution.* New York: Macmillan, 1988.

———, ed. *Essays on the Making of the Constitution.* 2d ed. New York: Oxford Univ. Press, 1987.

Lindsay, Thomas. "James Madison on Religion and Politics: Rhetoric and Reality." *American Political Science Review* 85 (1991): 1321-37.

Littell, Franklin Hamlin. "The Basis of Religious Liberty in American History." *Journal of Church and State* 6 (1964): 314-32.

————. *From State Church to Pluralism: A Protestant Interpretation of Religion in American History.* Garden City, N.Y.: Doubleday, 1962.

Little, David. "Roger Williams and the Separation of Church and State." In *Religion and the State: Essays in Honor of Leo Pfeffer,* edited by James E. Wood Jr. Waco, Tex.: Baylor Univ. Press, 1985.

————. "Thomas Jefferson's Religious Views and Their Influence on the Supreme Court's Interpretation of the First Amendment." *Catholic University Law Review* 26 (1976): 57-72.

Loveland, Anne C. *Southern Evangelicals and the Social Order, 1800-1860.* Baton Rouge: Louisiana State Univ. Press, 1980.

Lugo, Luis E., ed. *Religion, Public Life, and the American Polity.* Knoxville: Univ. of Tennessee Press, 1994.

Lutz, Donald S. "From Covenant to Constitution in American Political Thought." *Publius: The Journal of Federalism* 10, no. 4 (Fall 1980): 101-33.

Lynch, Joseph M. "Madison's Religion Proposals Judicially Confounded: A Study in the Constitutional Law of Conscience." *Seton Hall Law Review* 20 (1990): 418-77.

Maas, David E. "The Philosophical and Theological Roots of the Religious Clause in the Constitution." In *Liberty and Law: Reflections on the Constitution in American Life and Thought,* edited by Ronald A. Wells and Thomas A. Askew. Grand Rapids, Mich.: William B. Eerdmans, 1987.

————. "The Watchwords of 1774." *Fides et Historia* 18, no. 3 (1986): 15-34.

Maclear, James Fulton. "'The True American Union' of Church and State: The Reconstruction of the Theocratic Tradition." *Church History* 28 (1959): 41-62.

Malbin, Michael J. *Religion and Politics: The Intentions of the Authors of the First Amendment.* Washington, D.C.: American Enterprise Institute, 1978.

Marnell, William H. *The First Amendment: The History of Religious Freedom in America.* Garden City, N.Y.: Doubleday, 1964.

Marsden, George M. "America's 'Christian' Origins: Puritan New England as a Case Study." In *John Calvin: His Influence in the Western World,* edited by W. Stanford Reid. Grand Rapids, Mich.: Zondervan, 1982.

Marty, Martin E. *The Infidel: Freethought and American Religion.* Cleveland: Meridian, 1961.

————. "Living with Establishment and Disestablishment in Nineteenth-Century Anglo-America." *Journal of Church and State* 18 (1976): 61-77.

————. *Pilgrims in Their Own Land: 500 Years of Religion in America.* Boston: Little, Brown, 1984.

Mathews, Donald G. *Religion in the Old South.* Chicago: Univ. of Chicago Press, 1977.

————. "The Second Great Awakening as an Organizing Process, 1780-1830: An Hypothesis." *American Quarterly* 21 (1969): 23-43.

McBrien, Richard P. *Caesar's Coin: Religion and Politics in America.* New York: Macmillan, 1987.

McCarthy, Rockne. "Civil Religion in Early America." *Fides et Historia* 8, no. 1 (1975): 20-40.

McClellan, James. *Joseph Story and the American Constitution: A Study in Political and Legal Thought.* Norman: Univ. of Oklahoma Press, 1971.

————. "The Making and the Unmaking of the Establishment Clause." In *A Blueprint for Judicial Reform,* edited by Patrick B. McGuigan and Randall R. Rader. Washington, D.C.: Free Congress Research and Education Foundation, 1981.

McConnell, Michael W. "Coercion: The Lost Element of Establishment." *William and Mary Law Review* 27 (1986): 933-41.

———. "Free Exercise as the Framers Understood It." In *The Bill of Rights: Original Meaning and Current Understanding,* edited by Eugene W. Hickok Jr. Charlottesville: Univ. Press of Virginia,1991.

———. "The Origins and Historical Understanding of Free Exercise of Religion." *Harvard Law Review* 103 (1990): 1409-517.

McLoughlin, William G. "Essay Review: The American Revolution as a Religious Revival: 'The Millennium in One Country.'" *New England Quarterly* 40 (1967): 99-110.

———. "Isaac Backus and the Separation of Church and State in America." *American Historical Review* 73 (1968): 1392-413.

———. *New England Dissent, 1630-1833: The Baptists and the Separation of Church and State.* 2 vols. Cambridge, Mass.: Harvard Univ. Press, 1971.

———. "Religious Freedom and Popular Sovereignty: A Change in the Flow of God's Power, 1730-1830." *Union Seminary Quarterly Review* 38 (1984): 319-36.

———. *Revivals, Awakenings, and Reform: An Essay on Religion and Social Change in America, 1607-1977.* Chicago: Univ. of Chicago Press, 1978.

———. "The Role of Religion in the Revolution: Liberty of Conscience and Cultural Cohesion in the New Nation." In *Essays on the American Revolution,* edited by Stephen G. Kurtz and James H. Hutson. Chapel Hill: Univ. of North Carolina Press, 1973.

———. *Soul Liberty: The Baptists' Struggle in New England, 1630-1833.* Hanover, N.H.: Univ. Press of New England, 1991.

Mead, Sidney E. "American Protestantism during the Revolutionary Epoch." *Church History* 22 (1953): 279-97.

———. *The Lively Experiment: The Shaping of Christianity in America.* New York: Harper and Row, 1963.

———. *The Nation with the Soul of a Church.* New York: Harper and Row, 1975.

———. "Neither Church nor State: Reflections on James Madison's 'Line of Separation.'" *Journal of Church and State* 10 (1968): 349-63.

———. *The Old Religion in the Brave New World: Reflections on the Relation between Christendom and the Republic.* Berkeley: Univ. of California Press, 1977.

Meyer, Jacob C. *Church and State in Massachusetts: From 1740 to 1833.* Cleveland: Western Reserve Univ. Press, 1930.

Miller, Glenn T. *Religious Liberty in America: History and Prospects.* Philadelphia: Westminster, 1976.

Miller, Howard. "The Grammar of Liberty: Presbyterians and the First American Constitutions." *Journal of Presbyterian History* 54 (1976): 142-64.

Miller, Perry. "The Contribution of the Protestant Churches to Religious Liberty in Colonial America." *Church History* 4 (1935): 57-66.

———. *The Life of the Mind in America: From the Revolution to the Civil War.* New York: Harcourt, Brace and World, 1965.

Miller, William Lee. *The First Liberty: Religion and the American Republic.* New York: Alfred A. Knopf, 1986.

Moehlman, Conrad Henry. *The Wall of Separation between Church and State: An Historical Study of Recent Criticism of the Religious Clause of the First Amendment.* Boston: Beacon, 1951.

Monsma, Stephen V. *Positive Neutrality: Letting Religious Freedom Ring.* Westport, Conn.: Greenwood, 1993.

Moore, Frank, ed. *The Patriot Preachers of the American Revolution, 1766-1783.* New York, 1860.

Moore, LeRoy. "Religious Liberty: Roger Williams and the Revolutionary Era." *Church History* 34 (1965): 57-76.

———. "Roger Williams as an Enduring Symbol for Baptists." *Journal of Church and State* 7 (1965): 181-89.

Moore, R. Laurence. "The End of Religious Establishment and the Beginning of Religious Politics: Church and State in the United States." In *Belief in History: Innovative Approaches to European and American Religion,* edited by Thomas Kselman. Notre Dame, Ind.: Univ. of Notre Dame Press, 1991.

———. *Religious Outsiders and the Making of Americans.* New York: Oxford Univ. Press, 1986.

Moorhead, James H. "Between Progress and Apocalypse: A Reassessment of Millennialism in American Religious Thought, 1800-1880." *Journal of American History* 71 (1984): 524-42.

Morgan, Edmund S. "The Puritan Ethic and the American Revolution." *William and Mary Quarterly,* 3d ser., 24 (1967): 3-43.

———. *Roger Williams: The Church and the State.* New York: Harcourt, Brace and World, 1967.

Morris, B.F. *Christian Life and Character of the Civil Institutions of the United States, Developed in the Official and Historical Annals of the Republic.* Philadelphia: George W. Childs, 1864.

Murray, Iain H. *Revival and Revivalism: The Making and Marring of American Evangelicalism, 1750-1858.* Carlisle, Pa.: Banner of Truth Trust, 1994.

Nagel, Paul C. *This Sacred Trust: American Nationality, 1798-1898.* New York: Oxford Univ. Press, 1971.

Neuhaus, Richard John. *The Naked Public Square: Religion and Democracy in America.* Grand Rapids, Mich.: William B. Eerdmans, 1984.

Nichols, James Hastings. "John Witherspoon on Church and State." *Journal of Presbyterian History* 42 (1964): 166-74.

Niebuhr, H. Richard. "The Idea of Covenant and American Democracy." *Church History* 23 (1954): 126-35.

———. *The Kingdom of God in America.* New York: Harper and Brothers, 1937.

"Nineteenth Century Judicial Thought Concerning Church-State Relations." *Minnesota Law Review* 40 (1956): 672-80.

Noll, Mark A. *Christians in the American Revolution.* Washington, D.C.: Christian Univ. Press, 1977.

———. "The Church and the American Revolution: Historical Pitfalls, Problems, Progress." *Fides et Historia* 8, no. 1 (1975): 2-19.

———. *A History of Christianity in the United States and Canada.* Grand Rapids, Mich.: William B. Eerdmans, 1992.

———. "The Image of the United States as a Biblical Nation, 1776-1865." In *The Bible in America: Essays in Cultural History,* edited by Nathan O. Hatch and Mark A. Noll. New York: Oxford Univ. Press, 1982.

———. *One Nation under God?: Christian Faith and Political Action in America.* San Francisco: Harper and Row, 1988.

———, ed. *Religion and American Politics: From the Colonial Period to the 1980s.* New York: Oxford Univ. Press, 1990.

Noll, Mark A., Nathan O. Hatch, and George M. Marsden. *The Search for Christian America.* Westchester, Ill.: Crossway, 1983.

Noonan, John T., Jr. *The Believer and the Powers That Are: Cases, History, and Other*

Data Bearing on the Relation of Religion and Government. New York: Macmillan, 1987.

O'Brien, Charles F. "The Religious Issue in the Presidential Campaign of 1800." *Essex Institute Historical Collections* 107, no. 1 (1971): 82-93.

O'Brien, Francis William. "The States and 'No Establishment': Proposed Amendments to the Constitution since 1798." *Washburn Law Journal* 4 (1965): 183-210.

O'Neill, James M. "Nonpreferential Aid to Religion Is Not an Establishment of Religion." *Buffalo Law Review* 2 (1953): 242-66, 272-78.

———. *Religion and Education under the Constitution.* New York: Harper and Brothers, 1949.

Parsons, Wilfrid. *The First Freedom: Considerations on Church and State in the United States.* New York: Declan X. McMullen, 1948.

Perry, William Stevens. *The Faith of the Signers of the Declaration of Independence.* Tarrytown, N.Y.: William Abbatt, 1926.

———. *The Influence of the Clergy in the War of the Revolution.* N.p., 1891.

Peterson, Merrill D., and Robert C. Vaughan, eds. *The Virginia Statute for Religious Freedom: Its Evolution and Consequences in American History.* New York: Cambridge Univ. Press, 1988.

Pfeffer, Leo. *Church, State, and Freedom.* Boston: Beacon, 1953; rev. ed., 1967.

———. "The Deity in American Constitutional History." *Journal of Church and State* 23 (1981): 215-39.

———. "Madison's 'Detached Memoranda': Then and Now." In *The Virginia Statute for Religious Freedom: Its Evolution and Consequences in American History,* edited by Merrill D. Peterson and Robert C. Vaughan. New York: Cambridge Univ. Press, 1988.

———. "No Law Respecting an Establishment of Religion." *Buffalo Law Review* 2 (1953): 225-41, 267-72.

Plöchl, Willibald M. "Thomas Jefferson, Author of the Statute of Virginia for Religious Freedom." *Jurist* 3 (1943): 182-230.

Reichley, A. James. *Religion in American Public Life.* Washington, D.C.: Brookings Institution, 1985.

"Rethinking the Incorporation of the Establishment Clause: A Federalist View." *Harvard Law Review* 105 (1992): 1700-1719.

Rice, Charles E. *The Supreme Court and Public Prayer.* New York: Fordham Univ. Press, 1964.

Richey, Russell E., and Donald G. Jones, eds. *American Civil Religion.* New York: Harper and Row, 1974.

Riemer, Neal. "Covenant and the Federal Constitution." *Publius: The Journal of Federalism* 10, no. 4 (Fall 1980): 135-48.

———. "Madison: A Founder's Vision of Religious Liberty and Public Life." In *Religion, Public Life, and the American Polity,* edited by Luis E. Lugo. Knoxville: Univ. of Tennessee Press, 1994.

———. "Religious Liberty and Creative Breakthroughs: The Contributions of Roger Williams and James Madison." In *Religion in American Politics,* edited by Charles W. Dunn. Washington, D.C.: Congressional Quarterly Press, 1989.

Robbins, John W. "The Political Philosophy of the Founding Fathers." *Journal of Christian Reconstruction* 3, no. 1 (Summer 1976): 52-68.

Rohrer, James R. "Sunday Mails and the Church-State Theme in Jacksonian America." *Journal of the Early Republic* 7 (1987): 53-74.

Rothman, Rozann. "The Impact of Covenant and Contract Theories on Conceptions of the U.S. Constitution." *Publius: The Journal of Federalism* 10, no. 4 (Fall 1980): 149-63.

Rutland, Robert Allen. *The Birth of the Bill of Rights, 1776-1791.* Chapel Hill: Univ. of North Carolina Press, 1955.

Samson, Steven Alan. "Christianity in Nineteenth Century American Law." *Antithesis* 2, no. 2 (March-April 1991): 23-29.

―――. "The Covenant Origins of the American Polity." *Contra Mundum*, no. 10 (Winter 1994): 26-38.

―――. "Crossed Swords: Entanglements between Church and State in America." Ph.D. diss., Univ. of Oregon, 1984.

Sandler, S. Gerald. "Lockean Ideas in Thomas Jefferson's *Bill for Establishing Religious Freedom.*" *Journal of the History of Ideas* 21 (1960): 110-16.

Sandoz, Ellis. *A Government of Laws: Political Theory, Religion and the American Founding.* Baton Rouge: Louisiana State Univ. Press, 1990.

―――, ed. *Political Sermons of the American Founding Era: 1730-1805.* Indianapolis: Liberty, 1991.

Sanford, Charles B. *The Religious Life of Thomas Jefferson.* Charlottesville: Univ. Press of Virginia, 1984.

Schaff, Philip. *Church and State in the United States; or, The American Idea of Religious Liberty and Its Practical Effects.* New York: G.P. Putnam's Sons, 1888.

Schultz, Roger. "Covenanting in America: The Political Theology of John Witherspoon." *Journal of Christian Reconstruction* 12, no. 1 (1988): 179-289.

Schulz, Constance B. "'Of Bigotry in Politics and Religion': Jefferson's Religion, the Federalist Press, and the Syllabus." *Virginia Magazine of History and Biography* 91 (1983): 73-91.

Schwartz, Bernard. *The Bill of Rights: A Documentary History.* 2 vols. New York: Chelsea House, 1971.

―――. *The Great Rights of Mankind: A History of the American Bill of Rights.* New York: Oxford Univ. Press, 1977.

Singer, C. Gregg. *A Theological Interpretation of American History.* Rev. ed. Phillipsburg, N.J.: Presbyterian and Reformed Publishing Co., 1981.

Singleton, Marvin K. "Colonial Virginia as First Amendment Matrix: Henry, Madison, and Assessment Establishment." *Journal of Church and State* 8 (1966): 344-64.

Sky, Theodore. "The Establishment Clause, the Congress and the Schools: An Historical Perspective." *Virginia Law Review* 52 (1966): 1395-466.

Smith, Craig R. *To Form a More Perfect Union: The Ratification of the Constitution and the Bill of Rights, 1787-1791.* Lanham, Md.: Univ. Press of America, 1993.

Smith, Elwyn A. *Religious Liberty in the United States: The Development of Church-State Thought since the Revolutionary Era.* Philadelphia: Fortress, 1972.

―――, ed. *The Religion of the Republic.* Philadelphia: Fortress, 1971.

Smith, Gary Scott. *The Seeds of Secularization: Calvinism, Culture, and Pluralism in America, 1870-1915.* Grand Rapids, Mich.: Christian Univ. Press, 1985.

Smith, Rodney K. "Getting Off on the Wrong Foot and Back on Again: A Reexamination of the History of the Framing of the Religion Clauses of the First Amendment and a Critique of the *Reynolds* and *Everson* Decisions." *Wake Forest Law Review* 20 (1984): 569-643.

―――. "Nonpreferentialism in Establishment Clause Analysis: A Response to Professor Laycock." *St. John's Law Review* 65 (1991): 245-71.

―――. *Public Prayer and the Constitution: A Case Study in Constitutional Interpretation.* Wilmington, Del.: Scholarly Resources, 1987.

Smith, Timothy L. *Revivalism and Social Reform in Mid-Nineteenth-Century America.* New York: Abingdon, 1957.

Smylie, James H. "Madison and Witherspoon: Theological Roots of American Political Thought." *Princeton University Library Journal* 22 (Spring 1961): 118-32.

———. "Protestant Clergy, the First Amendment, and Beginnings of a Constitutional Debate, 1781-1791." In *The Religion of the Republic,* edited by Elwyn A. Smith. Philadelphia: Fortress, 1971.

———. "Protestant Clergymen and American Destiny." *Harvard Theological Review* 56, no. 3 (1963): 217-31.

Spiegel, Jayson L. "Christianity as Part of the Common Law." *North Carolina Central Law Journal* 14 (1984): 494-516.

Starr, Kenneth W. "The Relationship of Church and State: The Views of the Founding Fathers." Supreme Court Historical Society, *1987 Yearbook,* 24-37.

Stokes, Anson Phelps. *Church and State in the United States.* 3 vols. New York: Harper and Brothers, 1950.

Stout, Harry S. *The New England Soul: Preaching and Religious Culture in Colonial New England.* New York: Oxford Univ. Press, 1986.

———. "Religion, Communications, and the Ideological Origins of the American Revolution." *William and Mary Quarterly,* 3d ser., 34 (1977): 519-41.

Strout, Cushing. *The New Heavens and New Earth: Political Religion in America.* New York: Harper and Row, 1974.

Sutherland, Arthur. "Historians, Lawyers, and Establishment of Religion." In *Religion and the Public Order,* An Annual Review of Church and State, and of Religion, Law, and Society, no. 5, edited by Donald A. Giannella. Ithaca, N.Y.: Cornell Univ. Press, 1969.

Sweet, Douglas H. "Church Vitality and the American Revolution: Historiographical Consensus and Thoughts towards a New Perspective." *Church History* 45 (1976): 341-57.

Sweet, William Warren. *Religion in Colonial America.* New York: Scribner's, 1942.

———. *Religion in the Development of American Culture, 1765-1840.* New York: Scribner's, 1952.

———. *Revivalism in America: Its Origin, Growth and Decline.* New York: Scribner's, 1945.

———. *The Story of Religions in America.* New York: Harper and Brothers, 1930.

Swomley, John M. *Religious Liberty and the Secular State: The Constitutional Context.* Buffalo, N.Y.: Prometheus, 1987.

Teaford, Jon C. "Toward a Christian Nation: Religion, Law and Justice Strong." *Journal of Presbyterian History* 54 (1976): 422-37.

Thomas, George M. *Revivalism and Cultural Change: Christianity, Nation Building, and the Market in the Nineteenth-Century United States.* Chicago: Univ. of Chicago Press, 1989.

Thomas, John L. "Romantic Reform in America, 1815-1865." *American Quarterly* 17 (1965): 656-81.

Thornton, John Wingate, ed. *The Pulpit of the American Revolution; or, The Political Sermons of the Period of 1776.* Boston: Gould and Lincoln, 1860; New York: Da Capo, 1970.

Toolin, Cynthia. "American Civil Religion from 1789 to 1981: A Content Analysis of Presidential Inaugural Addresses." *Review of Religious Research* 25 (1983): 39-48.

Tuveson, Ernest Lee. *Redeemer Nation: The Idea of America's Millennial Role.* Chicago: Univ. of Chicago Press, 1968.

Van Der Slik, Jack R. "Respecting an Establishment of Religion in America." *Christian Scholar's Review* 13 (1984): 217-35.

Van Patten, Jonathan K. "In the End Is the Beginning: An Inquiry into the Meaning of the Religion Clauses." *Saint Louis University Law Journal* 27 (1983): 1-93.

———. "Standing in Need of Prayer: The Supreme Court on James Madison and Religious Liberty." *Benchmark* 3, nos. 1-2 (1987): 59-69.

Van Tyne, Claude H. "Influence of the Clergy, and of Religious and Sectarian Forces, on the American Revolution." *American Historical Review* 19 (Oct. 1913): 44-64.

Veit, Helen E., Kenneth R. Bowling, and Charlene Bangs Bickford, eds. *Creating the Bill of Rights: The Documentary Record from the First Federal Congress.* Baltimore: Johns Hopkins Univ. Press, 1991.

Veltri, Stephen C. "Nativism and Nonpreferentialism: A Historical Critique of the Current Church and State Theme." *University of Dayton Law Review* 13 (1988): 229-65.

Wald, Kenneth D. *Religion and Politics in the United States.* 2d ed. Washington, D.C.: Congressional Quarterly Press, 1992.

Way, H. Frank. "The Death of the Christian Nation: The Judiciary and Church-State Relations." *Journal of Church and State* 29 (1987): 509-29.

Weber, Donald. *Rhetoric and History in Revolutionary New England.* New York: Oxford Univ. Press, 1988.

Weber, Paul J. "James Madison and Religious Equality: The Perfect Separation." *Review of Politics* 44 (1982): 163-86.

———, ed. *Equal Separation: Understanding the Religion Clauses of the First Amendment.* Westport, Conn.: Greenwood, 1990.

Wells, Ronald A., and Thomas A. Askew, eds. *Liberty and Law: Reflections on the Constitution in American Life and Thought.* Grand Rapids, Mich.: William B. Eerdmans, 1987.

West, Ellis. "The Case against a Right to Religion-Based Exemptions." *Notre Dame Journal of Law, Ethics and Public Policy* 4 (1990): 591-638.

———. "The Right to Religion-Based Exemptions in Early America: The Case of Conscientious Objectors to Conscription." *Journal of Law and Religion* 10 (1993-94): 367-401.

West, John G., Jr. "The Politics of Revelation and Reason: American Evangelicals and the Founders' Solution to the Theological-Political Problem, 1800-1835." Ph.D. diss., Claremont Graduate School, 1992.

Whipple, Leon. *Our Ancient Liberties: The Story of the Origin and Meaning of Civil and Religious Liberty in the United States.* New York: H.W. Wilson, 1927.

White, Ronald C., Jr., and Albright G. Zimmerman, eds. *An Unsettled Arena: Religion and the Bill of Rights.* Grand Rapids, Mich.: William B. Eerdmans, 1990.

Whitehead, John W. *An American Dream.* Westchester, Ill.: Crossway, 1987.

Wills, Garry. *Under God: Religion and American Politics.* New York: Simon and Schuster, 1990.

Wilson, John F. *Public Religion in American Culture.* Philadelphia: Temple Univ. Press, 1979.

———, ed. *Church and State in America: A Bibliographical Guide. The Colonial and Early National Periods.* Westport, Conn.: Greenwood, 1986.

Wilson, John F., and Donald L. Drakeman, eds. *Church and State in American History: The Burden of Religious Pluralism.* 2d ed. Boston: Beacon, 1987.

Wilson, John K. "Religion under the State Constitutions, 1776-1800." *Journal of Church and State* 32 (1990): 753-73.

Witte, John, Jr. "How to Govern a City on a Hill: The Early Puritan Contribution to American Constitutionalism." *Emory Law Journal* 39 (1990): 41-64.

———. "The Theology and Politics of the First Amendment Religion Clauses: A Bicentennial Essay." *Emory Law Journal* 40 (1991): 489-507.

Wood, Gordon S. *The Creation of the American Republic, 1776-1787.* Chapel Hill: Univ. of North Carolina Press, 1969.

Wood, James E., Jr., ed. *Religion and the State: Essays in Honor of Leo Pfeffer.* Waco, Tex.: Baylor Univ. Press, 1985.

Wyatt-Brown, Bertram. "Prelude to Abolitionism: Sabbatarian Politics and the Rise of the Second Party System." *Journal of American History* 58 (1971): 316-41.

Wyndham, Mark. "The Historical Background to the Issue of Religious Liberty in the Revolutionary Era." *Journal of Christian Reconstruction* 3, no. 1 (Summer 1976): 152-71.

Zuckert, Catherine. "Not by Preaching: Tocqueville on the Role of Religion in American Democracy." *Review of Politics* 43 (1981): 259-80.

INDEX

Acts of the Apostles, 145

Acts of the General Assembly of the State of South-Carolina . . . , 79, 106

"An Act regulating the Post-office Establishment," 4-5, 26 n 20

"An Act to reduce into one the several acts establishing and regulating the Post-office Department," 5, 26 n 22, 65

Adams, Andrew N., 166 n 1

Adams, Anna, 187

Adams, Ann Richardson ("Anzie"), 167 n 15

Adams, Arlin M., 35 n 138

Adams, Bowen, 189

Adams, Henry, 163

Adams, Rev. Jasper, 23 n 8, 123-25, 126 n 9, 158, 159, 163-64, 166 n 1; birth of, 163, 172; on Christianity and civil government, 1, 3, 4, 14-18, 22, 39-58, 152, 153-56; on Christianity and common law, 12-14, 30 nn 87-88, 49, 137, 144, 153; on Christianity's impact on society, 1, 14-18, 39-58, 152-56, 160 n 14; on colonial America, 43-45, 151; death of, 164, 167 n 16, 168-76; death of first wife, 166 n 10; education of, 2, 163, 172, 175; on education, 44, 49, 51, 155, 158; as educator, 2, 164, 172-75; *Elements of Moral Philosophy,* 27 n 31, 165, 166 n 14, 173, 175; on establishment of religion, 1, 4, 14-18, 33 n 119, 40-50, 142-43, 154; on First Amendment, 15, 22, 31 n 99, 42, 46, 154; on George Washington, 31 n 92, 99, 155, 160 n 14; on Jefferson's "wall of separation," 17; letters in response to sermon, 113-22; marriage and death of daughter, 167 n 15; on "middle course," 18, 48, 152, 154; *Moral Causes of the Welfare of Nations,* 161 n 20, 165; notes on text of sermon, xvii-xix, 123, 177-79; poor health of, 163-64; as preacher, 2, 127, 173-75; as president of College of Charleston, 1, 2, 163-64, 168, 170, 173; as president of Geneva College, 163, 166 n 9, 168, 173; published works of, 164-65, 166 n 7, 166-67 n 14, 174;

references to, in "Immunity of Religion," 123-26, 125 n 5, 127-37, 140-44, 147-49; on references to Christianity in U.S. Constitution, 47 n 21, 63-65, 141; *Relation of Christianity to Civil Government,* xi, xii, 1, 23 nn 1, 9, 24 n 12, 25 n 15, 26 nn 17-18, 27 n 32, 29 n 73, 30 nn 74-76, nn 87-88, 31 nn 91-101, 32 nn 102-13, n 119, 39-104, 127, 160 nn 1, 3-6, 160-61 nn 8-19, 162 nn 34-35, 165, 173, 175; as scholar, 127, 164, 166 n 3, 166-67 n 14, 173, 175; second marriage of, 163, 166 n 10; on state constitutions, 45-49, 61-63, 137-44; on Sunday observance, 7, 45, 46, 48, 50, 54, 56, 63-66, 74-76, 79, 86, 86 n *, 148; as teacher, 127, 172-75; and Thomas Cooper controversy, 12; use of history in sermon, 14, 15, 16, 20, 24 n 12, 42-58, 153; as writer, 127, 174-75

Adams, John, 30 n 79, 69, 135, 166 n 1

Adams, John Quincy, 2, 166 n 1, 184

Adams, Samuel, 70

Address Delivered before the Citizens of Providence, . . . , 28 n 52

Africa, 50

Age of Jackson, 24 nn 12-13, 26 n 26, 28 n 50

Age of Reason, 146

Aitken, Robert, 71-72

Alabama, constitution of, 138

Aldrich, P. Emory, 31 n 90

Alexandria Seminary, 188

Alfred's laws, 145

Algiers, Dey of, 134

Alley, Robert S., 161 n 33

Allison, Patrick, 71

Almon, J., 43 nn 7-9, 59, 107

Alphabetical Digest of the Public Statute Law of South-Carolina, 75, 79, 106

American Bible Society, 179

American Bibliography, 105-6

American Board of Commissioners for Foreign Missions, 25 n 13

American Indians, 24 n 13, 43-44, 53, 59-60, 75, 95-97